Christmas &
Special Occasions

ROBERT CARRIER'S KITCHEN

Christmas & Special Occasions

Marshall Cavendish   London Sydney & New York

Editor	Roz Fishel
Editorial Staff	Caroline Macy
	Penny Smith
	Kate Toner
Art Editor	Ross George
Series Editor	Pepita Aris
Production Executive	Robert Paulley
Production Controller	Steve Roberts

Photography
Bryce Attwell: 51
Paul Bussell: 2, 16, 23, 35, 42, 56, 72, 74, 86, 95, 104, 106, 110
Alan Duns: 71, 87
Laurie Evans: 10, 15, 28, 30, 34, 36, 37, 54, 67 (above), 79, 80
John Hutchinson: 60 (above), 66 (above)
James Jackson: 8, 26, 38, 40, 41, 48 (below), 70, 76, 78, 90, 92, 102, 109
Chris Knaggs: 11, 12, 48 (above), 69, 82, 101
David Levin: 18, 19
Peter Myers: 22, 24, 32, 39, 44, 50, 58, 60 (below), 61, 63, 64,
67 (below), 73, 77, 93, 108
Paul Webster: 49
Paul Williams: 13, 20, 31, 46, 52, 68, 84, 88 (left and right), 94, 97, 100
Cover picture: **Paul Bussell**

Weights and measures
Both metric and imperial measurements are given. As these are not exact equivalents, please work from one set of figures or the other. Use graded measuring spoons levelled across.

Time symbols
The time needed to prepare the dish is given on each recipe. The symbols are as follows:

 simple to prepare and cook

 straightforward but requires more skill
or attention

 time-consuming to prepare or requires extra skill

 must be started 1 day or more ahead

On the cover: Christmas pudding, page 8

This edition published 1985
© Marshall Cavendish Limited 1985

Printed in Italy by
L.E.G.O. S.p.a. Vicenza

Typeset by Quadraset Limited, Midsomer Norton, Bath, Avon

Published by Marshall Cavendish House
58 Old Compton Street London W1V 5PA
ISBN 0 86307 264 X (series)
ISBN 0 86307 402 2 (this volume)

Contents

Certain celebrations — such as Christmas, Easter, weddings and birthday parties — call for suitably special foods. In this volume, *Christmas & Special Occasions*, I show you how to create a whole range of stunning spreads for festive events throughout the year, be they for formal or informal affairs; for children or for adults; for large crowds or, as in the case of Mother's Day, for just one particular person.

I begin with that most traditional occasion: Christmas. As well as all the delicious trimmings, I also cover such essentials as how to roast your turkey so that it is wonderfully succulent, and how to make a Christmas pudding that is utterly irresistible. My hot and cold punches, eggnogs and toddies will bring a touch of Christmas cheer to any gathering.

Christmas is a time for giving gifts, and an excellent way to show someone how much you care is to spend a little time making something just for them. Candied fruits and nuts, truffles and other delicacies — prettily wrapped — make very attractive presents which are really not difficult to prepare. Children will love the edible stocking fillers, which are colourful, simple to make and perfect starters for a day filled with gastronomic delights.

Early in the year comes Easter and my recipes cover a wide range of exciting European dishes, as well as our own more familiar fare, such as Hot cross buns, Simnel cake and Easter biscuits. And I show you how to make the most exquisite chocolate eggs and mouthwatering sweetmeats which children — and adults too! — will love.

If you're looking for fresh, entertaining ideas for children's birthday parties, this volume will prove invaluable. I suggest several quite different themes with accompanying menus, all of which should ensure a fun-filled and — most important for the organizer — smooth-running event.

Weddings vary enormously: for instance, should it be a big, formal celebration or a smaller, more relaxed gathering; should it be in the middle of the day, in the afternoon or in the evening; is finance the main deciding factor? My guidelines on how to choose the best kind of wedding for you, and which menu and drinks to serve, are intended to inspire you with ideas and confidence and help you towards a truly memorable day.

The most important thing about these special occasions is to make them as enjoyable as possible for your guests and also for yourself; my recipes and suggestions in this delightful volume will show you how you can achieve this.

Happy cooking and bon appétit!

Robert Carrier

Christmas

ORGANIZING CHRISTMAS

Get into the Christmas spirit early by making goodies like the pudding, cake and mincemeat well in advance. Not only do they taste better for maturing, but you'll give yourself plenty of time to enjoy the seasonal activities.

Christmas is such a busy, hectic time for the cook that anything that can be made ahead of time is a help. And it is a pleasant bonus that the fun-to-make, satisfying items, such as the Christmas pudding and Christmas cake, benefit most from being made early. So get in the festive mood weeks, if not months, in advance with a generously-stocked larder and freezer.

Start your festive cooking with the Christmas pudding and Christmas cake (see recipes). These classic treats are best if they are made at least 6 weeks in advance and the pudding can be made more than a year ahead. Mincemeat is another Christmas ingredient that very noticeably improves for being made early — the flavours mingle and combine, and the fruit absorbs the taste of a drop of the Christmas spirit!

Use your mincemeat to make up and freeze a batch of mince pies; they are marvellously useful as they can be heated through quickly, not only on Christmas Day but when friends drop in unexpectedly before or during the holiday. Mince pies with almond pastry (see recipe) are a little different from the traditional ones. Made with melt-in-the-mouth almond pastry, they are single crust pies, and each one is topped with a glistening pat of Brandy butter (see recipe). This deliciously flavoured butter can be stored, wrapped in cling film or foil, in the refrigerator or freezer for a couple of weeks or so until it is needed. Don't forget to serve some with the Christmas pudding too.

Cooking the Christmas turkey can only be done on the day it is to be eaten hot, but you can at least make the stuffing ahead. Try my Apricot and raisin stuffing (see recipe) and freeze it. To use, thaw it overnight — do not put it into the bird until a few hours before you are ready to cook it and remember not to pack it too tightly.

Fruit plays an important part in offsetting the richness of holiday fare, and Cranberry sauce (see recipe) is a perfect choice as an accompaniment for turkey and other poultry. In this recipe the whole fruits are cooked so that they keep their berry shape, colour and texture. You can store the sauce in either the refrigerator or freezer.

It is also a good idea to cook and freeze meals that can be eaten both before and after Christmas Day. Lamb with peppers is a casserole designed to be heated directly from frozen. Or try making Iced fudge mousse, a dessert which will turn a meal into a party.

There is no need to exhaust the pleasure of turkey by eating it for days after Christmas. You can freeze cooked turkey and then use it later in dishes such as Turkey mousse and Turkey asparagus Apollo (see recipes).

By using your freezer and larder sensibly, Christmas can be a time of delicious meals enjoyed by the whole family — including the well-organized cook.

Christmas pudding

In a cool, airy place this pudding can keep perfectly for over a year. It should be made at least 6 weeks before Christmas to allow it to develop a rich flavour.

🕐 🍴 7 hours, plus cooling and storing, then 2½ hours reheating

Makes 2 × 1 kg /2¼ lb puddings
175 g /6 oz wholewheat flour
5 ml /1 tsp salt
100 g /4 oz wholewheat breadcrumbs
175 g /6 oz shredded suet
175 g /6 oz Barbados sugar
5 ml /1 tsp ground cinnamon
1.5 ml /¼ tsp grated nutmeg
1.5 ml /¼ tsp ground allspice
450 g /1 lb seedless raisins
275 g /10 oz currants
275 g /10 oz sultanas
175 g /6 oz candied peel, chopped
50 g /2 oz blanched sweet almonds, chopped
50 g /2 oz blanched bitter almonds, chopped
2 eggs
60 ml /4 tbls molasses or black treacle
150 ml /5 fl oz prune juice
75 ml /5 tbls brandy or sweet sherry
butter, for greasing
sprig of holly, to decorate
Brandy butter (see recipe), to serve

1 In a large mixing bowl, mix together the flour, the salt, the breadcrumbs, the suet, the sugar and the spices.
2 Stir in the dried fruits, peel and almonds and mix well to distribute them evenly.
3 Beat together the eggs, the molasses or treacle, the prune juice and the brandy or sherry and stir into the mixture. Stir the mixture very well.
4 Thoroughly grease two 1 kg /2¼ lb pudding bowls and 2 sheets of greaseproof paper. Stand a trivet or piece of folded foil in each of 2 large saucepans and fill them ⅓ full with boiling water. Cover the pans and bring the water back to the boil.
5 Divide the mixture between the two pudding bowls. Cover them generously with greaseproof paper, making a pleat down the centre so the pudding has room to expand as it cooks. Cover each bowl with a piece of scalded calico cotton, or with foil, and tie securely with twine. Leave loops on either side of the bowl, for lifting it out.
6 Place the puddings in the saucepans and add more boiling water if necessary so that the level comes halfway up the sides of the bowls. Bring quickly to the boil again, cover and boil for 6 hours. Top up the pans with more boiling water from time to time.

Brandy butter, Mince pies with almond pastry and Christmas puddings

7 Remove the puddings from the pans and leave them to cool. Replace the coverings with clean, greased greaseproof paper and a clean cloth or foil. Store in a cool, dry place.
8 To serve, boil the puddings in the same way for 2½ hours. Turn out onto a heated serving dish and serve, decorated with the holly and accompanied by Brandy butter.

● Using a pressure cooker saves considerably on cooking time. Stand the puddings on the trivet, add about 1.4 L /2½ pt boiling water, put on the lid and boil for 30 minutes. Bring up to High pressure and pressure cook for 1½ hours. Reduce the pressure slowly. To reheat, cook for 30 minutes at High pressure.
● For a spectacular entrance, warm a little brandy, pour it over the pudding and set light to it as you bring it to the table. Put on the holly after the flames have died down.

Mincemeat

🕐 🍴 overnight soaking, 15 minutes, 2 days macerating, plus maturing

Makes 1.8 kg /4 lb
225 g /8 oz dried apricots, soaked overnight, drained and finely chopped
225 g /8 oz seedless raisins, chopped
225 g /8 oz currants
50 g /2 oz sultanas
100 g /4 oz mixed candied peel, chopped
100 g /4 oz blanched almonds, chopped
225 g /8 oz shredded suet

2.5 ml /½ tsp salt
5 ml /1 tsp mixed ground spice
2.5 ml /½ tsp ground cinnamon
1.5 ml /¼ tsp grated nutmeg
175 g /6 oz dark Barbados sugar
grated zest and juice of 1 orange
grated zest and juice of 1 lemon
2 medium-sized apples, peeled, cored and finely
    chopped
125 ml /4 fl oz brandy
60 ml /4 tbls sweet sherry

1 Mix all the ingredients together very thoroughly. Cover the bowl and leave the mixture for 2 days, stirring occasionally.
2 Pack the mincemeat into warmed, sterilized jars. Cover the top of the preserve with a disc of waxed paper and then cover the jars with plastic-lined screw-top lids (well-washed coffee jars are ideal).
3 Store the preserve in a cool, dry, airy place. Make it at least 2 weeks in advance for the flavours to blend. It can be stored for up to a year, and it improves with keeping.

Brandy butter

⏱ 15 minutes

Makes 350 g /12 oz
175 g /6 oz unsalted butter, at room
    temperature
75 g /3 oz light brown sugar
75 g /3 oz caster sugar
15 ml /1 tbls grated orange zest
90 ml /6 tbls brandy

1 In a bowl beat together the butter, light brown sugar, the caster sugar and the grated orange zest until the mixture is smooth and soft.
2 Add the brandy, a few drops at a time, and beat each addition thoroughly into the butter before adding more. Do not add too much of the spirit at a time or the mixture may separate.
3 Chill the brandy butter, wrap it tightly in cling film or foil and then store it in the refrigerator for up to 2 weeks. Or it will keep well in the freezer.

● This sweet-flavoured butter is a must with the Christmas pudding — and is equally good with mince pies.
● You can make dark rum butter in the same way as brandy butter, just substitute dark rum for the brandy.
● To make decorative pats of brandy butter, shape the butter into a roll. Refrigerate or freeze it and, when ready to use, cut it into 5 mm /¼ in slices. Cut decorative shapes from the slices with aspic cutters.

Mince pies with almond pastry

Make your mince pies in advance from a delicious combination of mincemeat and nutty almond pastry.

⏱ 50 minutes,
    plus 1 hour chilling

Makes 16 open pies
225 g /8 oz butter at room temperature, plus
    extra for greasing
100 g /4 oz caster sugar
2 egg yolks
350 g /12 oz flour, plus extra for dusting
100 g /4 oz ground almonds
a few drops of lemon juice
750 g /1½ lb Mincemeat (see recipe)
Brandy butter (see recipe), to serve

1 Cream together the butter and the sugar. Beat in the egg yolks a little at a time. Gradually stir in the flour and then stir in the ground almonds and the lemon juice.
2 Shape the dough into a ball and wrap in cling film or foil. Chill in the refrigerator for at least 1 hour.
3 Heat the oven to 190C /375F /gas 5.
4 On a lightly floured board, thinly roll out the dough and, using a 10 cm /4 in cutter, cut into 16 rounds. Grease fluted tartlet tins and line them with the pastry. Prick the bases of the pastry all over with a fork.
5 Line the tarts with foil and beans and bake 'blind' for 10 minutes.
6 Remove the linings, spoon in the mincemeat and return to the oven for a further 10 minutes. Remove from the oven and cool for a few minutes in their tins, then transfer to a wire rack to finish cooling.
7 Pack the pies in a rigid polythene container, cover and freeze.
8 To serve, reheat the Mince pies from frozen on a baking sheet in the oven at 180C / 350F /gas 4 for 10 minutes. Serve the pies topped with a small pat of brandy butter.

Cranberry sauce

This brilliant red sauce, which is so much a part of the Christmas meal, is also very good with cold turkey and other meats including smoked sausages.

 20 minutes, plus cooling

Makes about 850 ml /1½ pt
450 g /1 lb sugar
10 ml /2 tsp grated orange zest
450 g /1 lb cranberries, fresh or frozen

1 Put 425 ml /15 fl oz water into a saucepan, add the sugar and stir over a low heat until the sugar has dissolved. Bring to the boil and boil for 5 minutes.
2 Add the orange zest and the cranberries. Lower the heat and simmer, without stirring, for 5 minutes, until the berries are bright and translucent. Remove the sauce from the heat and allow it to cool.
3 Spoon the cold sauce into containers with lids. Store the sauce for up to 1 week in the refrigerator or for up to 6 months in the freezer. Serve with hot or cold meats.

Apricot and raisin stuffing

25 minutes, plus overnight soaking

Makes 750 g /1½ lb stuffing
225 g /8 oz dried apricots, chopped
225 g /8 oz seedless raisins
150 ml /5 fl oz cider
75 g /3 oz butter
1 medium-sized onion, finely chopped
175 g /6 oz fresh white breadcrumbs
grated zest of 1 orange
2.5 ml /½ tsp mixed ground spice
1.5 ml /¼ tsp ground allspice
salt and freshly ground black pepper
1 egg, beaten

1 Soak the apricots and raisins overnight in the cider.
2 Melt 25 g /1 oz of the butter and fry the onion over a moderate heat for 3–4 minutes until soft and translucent. Melt the remaining butter in the same pan and remove it from the heat.
3 Stir the breadcrumbs, the orange zest and the spices into the soaked fruit, stir in the softened onion and the melted butter, season with salt and pepper and bind the mixture with the beaten egg.
4 Allow the mixture to cool thoroughly, pack it into a rigid container, then cover it and freeze until it is needed.
5 To use, thaw at room temperature overnight and then pack the stuffing into the turkey just before roasting.

Lamb with peppers

1½ hours, plus freezing and reheating

Christmas cake

3½–4 hours, decorating the cake, plus 3 weeks drying

Makes a 23 cm /9 in cake
250 g /9 oz butter at room temperature, plus extra for greasing
250 g /9 oz Barbados sugar
6 medium-sized eggs, separated
grated zest and juice of 1 orange
60 ml /4 tbls molasses or black treacle
350 g /12 oz flour
5 ml /1 tsp ground mixed spice
2.5 ml /½ tsp ground cinnamon
2.5 ml /½ tsp ground ginger
a pinch of grated nutmeg
2.5 ml /½ tsp salt
5 ml /1 tsp bicarbonate of soda
350 g /12 oz currants
225 g /8 oz seedless raisins
225 g /8 oz sultanas
100 g /4 oz glacé pineapple, chopped
100 g /4 oz mixed candied peel, chopped
300 ml /10 fl oz milk
75 ml /5 tbls brandy
For the decoration
60 ml /4 tbls apricot jam, melted with 20 ml /1½ tbls water
Almond paste (see chart and recipe page 99)
Royal icing (see chart and recipe page 99)

1 Grease a 23 cm /9 in round deep cake tin and line the base and sides with a double thickness of greased greaseproof paper. Heat the oven to 140C /275 F /gas 1½.

Christmas cake

2 Beat together the butter and sugar until the mixture is light and fluffy. Beat in the egg yolks one at a time, then the orange zest, orange juice and molasses or treacle.
3 In a large bowl, sift half the flour with the spices and the salt. In another bowl, mix the remaining flour with the bicarbonate of soda and the dried fruits and peel. Mix together the milk and the brandy.
4 Gradually stir the spiced flour into the egg mixture. Stir in the floured fruit, alternating with the milk mixture, and beat well.
5 Whisk the egg whites until stiff peaks form and fold them into the mixture.
6 Turn the mixture into the tin and level the top, making a shallow depression in the centre so the cake rises evenly.
7 Bake for 2½–3 hours, or until a skewer inserted in the centre comes out clean. If the cake is browning too quickly cover it with crumpled foil.
8 Leave the cake in the tin to cool overnight. Remove it from the tin, close wrap it in 2 thicknesses of foil and store in an airtight tin until you decorate it.
9 About 3 weeks before you want to eat the cake, paint it with the melted apricot jam and then cover it with Almond paste.
10 When the Almond paste is completely dry, flat ice the cake with Royal icing. When this is dry, pipe the cake decoratively with more Royal icing. Make holly leaves and berries from the spare Almond paste, colouring some green and some red and yellow (see picture) and place on top of the cake.

Serves 4–6

1.4 kg /3 lb shoulder of lamb, boned and cubed
oil, for frying
500 g /1 lb onions, sliced
1 each of green, red and yellow peppers,
*   seeded, blanched and sliced*
250 g /8 oz button mushrooms, wiped
150 ml /5 fl oz chicken stock, home-made or
*   from a cube*
salt
freshly ground black pepper
To serve
150 ml /5 fl oz soured cream
15 ml /1 tbls finely chopped fresh parsley

1 Fry the lamb in a saucepan in a small quantity of oil until browned on all sides. Add the onions and fry until soft.
2 Add the peppers, mushrooms, stock and seasoning and bring to the boil. Cover and simmer for 45 minutes. Cool and then freeze in a casserole or freezer-proof container.
3 To serve: thaw completely, then cook for 1 hour at 170C /325F /gas 3, or cook from frozen for 2 hours. Swirl the soured cream over the top and sprinkle with parsley.

Turkey mousse

Making and cooling the sauce, then 20 minutes, plus 4–5 hours setting

Serves 4–8

275 g /10 oz cooked turkey meat, minced
2 eggs, separated
30 ml /2 tbls fresh dill, finely chopped
5 ml /1 tsp freshly grated nutmeg
2–3 dashes Tabasco sauce
salt and freshly ground black pepper
25 g /1 oz powdered gelatine
sliced tomatoes, onion and lettuce, to serve
For the sauce
50 g /2 oz butter
50 g /2 oz plain flour
275 ml /10 fl oz milk
salt and freshly ground black pepper

1 Melt the butter in a heavy pan. Blend in the flour and stir over a low heat for 2 minutes to make a roux.
2 Gradually add the milk, stirring the roux constantly. Bring the mixture to the boil, stirring, and simmer it for 4–5 minutes until the sauce has thickened and no longer tastes of flour. Season and cool.
3 Mix the turkey with the cooled sauce. Beat in the egg yolks, dill, nutmeg, Tabasco and salt and pepper to taste.
4 Sprinkle the gelatine over 45 ml /3 tbls cold water in a small bowl and set the bowl in a pan of barely simmering water until the gelatine dissolves.
5 Pour a little of the melted gelatine into an 850 ml /1½ pt ring mould and swirl it around so that the mould is evenly coated. Put the mould into the refrigerator to chill.
6 Add the remaining gelatine to the turkey mixture, beating well. Whisk the egg whites until stiff, then fold gently into the turkey mixture. Pour into the chilled mould and leave in the refrigerator for 4–5 hours to set.
7 When ready to serve, dip a tea-towel into very hot water, wring out and place over the mould for a few seconds. Place a plate over

the mould and invert quickly, tapping the top of the mould to dislodge the mousse.
8 Pile the sliced tomatoes and onion into the centre of the mousse, surround with shredded lettuce and serve.

Turkey and asparagus Apollo

20 minutes

Serves 4

350 g /12 oz canned asparagus spears
about 350 ml /12 fl oz chicken stock,
*   home-made or from a cube*
40 g /1½ oz butter
40 g /1½ oz flour
150 ml /5 fl oz thin cream
10 ml /2 tsp lemon juice
salt and freshly ground black pepper
350 g /12 oz cooked turkey meat
2 hard-boiled eggs

1 Drain the liquid from the asparagus and make it up to 425 ml /15 fl oz with chicken stock. Reserve some of the best spears for garnishing and chop the rest into 25 mm / 1 in lengths.
2 Melt the butter in a saucepan and stir in the flour; cook gently for a minute. Add the measured liquid and beat briskly until the mixture is smooth and boiling. Stir in the cream and the lemon juice, then season and simmer gently for 5 minutes.
3 Cut the turkey into bite-size cubes and reheat it thoroughly in the sauce.
4 Slice one of the eggs thinly and reserve it for garnishing. Coarsely chop the other egg

and stir it into the sauce with the asparagus pieces. Heat through and check seasoning.
5 Turn the mixture into a heated shallow serving dish. Arrange the egg slices in the centre with the reserved asparagus spears radiating outwards. Serve hot.

Iced fudge mousse

45 minutes, then freezing and softening

Serves 6

150 g /5 oz soft dark brown sugar
25 g /1 oz butter
4 egg yolks
5 ml /1 tsp vanilla essence
225 ml /8 fl oz thick cream
fresh fruit or 1 large can of fruit, to serve

1 In a thick-based saucepan, heat the sugar and the butter over a moderate heat until the sugar has dissolved in the butter. Boil and stir it for 1–2 minutes, then stir in 100 ml / 4 fl oz water. Cook without stirring until the mixture is thick and smooth.
2 In a small heatproof bowl, beat the egg yolks until well blended. Stir in the sugar mixture. Put the bowl over a pan of simmering water and beat the mixture vigorously until it is light and fluffy. Cool.
3 Add the vanilla essence to the cream and whip until thick. Fold this into the cooled sugar mixture and then pour it into a freezer-proof mould. Cover, label and freeze.
4 About 30 minutes before it is needed, gently unmould the mousse onto a plate and decorate with slices of fresh or canned fruit.

Turkey mousse

PERFECT TURKEY

Succulent turkey, surrounded by glazed parsnips, tasty Brussels sprouts and golden roast potatoes — or try these attractive Potatoes with flair — will be sure to win the cook praise from everybody at the table.

Christmas lunch is eagerly looked forward to by everyone except possibly the poor cook! The most difficult task is co-ordinating the turkey and its accompaniments so they are all ready at exactly the right moment. However, armed with the timetable over the page, and with many of the dishes cooked, or part-cooked, the day before, you will be able to relax and enjoy the day like everybody else around you.

If you have a cooker with two ovens or a closed grill, then you have a lot of useful extra space to keep dishes warm till you are ready to serve the meal. Assuming, however, that you have only one oven and an open grill, then split-second timing and putting the various dishes in the correct place in the oven are essential.

If you are cooking for ten or twelve people, do enlist some help in the kitchen rather than trying to cope with everything yourself. One extra pair of willing, helpful hands is worth far more than a second oven!

Christmas roast turkey

🕐🍴 preparing the chestnuts, then 5–5½ hours

Potatoes with flair

Serves 20–24
6.8 kg /15 lb turkey, dressed weight
1 large lemon, cut in half
salt and freshly ground black pepper
14 thin slices of streaky bacon
275 g /10 oz butter
150 ml /5 fl oz dry white wine
1.5 kg /3½ lb potatoes, parboiled
5 ml /1 tsp Dijon mustard
turkey giblets and liver, sautéed in a little
  butter until cooked, and chopped
Cranberry sauce, to serve (see page 10)
For the stuffing
Apricot and raisin stuffing (see page 10)
450 g /1 lb fresh chestnuts
2.5 ml /½ tsp coarse salt

1 Prepare the chestnuts the day before. Heat the grill to high. Slit each chestnut down the middle on the flat side of the nut, lay them on a baking sheet slit side up and put them under the grill for 5–6 minutes. Watch them carefully to see they do not burn. When the skins split, remove the nuts.
2 Peel the shells, then rub off the skins.
3 Bring a pan of water to the boil, drop in the chestnuts and boil for 10 minutes until the outsides are soft. Drain, sprinkle with the salt; keep covered in a cool place.
4 Heat the oven to 220C /425F /gas 7. With a damp cloth, wipe the turkey inside and out, then dry with absorbent paper. Pack the Apricot and raisin stuffing inside the

bird. Put the chestnuts inside the cavity as well, then truss the bird.
5 Rub the skin all over with the cut lemon, then sprinkle with salt and freshly ground black pepper and lay the bacon rashers over the breast. Place in the roasting tin.
6 Melt 225 g /8 oz butter in a small saucepan until it is just bubbling. Pour it over the turkey, then add the dry white wine to the tin and cover the bird loosely with foil.
7 Place it in the oven. After 15 minutes, turn the oven down to 170C /325F /gas 3 and cook for a further 2¾ hours, basting every 20–30 minutes with the juices.
8 Remove 310 ml /14 tbls of the cooking juices. Melt the remaining butter, put it into a second roasting pan with 90ml /6 tbls of the turkey juices, keeping the remainder for the parsnips. Heat it until it is sizzling, then add the parboiled potatoes, baste thoroughly and put it on the bottom shelf of the oven. Cook the turkey and potatoes for a further 1½ hours, basting every 20 minutes.
9 Remove the foil and bacon slices from the breast for the last 30 minutes of cooking to allow the breast to brown. The turkey is cooked if the juices run clear from its thickest part when pierced with a skewer.
10 Transfer the turkey and the potatoes to a warmed serving platter, loosely re-cover with foil and return to the oven, turned off.
11 Skim the fat from the pan juices and add the mustard and chopped giblets and liver with 60 ml /4 tbls water to the roasting tin. Bring to the boil and boil for 2–3 minutes. Pour into a sauce-boat.
12 Serve the turkey with Cranberry sauce, handed separately.

● Allow 43 minutes per kg /20 minutes per lb for well-done meat. Weigh the bird after you have stuffed it.

Potatoes with flair

🍴 1 hour 20 minutes

Serves 4
450 g /1 lb waxy or all-purpose potatoes
15 ml /1 tbls dripping, or 15 ml /1 tbls oil
  and 15 g /½ oz butter
salt and freshly ground black pepper

1 Heat the oven to 200C /400F /gas 6.
2 Peel the potatoes and cut them into even shapes, about 6 cm /2½ in long. Slice each one across the width at 5 mm /¼ in intervals, cutting almost to the base but leaving the slices joined. Rinse the potatoes in cold water and dry them thoroughly. Do not parboil these potatoes — they will start to break up.
3 Put the dripping, or oil and butter, in a roasting tin and melt it over a low heat. When the fat is almost smoking hot, add the potatoes. Turn them carefully in the fat until they are evenly coated. Season them generously with salt and pepper.
4 Roast the potatoes in the oven, turning them occasionally, for 50–60 minutes until they are crisp and golden but feel soft when pierced with a fork.

Christmas roast turkey

Christmas countdown

Four days before Christmas
Apricot and raisin stuffing: if not already prepared and frozen, begin to make it now and freeze it: soak the apricots and raisins in cider overnight. (Or, see **The night before**.)

Three days before Christmas
Cranberry sauce: make and refrigerate.
Apricot and raisin stuffing: make. Freeze.
Roast turkey: if cooking a frozen turkey, start defrosting it now.

Two days before Christmas
Roast turkey: remove giblets. Cook giblets, chop and refrigerate, keeping them covered.

The day before Christmas
Vegetables: peel the potatoes, parsnips and Brussels sprouts. Cover with cold water. Refrigerate.
Chestnuts: put under the grill to split their skins, peel and skin. Parboil, drain, cool and keep covered in a cool place.
Apricot and raisin stuffing: if frozen, remove it from the freezer and defrost it.

The night before the meal
Roast turkey: take the turkey out of the refrigerator, cover it loosely with foil and leave it to come to room temperature.
Apricot and raisin stuffing: if not already made, soak the apricots and raisins in cider overnight.

Six hours before the meal
Apricot and raisin stuffing: make the stuffing and allow it to cool.

Five and a half hours before the meal
Roast turkey: stuff the bird with Apricot and raisin stuffing and whole chestnuts. Truss the turkey. Melt the butter for basting. Heat the oven.

Five hours before the meal
Roast turkey: put the turkey in the oven.

Three hours before the meal
Cranberry sauce: remove it from refrigerator. Put it into a serving bowl.

Two hours before the meal
Giblets: remove them from the refrigerator.
Vegetables: drain the vegetables and re-cover with fresh cold water.

One and three-quarter hours before the meal
Vegetables: parboil the potatoes. Blanch the parsnips, drain them and refresh them under cold water, then keep them covered with cold water till ready to cook.

One and a half hours before the meal
Vegetables: put the potatoes in a roasting pan, baste with some of the turkey juices and roast on the bottom shelf.

One hour before the meal
Vegetables: cook Brussels sprouts until they are *al dente*.

Forty minutes before the meal
Vegetables: cook the parsnips.

Thirty minutes before the meal
Roast turkey: remove the foil and bacon.

Twenty minutes before the meal
Chipolatas and bacon rolls: heat the grill to high. Cook the chipolatas; turn after 5 minutes.
Vegetables: turn and baste the parsnips, add the orange juice and sugar.

Fifteen minutes before the meal
Roast turkey: remove it from the oven, put it on a warmed serving platter with the potatoes. Cover it with foil, return it to the turned-off oven with the door ajar. Skim fat off the cooking juices and make the gravy. Keep warm.
Vegetables: bring the water for the Brussels sprouts to the boil.

Ten minutes before the meal
Chipolatas and bacon rolls: put the chipolatas in a warmed serving dish at the bottom of the oven. Grill the bacon — turn the bacon after 3 minutes.

Five minutes before the meal
Chipolatas and bacon rolls: roll up the bacon rashers, spear them with cocktail sticks and put them in the dish with the chipolatas.
Vegetables: steam the Brussels sprouts.

Just before the meal
Vegetables: put Brussels sprouts and parsnips into serving dishes.

Roast glazed parsnips

🕭 1 hour

Serves 10
1.4 kg /3 lb parsnips
25 g /1 oz butter
120 ml /8 tbls pan juices from the Roast turkey
juice of 1 orange
15 ml /1 tbls soft brown sugar
salt and freshly ground black pepper

1 Peel the parsnips and cut them lengthways into 12 mm /½ in thick slices.
2 Bring a large saucepan of water to the boil, add the parsnips and cook for 5 minutes. Drain and refresh under cold water. (Keep in a bowl of cold water, in a cool place, till ready to proceed.)
3 Forty minutes before the meal put the butter, with the pan juices from the turkey, into a roasting tin. When it is bubbling add the parsnips, turning them over 2 or 3 times so that they are covered in fat. Cook over a medium heat for 20 minutes, turning them halfway through the cooking time.
4 Pour the orange juice over the parsnips and sprinkle on the brown sugar, then continue to cook them for a further 20 minutes, turning occasionally.
5 Season and serve immediately.

Steam-finished Brussels sprouts

🕭 35 minutes

Serves 10
1.4 kg /3 lb Brussels sprouts
salt and freshly ground black pepper
juice of 1 lemon

1 Choose sprouts that are evenly-sized if possible, otherwise divide them into large ones and small ones.
2 Bring a large pan of salted water to the boil, add the large sprouts to the pan and boil for 6 minutes, then add the small ones. Continue cooking for a further 6 minutes. The sprouts should be very slightly hard when pierced with a knife.
3 Drain and refresh them under cold water, then put them into a bowl, sprinkle with the lemon juice and leave until completely cold. Cover the bowl with cling film. Put the sprouts aside until just before the meal.
4 Fifteen minutes before the meal bring a large saucepan of water to the boil. Five minutes before the meal put the sprouts into a steamer and put it over the water. Steam for 2½ minutes, then turn the top sprouts to the bottom; steam for another 2½ minutes.
5 Transfer the sprouts to a warmed serving dish, season with salt and freshly ground black pepper and serve.

Chipolatas and bacon rolls

🕭 20 minutes

Serves 10
700 g /1½ lb chipolata sausages
700 g /1½ lb streaky bacon (about 20 rashers)
freshly ground black pepper

1 Heat the grill to high.
2 Prick the sausages with a fork on both sides and put them on the grill rack. Cook for 5 minutes then turn over. Cook for a further 5 minutes. Remove them to a warmed serving platter and put it at the bottom of the oven. (By this time the turkey and potatoes will be ready on a serving dish and keeping warm in the turned-off oven, so the chipolatas will fit at the bottom.)
3 Put the bacon rashers on the grill rack, slightly overlapping if necessary. Season them with pepper. Cook the rashers for 2–3 minutes, turn them over and cook for a further 2 minutes.
4 Roll up the bacon rashers, spear them with cocktail sticks and put them on the dish with the chipolatas. Serve immediately.

● Try rolling up the bacon when it is still raw and threading it onto skewers before grilling it, you may find it easier to manage than after it has been cooked.

FESTIVE GOOSE

In Europe goose is often served on Christmas Day. This recipe makes the most of a beautiful bird, with a stuffing of bacon, apple and walnut. Serve it with potatoes cooked in the juices of the goose.

Geese are larger than ducks, but the proportion of bone to meat is higher. Geese are also very fatty, with light pink flesh which becomes pale brown when it is cooked. The flavour is faintly gamey. The best bird to roast is a gosling — a young goose not more than six months old. It should have a plump breast, soft yellow feet and a yellow bill. Geese are not seasonal, but they are at their best from winter to late spring and, in fact, it can be almost impossible to obtain a fresh goose during the summer months.

Roast goose is traditionally served with a variety of stuffings and sauces. Potato and onion or chestnut and apple stuffing absorbs the fat effectively, and the sharpness of apple or Cranberry sauce (see page 10) also offsets the richness of the meat.

In Poland and Germany roast goose is very popular. The Germans baste the skin with beer about 15 minutes before the end of the cooking time to make it crisp, and the usual accompaniment for the goose is red cabbage or sauerkraut.

Redcurrant-stuffed apples are delicious as a garnish for goose, served as an alternative to conventional stuffing. Poach 4 apples, peeled, halved and cored, in 250 ml /4 oz sugar until they are tender but not disintegrating. Arrange the apple halves attractively around the goose on the heated serving dish and just before serving fill the cavity of each apple with 5 ml /1 tsp redcurrant jelly.

Festive goose

⏲ bringing to room temperature, then 3 hours 20 minutes

Serves 6–8
4.5 kg /10 lb goose, dressed weight
salt and freshly ground black pepper
1.4 kg /4 lb potatoes
2 medium-sized onions
30 ml /2 tbls flour
300 ml /10 fl oz hot vegetable stock,
*   home-made or from a cube*
bouquets of watercress, to garnish
For the stuffing
50 g /2 oz butter
1 medium-sized onion, chopped
½ garlic clove, crushed
2 eating apples, peeled, cored
*   and chopped*
225 g /8 oz streaky bacon, chopped
75 g /3 oz fresh white breadcrumbs
50 g /2 oz walnuts, chopped
15 ml /1 tbls clear honey
1 egg, beaten
salt
freshly ground black pepper

1 Remove the long wing pinions (and the feet if they have been left on) and any remaining feathers and quills from the goose.

Leave it to come to room temperature.
2 To make the stuffing: melt the butter in a heavy-based saucepan over a moderate heat. Add the chopped onion and fry for 5–6 minutes, stirring, until soft and translucent. Add the garlic, apple and bacon and cook, stirring occasionally, for 15 minutes. Remove it from the heat, add the rest of the stuffing ingredients, mix them in well and season with salt and freshly ground black pepper to taste. Leave until it is cold.
3 Heat the oven to 180C /350F /gas 4.
4 Pack the stuffing — not too tightly — inside the goose. Secure the vent with a skewer. Prick the goose all over with a fork and season with salt and freshly ground black pepper. Put on a rack in a roasting tin and place in the oven.
5 Meanwhile, thinly slice the potatoes and onions. When the goose has been cooking for 1¾ hours, remove it from the oven and drain

off all but 60 ml /4 tbls of the fat. Toss the potatoes and onions in the remaining fat and arrange them in a layer on the base of the tin. Put the goose on the rack above the potatoes and replace it in the oven.
6 Cook for another 45 minutes, basting the goose and turning the potatoes several times. Remove it from the oven and using a slotted spoon, transfer the potatoes and onion to another ovenproof dish. Return the goose to the oven and put the potatoes on the top shelf. Cook the goose and the potatoes for a further 20 minutes.
7 Remove the goose from the oven, put it on a heated serving dish and keep it warm. Transfer the potatoes to a serving dish and keep them warm.
8 To make the gravy: drain off the excess fat from the roasting tin, sprinkle the flour over the remaining juices and stir well. Cook for 5–6 minutes to form a roux. Gradually add the hot stock, stirring constantly. Bring the gravy to the boil, season well with salt and freshly ground black pepper and pour it into a heated sauce-boat.
9 Serve the goose, garnished with bouquets of watercress, and the roast potatoes, and hand the sauce-boat separately.

Festive goose

CHRISTMAS CHEER

Spicy drinks, packed with alcoholic punch and served hot or cold, will liven up any party. On a smaller scale, the eggnogs and toddies make perfect pick-me-ups and marvellous night-caps.

A recipe for any mixed drink is only a guide-line: you can vary it as much as you like, but do sample it first, for safety!

The wine or spirit used as the base for a mixed drink does not have to be expensive but you must use fresh fruit and juices. Do not boil the drink if you have to heat it, as this will spoil the flavour.

Make the drink the centre of attention and serve it from a punch bowl or large jug. A few drops of food colouring can be added to make the drink more attractive if necessary. Fruit makes a good garnish, but do not overdo it and turn the drink into a fruit salad. You will need a ladle that pours well for serving the drink; and for the hot punches, you will need to provide glasses with handles or mugs.

There are many strange names for mixed drinks, but the most common is punch. It is said to be an English coinage of a Hindi word for a drink which had five ingredients. It was adopted by the British in India and made of tea, water, sugar, citrus juice and spirit. Interestingly too, the word 'puncheon' was used for a large cask that transported Caribbean rum. Nowadays, most wine- or spirit-based mixed drinks are called punches.

Mulls are made with warmed wine, beer or cider, but they are not quite as alcoholic as punches. You can easily invent your own mulls, but beware — in the 17th century the verb 'mull' also meant 'to stupefy'!

Possets are made of milk curdled with wine, ale or other alcohol and were originally used as cures for colds and other ailments. Nogs always include eggs and are traditionally used as a pick-me-up.

Toddies and grogs are both made from spirits: toddy was a popular night-cap in 18th century Scotland and grog was named after the 18th century Admiral 'Grogram' Vernon who ordered the dilution of the Royal Navy's daily rum ration. His nickname came from his grogram (coarse silk) coat. Toddies and grogs are made individually.

According to legend, a 5th century Saxon princess, Rowena, presented a gold cup to a British king with the words 'waes hale' (good health). Centuries later the wassail bowl became an old-English punch associated with Christmas and Twelfth Night — and general riotous carousing.

Atholl brose

There are many variations of this toddy and the ones that include oatmeal are more of a meal than a drink. Traditionally, Atholl brose should be stirred with a silver spoon.

Makes 1 drink
50 ml /2 fl oz Scotch whisky
25 ml /1 fl oz clear honey
boiling milk, to taste

1 Mix the whisky and honey in a warmed glass. Top with boiling milk and stir.

English bishop

This punch may have gained its name from the historical association of bishops with claret, as generally the recipes called for red wine. This is a robust version which is made with port.

Makes 6–8 drinks
12 cloves
1 medium-sized orange
75 cl bottle port
75 ml /3 fl oz dark rum
75 ml /3 fl oz brandy
5 ml /1 tsp allspice
5 ml /1 tsp freshly grated nutmeg
soft brown sugar, to taste

1 Stick the cloves into the orange and bake it until brown. Meanwhile, gently heat the port in a pan.
2 Cut the browned orange into quarters and place it in a warmed bowl. Pour the warmed port on top of the orange quarters and stir in the spices, rum and brandy. Sweeten with sugar, if necessary.

Cider wassail bowl

Hot butter rum toddy

 10 minutes

Serves 1
2 cloves
2 allspice berries
25 mm /1 in piece cinnamon stick
5 ml /1 tsp sugar, or more if necessary
boiling water
50 ml /1 fl oz dark rum
a small knob of butter

1 Put the cloves, allspice berries, cinnamon stick and sugar into a 150 ml /5 fl oz tumbler. Pour in a little boiling water and leave to stand for 5 minutes.
2 Pour in the rum and add the knob of butter. Fill the glass with boiling water and stir to dissolve the butter. Add more sugar to taste, if necessary, and serve the hot butter rum toddy at once.

Champagne fruit punch

Serve this celebration punch at the start of your Christmas party.

15 minutes,
then 3–4 hours macerating

Makes 25–30 servings
450 /1 lb canned pineapple cubes, drained and the juice reserved
150 ml /5 fl oz cognac
2 × 75 cl bottles dry white burgundy
10 ml /2 tsp lemon juice
ice cubes, to serve
1 × 75 cl bottle of champagne

1 Put the pineapple cubes into a large bowl or jug. Pour in the cognac and 1 bottle of burgundy. Add the lemon juice and pineapple juice to taste. Place in the refrigerator to macerate for 3–4 hours.
2 Remove from the refrigerator and add the ice. Pour in the second bottle of burgundy, then the champagne, and serve.

Glögg

This mulled wine is drunk in Germany where it is called Glühwein, and it is very popular in Sweden, too.

Makes 12–14 drinks
75 cl bottle medium-sweet sherry
75 cl bottle brandy
½ × 75 cl bottle red wine
15 ml /1 tbls ground cinnamon
2.5 ml /½ tsp Angostura bitters
175–200 g /6–7 oz almonds, blanched
75–100 g/3–4 oz raisins

1 Mix all the ingredients in a large pan and heat slowly. Put about 6 raisins and almonds in each mug and pour on the hot drink.

Auld man's milk

Rum or brandy may be used in this recipe instead of whisky, but Scotch whisky is the customary ingredient.

Makes 12–14 drinks
10 medium-sized eggs, separated
300 g /11 oz sugar
1.5 L /2½ pt milk
5 ml /1 tsp ground cinnamon
75 cl bottle Scotch whisky

1 Beat the egg yolks with the sugar, then blend with the milk and cinnamon. Add the whisky and heat gently. Whisk the egg whites, then fold them into the mixture.

Cider wassail bowl

This traditional Christmas drink will warm you through and put you in a party mood.

 20 minutes

Makes 15–20 drinks
5 ml /1 tsp whole cloves
5 ml /1 tsp whole allspice berries
2 cinnamon sticks
2.3 L /4 pt cider
275 ml /10 fl oz brandy
30–45 ml /2–3 tbls soft dark brown sugar
apple quarters stuck with cloves

1 Place the cloves, the allspice berries and the cinnamon sticks in a piece of muslin and tie it up to make a spice bag.
2 Pour the cider and brandy into a large heavy-based saucepan. Add the brown sugar to taste. Add the muslin bag of spices.
3 Bring it to the boil, stirring gently until the sugar has dissolved. Lower the heat and simmer it for 10–15 minutes.
4 Add the apple quarters and continue simmering for 1–2 minutes, then pour the drink and the apple quarters into a warmed punch bowl. Discard the spice bag.
5 To serve, ladle the hot drink into warmed glasses, leaving the apple quarters behind in the bowl.

Christmas eggnog

5 minutes

Serves 1
1 egg
15 ml /1 tbls sugar
25 ml /1 fl oz calvados or brandy
25 ml /1 fl oz dark rum
thick cream
freshly grated nutmeg

1 In a shaker, combine the egg, the sugar, the calvados or brandy, and the rum. Cover and shake.
2 Strain the mixture into a glass.
3 Top it with thick cream. Sprinkle the top with freshly grated nutmeg to taste and serve it as soon as possible.

Negus

Dr Johnson's special punch

Serve this punch at an evening party or during a cold, wintry afternoon.

Makes 14–16 drinks
12 cubes of sugar
1 medium-sized orange
2 × 75 cl bottles red wine
200 ml /7 fl oz brandy
200 ml /7 fl oz Cointreau
freshly grated nutmeg

1   Rub the sugar cubes on the orange. Slice the orange and place it in a pan. Add the wine and heat it slowly, stirring in the flavoured sugar.
2   When the mixture is hot, remove it from the heat and add the brandy and Cointreau. Ladle it into punch cups and then sprinkle it with nutmeg.

Hot nog

Makes 6–8 drinks
2 medium-sized eggs
30 ml /2 tlbs sugar
150 ml /5 fl oz whisky, rum or brandy
1 L /1¾ pt very hot milk
freshly grated nutmeg

1   Beat the eggs with the sugar and spirit. Vigorously stir in the hot milk.
2   Pour it into mugs and then sprinkle with nutmeg.

● For a wine nog, replace the spirit with 300 ml /10 fl oz wine.

Tea punch

Makes 16–18 drinks
½ × 75 cl bottle dark rum
½ × 75 cl bottle brandy
250 g /9 oz soft brown sugar
juice of 1 large lemon
1.5 L /2½ pt strong tea, boiling hot

1   Pour the rum and brandy into a well-warmed bowl. Add the sugar and lemon and set alight
2   Pour on the tea to put out the flames and serve it immediately.

Christmas rum punch

15 minutes,
plus 2–4 hours macerating

Makes 15–20 drinks
juice of 2 oranges
juice of 2 lemons
1 × 75 cl bottle dark rum
50–100 ml /2–4 fl oz Grand Marnier
225 g /8 oz canned pineapple cubes, with their juice
100 g /4 oz maraschino cherries, with their juice
1 orange, thinly sliced
1 lemon, thinly sliced
15–30 ml /1–2 tbls sugar
1½–2 L /2½–3½ pt soda water
ice cubes, to serve

1   In a large jug mix the orange and lemon juice, dark rum and Grand Marnier.
2   Add the pineapple cubes and juice, and the maraschino cherries and juice. Stir well.
3   Add the orange and lemon slices. Place

the jug or bowl in the refrigerator and leave the mixture to macerate for 2–4 hours.
4   Remove it from the refrigerator and add sugar to taste. Stir well to dissolve the sugar, then add soda water to taste.
5   Add the ice cubes to the punch and then serve it immediately.

Rum toddy

Makes 1 drink
50 ml /2 fl oz dark rum
50 ml /2 fl oz lemon juice
10 ml /2 tsp soft brown sugar
strained hot tea, to taste
freshly grated nutmeg

1   Pour the rum, lemon and sugar into a glass. Top with hot tea, stir it and sprinkle with a little nutmeg.

Negus

Makes 12–14 drinks
1 large lemon
12 cloves
2 × 75 cl bottles port (or 1 bottle red wine and 1 bottle port)
125 ml /4 fl oz brandy
the peel of 3 lemons
10 ml /2 tsp freshly grated nutmeg
30 ml /2 tbls soft brown sugar
4 cinnamon sticks
300 ml /11 fl oz boiling water

1   Stick the cloves into the lemon and place it in a large pan. Add the other ingredients and heat slowly, testing to see if more sugar is needed.

Ale posset

Makes 8–10 drinks
1 slice brown bread, toasted
1 L /1¾ pt boiling milk
2 medium-sized egg yolks, beaten
25 g /1 oz butter, melted
30 ml /2 tbls soft brown sugar
1 L /1¾ pt draught brown ale or Guinness

1   Place the toast in a large bowl and pour on the boiling milk.
2   Whisk the yolks with the butter and sugar. Strain the milk onto the egg mixture and blend. Transfer it to a pan, add the ale and warm it gently.

Cider mull

Makes 10–12 drinks
10 cloves
15 ml /1 tbls ground cinnamon
2.5 ml /½ tsp ground allspice
2.5 ml /½ tsp freshly grated nutmeg
50 g /2 oz soft brown sugar
2 × 1 L bottles still cider

1   Simmer the cloves, spices and sugar in 150 ml /5 fl oz water for 20 minutes. Strain into a pan and add the cider. Warm slowly and sweeten with more sugar if you wish.

Edible Christmas Gifts

EUROPEAN BAKING

Add a Continental flavour to your festivities with these traditional yule-tide delicacies which will make unusual Christmas gifts — mouthwatering cakes and pastries, and little biscuits to hang on your tree.

Traditions in European Christmas bakery, particularly in the northern countries, are very similar. Though the cakes and pastries vary from region to region, the basic ingredients of honey and spices, fruit and nuts appear time and again.

The eve of St Nicholas's Day (December 5–6) is a family festival in the Netherlands. Red-robed St Nicholas, sitting astride his white horse and accompanied by his attendant, Black Peter, appears with a sack on his back — this holds the presents for the good children; the naughty children, it is said, are taken away in the sack. Soft, chewy biscuits called Spicy Dutchmen (see recipe), initial-shaped biscuits called *sprits* and doughnuts flavoured with raisins and candied peel, are made and eaten at this time.

The Swedish festival of light, St Lucia's Day, falls on December 13. The youngest girl in each family dresses in a long white gown and a crown of lingonberry greens ringed with candles and takes trays of saffron yeast buns (see recipe for Swedish plaited saffron bread) and coffee to her parents very early in the morning.

Festivities in Sweden continue until Christmas Eve and beyond, as they do throughout all of Scandinavia. In these countries, Christmas Eve is the main occasion for a feast of traditional foods, almost invariably including porridge — and one person in each home will find buried in his or her portion a blanched almond, to bring good luck in the year to come. Christmas baking in Scandinavia is lavish and elaborate and features spiced biscuits which are often made into gingerbread houses; rich, buttery biscuits often containing almonds; aromatic yeasted loaves studded with candied fruits, and doughnuts.

In Germany, too, baking always starts several weeks before Christmas. For days every home is scented with the spicy fragrances of cinnamon, nutmeg, aniseed and bitter almonds, and the sharp tang of ginger and orange and lemon. Currants and sultanas are carefully inspected, washed and dried; candied fruits are chopped small and almonds are slivered. Cinnamon stars (see recipe) and Spiced chocolate biscuits (see recipe) are among the hundreds of biscuits baked in every conceivable shape. Marzipan hearts are hung from Christmas trees. Stollen (see recipe), the fruity yeast rolls folded to represent the infant Jesus wrapped in swaddling clothes, are served to guests and given as presents.

The topping for Dresden Christmas Stollen includes vanilla sugar, which can be easily made by burying a length of vanilla pod in a jar of caster sugar. Stored there for a couple of weeks, it will impregnate the sugar with a delicate vanilla flavour.

In Hungary, Christmas Eve dinner is a fairly simple meal of fish, followed by nuts dipped in honey, honey biscuits and *Beigli*, a Christmas roll filled with a poppyseed or ground walnut paste. In contrast, Poland's lavish feast stretches to 12 courses. It features carp or pike, and includes honey cakes and *Makownik*, another yeasted poppyseed cake.

An eye-catching addition to the Christmas table in most French households is *Bûche de Noël* (see recipe) — a Swiss roll filled with butter cream, coated with chocolate or mocha butter cream and decorated to look like a log. In Provence it is traditional to serve 13 desserts in memory of the Last Supper. These include nougat, griddle cakes scented with orange-flower water and a crown-shaped yeast cake.

Northern Italy follows the familiar Teutonic traditions with decorated Christmas trees and *panettoni*, round fruited yeast breads. But as one moves south, certain sweetmeats such as the Sienese *panforte*, a spiced honey and nut confection, nougat-like *torrone*, and the Neapolitan *struffoli* have a distinctly Middle Eastern character about them.

Dresden Christmas Stollen and
Swedish plaited saffron bread

Swedish plaited saffron bread

This versatile dough can also be made into buns in various shapes; the following recipe makes about 15 small buns.

 1¾ hours, plus 2¼ hours rising and cooling

Makes 2 loaves

2.5 ml /½ tsp saffron strands
10 ml /2 tsp caster sugar
250 ml /9 fl oz milk, warmed to blood heat
400 g /14 oz strong plain flour, sifted and warmed
25 g /1 oz fresh yeast
75 g /3 oz butter, melted
a pinch of salt
1 medium-sized egg yolk
100 g /4 oz sugar
50 g /2 oz raisins
40 g /1½ oz chopped mixed peel
25 g /1 oz chopped blanched almonds
oil, for greasing
flour, for dredging
1 medium-sized egg, lightly beaten, to glaze
raisins or chopped blanched almonds and coarse sugar (preserving sugar or coffee crystals), to decorate

1 Heat the oven to 140C /275F /gas 1. Dry the saffron strands in the oven for 10 minutes, then pound them to a powder with 5 ml /1 tsp caster sugar.

2 Make a sponge batter as for Dresden Christmas Stollen (see recipe) using 125 ml / 4 fl oz milk, 100 g /4 oz flour, 25 g /1 oz fresh yeast and 5 ml /1 tsp caster sugar. Leave to ferment.
3 Mix the crushed saffron with the rest of the milk, then add the melted butter.
4 Sift the remaining flour with the salt into a bowl, make a well in the centre and pour in the milk and butter mixture, the egg yolk, sugar, fruit and nuts. Draw some of the flour from the sides and mix it in, then add the foaming sponge mixture.
5 Blend well, then knead hard until the dough is very smooth and elastic and comes away cleanly from the sides of the bowl.
6 Lightly oil a large polythene bag. Place the ball of dough in it and fasten the bag tightly, leaving room for the dough to expand. Leave in a warm, draught-free place until it has doubled in bulk, about 1½ hours.
7 Turn the dough out onto a floured surface, knead for a few minutes until smooth, then cut in half. Replace one piece in the bag while you shape the other.
8 Cut the piece of dough in 2 equal pieces and roll each into a rope about 45 cm /18 in long. Plait the 2 pieces together very lightly and loosely. Tuck the ends underneath. Shape the remaining dough, place the loaves on greased baking sheets, cover with a clean dry cloth and leave in a warm place until they have doubled in bulk, about 40 minutes. Heat the oven to 200C /400F /gas 6.
9 Brush the risen dough plaits with lightly beaten egg and scatter with raisins or with a combination of chopped almonds and coarse sugar. Bake for 20–25 minutes, then cool on a wire rack. The loaves will keep fresh for up to 1 week if tightly wrapped in foil.

Dresden Christmas Stollen

There are several local variations on this German fruit bread, but this version is popular all over the country.

3 hours, plus rising, then cooling and 1 day maturing

Makes 2 loaves

600 ml /1 pt milk, warmed to blood heat
1 kg /2¼ lb strong plain flour, sifted and warmed
100 g /4 oz fresh yeast
200 g /7 oz caster sugar
2.5 ml /½ tsp ground cardamom
2.5 ml /½ tsp ground mace
450 g /1 lb butter, melted and cooled
grated zest of 1 lemon
10 ml /2 tsp salt
oil, for greasing
flour, for dredging
450 g /1 lb raisins
150 g /5 oz sultanas
250 g /9 oz mixed candied peel, chopped
150 g /5 oz almonds, blanched and chopped
For the topping
100 g /4 oz unsalted butter, melted
100 g /4 oz sugar
30 ml /2 tbls vanilla sugar (see introduction)
125 g /4 oz icing sugar

1 First make a sponge batter: in a large jug or bowl, mix together the warmed milk and 65 g /2½ oz flour. Crumble in the yeast, stir, then add 5 ml /1 tsp caster sugar. Stir well to disperse any lumps, cover and leave in a warm place for about 10 minutes, by which time it should have at least doubled in volume.
2 Sift the remaining flour with the cardamom and mace into a large bowl. Make a well in the centre and pour in the melted butter. Draw a little of the flour from the sides and mix it in, then add the foaming batter. Beat well and add the remaining sugar, lemon zest and salt.
3 Continue beating, then knead hard, either in the bowl or on a floured surface, until the dough is very smooth, firm and elastic and comes away cleanly from the sides of the bowl.
4 Lightly oil a large polythene bag. Place the ball of dough in it and fasten the bag tightly, leaving room for the dough to expand. Leave it to rise in a warm, draught-free place until it is doubled in bulk, about 1½ hours.
5 Turn the dough out onto a floured surface, knead for a few moments, then pull the sides over into the centre, turn it over and replace it in the bag. Seal and leave to rise in a warm place for at least 30 minutes until doubled in bulk.
6 Meanwhile, heat the oven to 100 C /200F / gas low. Dust the fruit with a little flour and combine them with the almonds, then warm them gently in the oven before kneading them into the dough. Thoroughly grease a large baking sheet.
7 Turn the risen dough out onto a well-floured work surface. Flatten it slightly and scatter the fruit and nut mixture over it. Knead carefully, making sure it is evenly distributed. Divide the dough into 2 equal pieces, leaving one covered in the bag while you shape the other.
8 Roll out the piece of dough to a slightly flattened oval shape a little smaller than the baking sheet. Transfer it to the greased sheet, laying it slightly to one side. Next, on one side only, press lightly with a rolling pin across the full width of the pastry from the centre outwards.
9 Lightly brush the thinner half with water and fold this over the thicker half, leaving a margin of about 5 cm /2 in. Press together well. Repeat with the remaining piece of dough. Cover the Stollen with a dry cloth and leave them to rise again, until doubled in bulk, about 40 minutes.
10 Heat the oven to 200C /400F /gas 6. Brush the risen Stollen with 50 g /2 oz melted butter and bake for 45–60 minutes until well browned. Cover with foil if they begin to brown too early.
11 Remove the Stollen from the oven and place on a wire rack. While hot, brush with the remaining melted butter and dredge with a mixture of the 3 sugars to form a thick sugary crust. Leave to cool.
12 When the loaves are cold, wrap them tightly in foil and leave them to mature for a day before cutting.

● These loaves will keep fresh for several weeks if wrapped tightly in foil.

Spicy Dutchmen

Called *Taai-taai*, these biscuits are crisp outside and chewy and soft inside.

🕐 🍴 45 minutes, 2–3 days maturing, then 50 minutes, plus cooling

Makes 10
125 g /4 oz clear honey
125 g /4 oz glucose powder
125 g /4 oz flour, plus extra for dredging
140 g /4½ oz rye flour
5 ml /1 tsp bicarbonate of soda
7.5 ml /1½ tsp cinnamon
2.5 ml /½ tsp freshly grated nutmeg
2.5 ml /½ tsp ground aniseed
75 g /3 oz preserved ginger, drained and finely chopped
butter, for greasing
1 medium-sized egg, beaten, to glaze
angelica and glacé cherries, to decorate

1   Put the honey, glucose and 25 ml /1 fl oz water in a saucepan. Bring to the boil, then boil gently until the glucose has dissolved. Set aside to cool.
2   Sift the flours together into a bowl, make a well in the centre and pour in the cooled honey mixture. Gradually draw the flour in from the sides, kneading very thoroughly to form a smooth, bread-like dough.
3   Wrap the dough in foil and leave it in a cool dark place for 2–3 days to rest and mature.
4   Heat the oven to 170C /325F /gas 3.

Dissolve the bicarbonate of soda in 15 ml / 1 tbls water. Knead it into the dough, together with the spices and the ginger.
5   Roll the dough out on a floured board to a thickness of 5 mm /¼ in. Using a 14 cm / 5½ in gingerbread man or woman cutter, cut out shapes.
6   Grease and flour a baking sheet. Place the shapes on it, spaced well apart, and brush them lightly with the beaten egg. Bake for 20 minutes.
7   While the biscuits are still hot, stick on small pieces of angelica and glacé cherry to make eyes and mouths. Cool them completely on a wire rack and then keep them stored in an airtight tin.

Cinnamon stars

In Germany these decorative biscuits are called *Zimtsterne*.

🍴 50 minutes, plus cooling

Makes about 50
175 g /6 oz flour, sifted twice, plus extra for dredging
90 g /3½ oz butter, in small pieces, plus extra for greasing
90 g /3½ oz caster sugar
15 ml /1 tbls cinnamon
2 medium-sized egg yolks, lightly beaten
1 medium-sized egg white, lightly beaten
coarse sugar (preserving sugar or coffee crystals) or silver cake balls, to decorate

1   Sift the twice-sifted flour onto a cool pastry board. Drop the small pieces of butter into the flour and quickly and lightly rub them together with your fingertips until the mixture resembles coarse crumbs.
2   Mix in the sugar and cinnamon, then the egg yolks, until the dough is smooth. Heat the oven to 180C /350F /gas 4.
3   Roll out the dough on a floured surface to a thickness of 3 mm /⅛ in. Using a star-shaped biscuit cutter, stamp out shapes. Transfer the biscuits to a lightly greased baking sheet and brush the tops of the biscuits with the lightly beaten egg white.
4   Using a cocktail stick or skewer, pierce a hole in the top of each star. Scatter a little sugar on top or stud then with silver balls.
5   Bake them for 10–12 minutes until lightly golden, then cool them on wire racks.

German marzipan hearts

Hang these jewel-like sweetmeats from your Christmas tree. You can use differently shaped biscuit cutters to make diamonds, triangles and half moons.

🍴 40 minutes, plus cooling

Makes about 15
125 g /4 oz finely ground almonds
125 g /4 oz sifted icing sugar, plus extra for dredging
15 ml /1 tbls rose-water
2 drops pure bitter almond essence
food colouring (optional)
1 medium-sized egg yolk, beaten, to glaze
For the decoration
glacé cherries, in small pieces
candied angelica, in small pieces

1   Make the marzipan. Knead the almonds, the sugar, the rose-water and the almond essence together into a fine, smooth paste.
2   Dust your work surface with sifted icing sugar and roll out three-quarters of the paste to a thickness of 5 mm /¼ in. Use a heart-shaped biscuit cutter to cut shapes.
3   Using the palms of your hands, roll the rest of the marzipan into a long, thin rope. Brush the edge of each heart with a little beaten egg yolk, then stick on a length of marzipan rope to make a raised edge. Heat the grill to high.
4   Using a cocktail stick, lightly indent a pattern on the raised edge of each heart, then pierce a hole near the top of the heart so a string can be threaded through.
5   If wished, brush the raised edges of the hearts with food colouring. Lightly brush all surfaces with beaten egg yolk and toast carefully under the hot grill, watching constantly, until the centres of the hearts are slightly golden and the edges are brown.
6   Decorate the hearts while they are still warm with cherries and angelica, using dabs of egg yolk to stick them on.
7   Tie lengths of thin string or sturdy thread through the holes when cool.

Spicy Dutchmen

Spiced chocolate biscuits

You can make these rich iced biscuits — *Lebkuchen* — into either squares or heart shapes; hung from your Christmas tree they will make delightful ornaments.

 40 minutes, overnight setting, then 1 hour, plus cooling

Makes 70–80
4 medium-sized egg whites
250 g /9 oz icing sugar, sifted
225 g /8 oz unblanched almonds
65 g /2½ oz plain chocolate, grated
50 g /2 oz mixed candied orange and lemon peel, finely chopped
5 ml /1 tsp ground cinnamon
5 ml /1 tsp ground cloves
1 large packet rectangular ice-cream wafers
For the icing
50 g /2 oz plain chocolate
50 g /2 oz icing sugar

1 In a large, spotlessly clean bowl, whisk the egg whites until they stand in firm, snowy peaks. Sift a third of the icing sugar over them and whisk in well, then add the remaining sugar in 2 batches, whisking hard after each addition. Continue whisking until the mixture thickens to a firm, glistening white mass. This takes about 15 minutes by hand and 7–8 minutes if you are using an electric mixer.
2 Put the unblanched almonds in a blender and grind them coarsely. Put them in a bowl and stir in the grated chocolate, candied peel, cinnamon and cloves, making sure the pieces of peel are well separated and coated.
3 Tip the nut mixture over the egg white and sugar mixture and, using a large metal spoon, gently fold together.
4 Using a sharp, pointed knife, cut each ice-cream wafer in half to form squares, or cut them into 2 heart shapes.
5 With a round-ended knife or small spatula, pile the nut mixture onto each wafer, tapering it up from the sides to a height of about 15 mm /½ in in the middle. Place the biscuits close together on baking sheets and leave them to dry overnight.
6 Heat the oven to 180C /350F /gas 4. Bake the biscuits for 25 minutes or until they are a pale golden brown.
7 While the biscuits are cooking, make the icing: melt the chocolate with 22.5 ml /1½ tbls water, then stir until combined.
8 Sift the icing sugar into a bowl and gently stir in 15 ml /1 tbls hot water. Stir the warm chocolate into the sugar to make a smooth mixture which will coat the back of a spoon. Cover the bowl with a damp cloth and stand in a cool place until you are ready to ice the biscuits.
9 When the biscuits are done, place them on wire racks. As soon as they are cool enough to handle, dip them in the chocolate icing, holding them by their bases.
10 If you are going to hang the biscuits from your Christmas tree, pierce a hole through each one with a skewer while they are still warm.

Bûche de Noël

This traditional Christmas yule log gateau from France is dusted with a little icing sugar and garnished with a sprig of holly for a stylish, festive look.

2¼ hours, plus chilling

Serves 8
butter and flour, for the tin
3 eggs
75 g /3 oz sugar
65 g /2½ oz flour
15 g /½ oz cocoa powder
45 ml /3 tbls apricot jam
15 ml /1 tbls kirsch
30–45 ml /2–3 tbls icing sugar
For the vanilla butter cream
175 g /6 oz butter, softened
4 ml /¾ tsp vanilla essence
22.5 ml /1½ tbls Grand Marnier
350 g /12 oz icing sugar, sifted
For the chocolate butter cream
225 g/8 oz unsweetened chocolate
350 g /12 oz icing sugar, sifted
175 g /6 oz butter, softened

1 Heat the oven to 180C /350F /gas 4. Butter a Swiss roll tin, line with greaseproof paper. Lightly butter and flour the tin.
2 In a bowl over simmering water whisk the eggs and sugar until thick and light. Remove from heat and whisk until cool.
3 Sift the flour and the cocoa powder 3 times and fold lightly, but thoroughly, into the mixture with a large metal spoon. Pour the batter into the prepared tin and bake for

Bûche de Noël

25 minutes. Lay a damp cloth on a table; cover with a sheet of greaseproof paper and turn the cake out onto the paper; carefully peel off the lining paper. Trim the edges. Lay a fresh sheet of greaseproof paper in its place. Roll up the cake starting at one of the short sides with the paper inside. Leave to cool.
4 To make the vanilla butter cream, cream the softened butter with the vanilla essence and Grand Marnier and gradually beat in the sifted icing sugar a little at a time, whisking until smooth. To make the chocolate butter cream, melt the chocolate in the top part of a double boiler. Gradually add the icing sugar and the butter and whisk until smooth.
5 Unroll the cake, remove the greaseproof paper and spread it with most of the vanilla butter cream. Roll up the cake, wrap in cling film and chill until the butter cream becomes firm. When ready to decorate, remove the cling film. Diagonally cut off a slice at one end — this will form a branch.
6 Heat together the apricot jam and kirsch until they are runny. Brush both ends of the cake with this apricot glaze. With the apricot glaze, attach the cut-off slice to the side of the cake to look like a branch. Ice both ends of the cake and the end of the branch with the reserved vanilla butter cream. Smooth these over and, using chocolate butter cream and a 3 mm /⅛ in nozzle, pipe lines to show the rings of the tree.
7 Ice the cake and the branch with the remaining chocolate butter cream. Using a fork, mark the icing to look like bark. Dust the bark lightly with icing sugar and decorate with a sprig of holly.

CANDYING

Candied fruit or nuts make unusual presents and, although they are very expensive to buy in the shops, they can be made quite cheaply at home. Once candied, the fruit or nuts are then given a glacé or crystallized finish.

Although the method for candying fruit or nuts stretches over quite a number of days, in fact it only takes up a little of your time each day. For the rest of the time the fruit or nuts are left to soak in the syrup.

It is only worth candying food that is in prime condition: just-ripe or canned fruit and fresh chestnuts. Take your time and follow the instructions carefully. If you try to hurry the process, the fruit may be tough to eat.

Canned fruit is much easier to candy than fresh fruit as it has already been processed in syrup. Choose canned fruit that has a strong flavour, such as pineapple, apricots or peaches. Fresh fruit takes longer to candy; choose plump, fresh, just-ripe fruit such as cherries, plums and pears. Only candy one sort of fruit at a time in the syrup, otherwise the flavours will be masked or the stronger flavour will predominate.

Apart from making perfect presents, crystallized and glacé fruit or nuts provide a special treat for the end of a dinner party. They also make lovely cake decorations and add a professional touch to many desserts. The syrup that is left over from candying is like clear honey and is worth saving. It can then be used in several ways: included in a fresh fruit salad, poured over ice cream or used for cooking stewed fruit.

Packing

Pack candied fruit in a box, dividing the layers with waxed paper. Separate the individual pieces of fruit from each other with waxed paper too. If you are giving the fruit as a present, you can arrange it in little sweet paper cases. Do not make the box airtight, otherwise candied fruit becomes mouldy after a time. Different types of fruit can be packed in one box to give variety.

Marrons glacés, on the other hand, should be stored in an airtight container of some sort if they are to be kept for any length of time.

You should also wrap the individual marrons glacés in foil, so that they do not become hard in texture.

If stored correctly, candied fruit and nuts will keep for 6 months or even longer, but avoid storing the boxed fruit in a damp place, otherwise it may become sticky.

Candied canned fruit

⏱🔪🔪🔪 11 days, averaging 10 minutes a day

Makes 500 g /1 lb candied fruit
500 g /1 lb canned fruit
550–800 g /1¼–1¾ lb sugar

1 Drain the fruit, reserving the syrup. All the fruit should be about the same size — remove any damaged pieces or very small or very large pieces. Weigh out 500 g /1 lb fruit and put it into a heatproof bowl.
2 Measure the syrup and make it up to 300 ml /10 fl oz with water, if necessary.
3 Put the syrup into a saucepan and add 250 g /8 oz sugar. Heat gently, stirring until the sugar has dissolved. Bring the syrup to

Home-made candied fruit and nuts make unusual gifts

Candying canned and fresh fruit

Time	Ingredients	Method	Soaking time
Day 1	Canned fruit: 500 g /1 lb fruit 250 g /8 oz sugar 300 ml /10 fl oz canned syrup	Dissolve the sugar in the drained syrup, boil it, then pour it over the fruit.	24 hours
	Fresh fruit: 500 g /1 lb fruit 200 g /6 oz sugar 300 ml /10 fl oz water	Prepare the fruit; poach it until tender. Drain, reserving cooking water. Dissolve the sugar in 300 ml /10 fl oz cooking water, boil then pour it over fruit.	24 hours
Day 2	50 g /2 oz sugar	Dissolve the sugar in the syrup, boil it and pour it over the fruit again.	24 hours
Day 3	50 g /2 oz sugar	Dissolve the sugar in the syrup, boil it and pour it over the fruit again.	24 hours
Day 4	50 g /2 oz sugar	Dissolve the sugar in the syrup, boil it and pour it over the fruit again.	24 hours
Day 5	Fresh fruit: 50 g /2 oz sugar	Dissolve sugar in syrup, boil; pour on fruit.	24 hours
	Canned fruit: 75 g /3 oz sugar	Dissolve sugar in syrup, add fruit, boil for 3–4 minutes, return it to the bowl.	48 hours
Day 6	Fresh fruit: 50 g /2 oz sugar	Dissolve sugar in syrup, boil; pour on fruit.	24 hours
Day 7	Fresh fruit: 50 g /2 oz sugar	Dissolve sugar in syrup, boil; pour on fruit.	24 hours
	Canned fruit: 75 g /3 oz sugar	Dissolve sugar in syrup, add fruit, boil for 3–4 minutes, cool. Test syrup, reboil if it is not thick enough. Return to the bowl.	3–4 days
Day 8	Fresh fruit: 75 g /3 oz sugar	Dissolve sugar in the syrup, add fruit, boil for 3–4 minutes, return to the bowl.	48 hours
Day 10	Fresh fruit: 75 g /3 oz sugar	Dissolve sugar in syrup, add fruit, boil for 3–4 minutes. Cool. Test syrup, reboil if not thick enough. Return to the bowl.	3–4 days
Day 11	Canned fruit	Place the fruit on the rack, drain then dry.	
Day 14	Fresh fruit	Place the fruit on the rack, drain then dry.	

the boil and then pour it over the fruit. The fruit must be completely immersed in the syrup. If there is not enough syrup, make some more by dissolving 250 g /8 oz sugar in 200 ml /7 fl oz water.

4 Leave the fruit to stand in a warm place for 24 hours.

5 Drain the syrup off the fruit into a saucepan. Add 50 g /2 oz sugar and heat gently until the sugar has dissolved. Bring it to the boil and pour it over the fruit again. Leave the fruit to stand in a warm place for 24 hours.

6 Repeat step 5 twice more.

7 On the fifth day, strain the syrup into a saucepan and add 75 g /3 oz sugar. Heat gently, stirring until the sugar has dissolved. Add the fruit to the syrup in the saucepan and bring gently to the boil. Boil for 3–4 minutes. Carefully pour the syrup and fruit into the bowl again. Leave the fruit in a warm place for 48 hours.

8 Repeat step 7 but this time leave the syrup and fruit to cool. Different canned fruit are processed in syrups of different strengths and you should test the cooled syrup to see if it is the consistency of thick honey. If it is, leave the fruit and syrup in the bowl for a further 3–4 days. If it is not, boil the fruit and syrup together again until the syrup has thickened and the fruit is plump, then pour it into the bowl again and leave for 3–4 days — the longer the time you leave it, the sweeter the fruit will be.

9 After 3–4 days, carefully remove the fruit from the syrup and place it on a wire rack; leave the fruit to drain.

10 When all the excess syrup has drained off, the fruit must be dried. This can be done in a very cool oven for 3–4 hours; the temperature must be as low as possible. If the fruit becomes overheated it will become caramelized and the flavour will be spoiled so make sure that the oven is never too hot and that the fruit, or the rack it stands on, does not touch the sides of the oven. For economy, use the heat left in the oven after baking — turn the oven off and put in the fruit for as long as the heat remains in the oven. Do this over 2–3 days, depending on how often you use the oven.

11 The candied fruit is now ready to eat, or to be given a crystallized or glacé finish (see recipes).

● Fresh fruit is candied in the same way as canned, but the process takes longer and more sugar is needed. The chart above gives the times and amounts of sugar needed and compares the process to that of candying canned fruit.

Crystallized finish

 40 minutes, plus drying

Makes 500 g /1 lb

500 g /1 lb candied fruit (see recipe), well dried
sugar

1 Prepare a small pan of boiling water and a bowl of sugar. Spear the fruit, a piece at a time, on a skewer or a fork then dip it in the boiling water. Allow any excess water to drain off then dip the fruit into the sugar.

2 Press the sugar lightly onto the fruit and then place it on a wire rack to dry at room temperature for a few hours.

Glacé finish

 40 minutes, plus drying

Makes 500 g /1 lb fruit

500 g /1 lb candied fruit (see recipe), well dried
500 g /1 lb sugar

1 Put the sugar and 150 ml /5 fl oz water into a saucepan and stir until the sugar has dissolved. Bring the syrup to the boil, then remove from the heat and cover with a piece of cling film. Prepare a pan of boiling water.

2 Pour a little of the syrup into a small heatproof bowl. Spear the candied fruit, one piece at a time, on a skewer or fork. Dip each first into boiling water, drain, then dip into the bowl of hot syrup. Place the fruit on a wire rack to drain.

3 As the syrup in the bowl becomes cloudy, discard it and replenish the bowl with fresh syrup from the saucepan.

4 Dry the fruit, on the rack, as for candied fruit but turn the fruit over occasionally so that it dries evenly.

Marrons glacés

 4 days, averaging 20 minutes a day

Makes about 1 kg /2¼ lb

1 kg /2¼ lb chestnuts in their shells or 500 g /1 lb canned chestnuts, drained
500 g /1 lb sugar
500 g /l lb glucose
6–8 drops vanilla essence

1 To prepare the chestnuts, snip off the tops, then boil them for 2–3 minutes. Peel off the shell and the brown inner skin. Put them in a pan with cold water to cover, then bring them very slowly to the boil and simmer gently until the chestnuts are tender. Drain them.

2 Put the sugar, glucose and 350 ml /12 fl oz water into a saucepan and heat gently, stirring, until the sugar and glucose are dissolved. Add the prepared chestnuts (including any broken ones). If the syrup does not cover the chestnuts, make more.

3 Bring the syrup to the boil, then remove the pan from the heat. Cover it and leave it in a warm place for 24 hours.

4 Uncover the pan, and bring the syrup to the boil again, with the chestnuts still in it. Cover the pan again and leave it in a warm place for 24 hours.

5 Add the vanilla essence to the syrup. Uncover the pan, bring it to the boil again, then cover and leave for 24 hours.

6 Lift the chestnuts out of the syrup and place them on a rack. Some more may have broken up — press these bits into balls.

7 Dry the chestnuts in the lowest of ovens for 3–4 hours. Finally, give them a glacé finish (see recipe).

STOCKING FILLERS

Adults and children alike enjoy the excitement of finding a full stocking at the end of their bed on Christmas morning — so here are some simple and sophisticated ideas for good stocking fillers.

To find something delightful in a Christmas stocking is fun, but to find something you can eat is better still. Many of these stocking fillers are quick and easy to make. They use convenient ingredients and materials — such as ribbons, bought sweets, marzipan and icing. Royal icing is used for sticking things together. Make it by whisking 1 egg white until it is frothy, then gradually add 225 g / 8 oz icing sugar, a little at a time, whisking well between each addition. Add 2.5 ml / ½ tsp lemon juice and mix thoroughly.

Marzipan stocking fillers
Use bought marzipan for speed and convenience, and add a few drops of food colouring to make Christmas people and animals — Father Christmas, angels, the baby in a manger, or reindeer and lambs. Marzipan and food colouring can also be used to make fruit or holly sprigs and mistletoe which look very pretty if they are tied together with colourful ribbon (see Marzipan baubles).

Pastry, biscuits and cakes
Bought shortcrust pastry, or your own favourite biscuit dough, can be cut out to look like stars or bells, candles or angels, Christmas trees and holly leaves. Use special biscuit cutters or make your own templates with cardboard. Use a sharp knife to cut out the shape, making sure you don't drag the knife as this results in uneven edges. Bake the biscuits and then decorate them with coloured glacé icing.

Small, bought Swiss rolls, chocolate-flavoured or plain, will make pretty crackers if you wrap them in tissue or shiny paper.

Pretty parcels
Make little red felt sacks. Fill the sacks with pieces of fudge or chocolate coins and tie them at the top with gold or silver thread.

Nylon net, cut into squares and wrapped around a handful of sugared almonds, looks lovely tied with narrow coloured ribbon.

To make little cake parcels, cut bought or home-made madeira cake into small squares. Cover them with coloured icing and tie a ribbon around the cake, finishing with a bow at the top.

Jewellery
Little girls will love jewellery to wear and eat. Dolly mixtures or other soft sweets threaded onto cotton will make fun necklaces and bracelets.
● For an 'expensive' look, foil-covered chocolate coins can be threaded onto cotton to make a beautiful necklace.
● To make a ring, cover a polythene bag tie with shiny gold or silver paper and shape it into a finger-sized circle. Using a small dot of Royal icing, stick on a small round sweet for the 'jewel', or use several tiny sweets to make a more elaborate 'jewel' cluster.

Decorated ribbons

⎸ making the Royal icing,
⎸ then 15 minutes, plus drying

colourful ribbon, about 4 cm /1½ in wide
sugar-coated coloured sweets
Royal icing (see introduction)

1 Cut lengths of ribbon and position the sweets at 25 mm /1 in intervals along it.
2 Stick in place with a dot of Royal icing. Use the decorated ribbons to make headbands or to adorn the Christmas tree.

Marzipan baubles

🕐⎸ 1 hour making and decorating,
plus at least 24 hours drying

marzipan
desiccated coconut
food colouring (red, green and 3 other colours)
sieved apricot jam
narrow ribbon
icing sugar, for dusting
Royal icing (see introduction)

1 Break off small pieces of marzipan and roll them into balls. Place the balls on greaseproof paper and leave to harden for 24 hours.
2 Divide the desiccated coconut among 3 small bowls. Add a few drops of food colouring (not red or green) to each bowl.
3 Warm the sieved apricot jam. Brush it all over the marzipan balls.
4 Roll each marzipan ball in coloured coconut. Press the coconut gently into the marzipan until it sticks. Leave it to dry.
5 Tie a piece of ribbon around each bauble, parcel-style, leaving enough ribbon at the top to make a loop for hanging up the bauble.
6 Colour a little marzipan with the green food colouring. Lightly dust a work surface with a little icing sugar and roll out the green marzipan. With a sharp knife, cut out small holly leaves.
7 Colour a little more marzipan with red and roll it into small holly berry shapes.
8 Using a small dot of Royal icing, attach 1 or 2 leaves and berries to the ribbon which decorates each bauble.

Garden rake

⎸ making the Royal icing,
⎸ then 15 minutes, plus drying

narrow coloured ribbon
1 narrow wooden stick
Royal icing (see introduction)
1 triangular ridged chocolate and honey bar, ½ the length of the wooden stick

1 Twist the ribbon around the wooden stick. Attach it with dots of Royal icing.
2 Attach the stick to the centre of the unridged side of the chocolate bar with a dot of Royal icing. Hold it firmly in place for 1 minute, then make sure the icing has completely dried before moving the rake.

Traffic lights

⎸ making the Royal icing,
⎸ then 5 minutes, plus drying

1 black, liquorice-flavoured, oblong chewy lollipop
1 round red sweet
1 round yellow sweet
1 round green sweet
Royal icing (see introduction)

1 Stick the red, yellow and green sweets to one long flat side of the lollipop at regular intervals with Royal icing.

Sweetie Christmas tree

⎸ making the Royal icing,
⎸ then 10 minutes, plus drying

10 cm /4 in green thin card circle
Royal icing (see introduction)
15 cm /6 in wooden stick
chocolate cup cake
foil-wrapped sweets or sugar-coated coloured sweets, to decorate

1 Form the card into a cone shape and glue it together with Royal icing.
2 Put a dot of Royal icing at one end of the wooden stick and place it inside the cone to make the trunk of the tree.
3 Carefully but firmly push the other end of the stick into the chocolate cup cake, to plant the tree.
4 Using small dots of Royal icing, stick the sweets to the tree. You can either cover it completely or arrange the sweets in a pretty pattern.

Father Christmas biscuits

40 minutes,
plus cooling and decorating

Makes 10 biscuits
butter, for greasing
75 g /3 oz flour, plus extra for dusting
a pinch of salt
50 g /2 oz butter
30 ml /2 tbls icing sugar
15 ml /1 tbls caster sugar
For the glacé icing
225 g /8 oz icing sugar
a few drops of red food colouring
For the decoration
tiny pieces of liquorice
small white marshmallows
thin red card

1 Heat the oven to 190C /375F /gas 5. Lightly butter a baking sheet.
2 Sift the flour and the salt into a large bowl. Dice the butter into the flour and salt mixture. Lightly rub it in with your finger-tips, until it resembles fine breadcrumbs.
3 Sift the icing sugar into the flour mixture and add the caster sugar. Fold it in with a metal spoon. Then, using your hand, work the mixture to a dough and knead it until it is smooth.
4 Roll the dough out on a lightly floured board to a thickness of 5 mm /¼ in. Cut the dough into round biscuit shapes using a floured 6.5 cm /2½ in biscuit cutter.
5 Put the biscuit shapes onto the prepared baking sheet, 15 mm /½ in apart, and bake for 12–15 minutes or until they are lightly golden and firm to the touch. With a palette knife, transfer the biscuits to a wire rack and leave them to get cold.
6 To make the glacé icing, sift 225 g /8 oz icing sugar into the top of a double boiler, or into a bowl standing in a pan of water. Add 50 ml /3 tbls water and stir over a low heat until the mixture is smooth and coats the back of a spoon.
7 Reserving a little glacé icing for sticking and decorating, colour the remainder with a few drops of red food colouring to make it pink. Using a palette knife, cover one side of the biscuits, then leave the icing to harden slightly.
8 Using a piping bag fitted with a small plain nozzle, pipe the remaining white icing to make 2 eyes, 1 nose and 1 mouth on each pink biscuit 'face'. Finish the eyes with tiny pieces of liquorice.
9 To make the beard, stick several small white marshmallows onto the edge of the biscuit beneath the mouth. Stick 2 marsh-mallows on each biscuit for eyebrows.

Choose from this selection of edible gifts to make novel stocking fillers

10 Cut red card triangles to make hats and stick these to the top of the biscuits, using small dots of icing.
11 Stick a small marshmallow pom-pom to the top of each hat with a little icing. Leave until the icing 'glue' has hardened.

Potted Stilton dates

45 minutes,
plus wrapping and packing

Makes 25–30 stuffed dates
450 g /1 lb large fresh dates
125 g /4 oz Stilton
25 g /1 oz unsalted butter
1.5 ml /¼ tsp ground allspice
1.5 ml /¼ tsp ground cardamom

1 Slit the dates lengthways and remove the stones.
2 Using a fork, blend together the Stilton and the butter and spices.
3 Put 1.5 ml /¼ tsp of the cheese mixture into each date cavity, pressing it in well so that you can close the date again. Put them in the refrigerator to chill.
4 Line small squares of coloured transpa-rent wrapping paper with slightly smaller squares of foil-lined paper. Put the dates in the papers and wrap them as though they are toffees, twisting the ends of the paper to seal them. Chill them until they are needed.

Fudge nut crunchies

🔪🔪 1¼ hours, then 4–5 hours setting, plus wrapping and packing

Makes about 45 × 25 mm /1 in squares
50 g /2 oz butter, plus extra for greasing
15 ml /1 tbls golden syrup
225 g /8 oz sugar
30 ml /2 tbls condensed milk
7.5 ml /1½ tsp vanilla essence
1.5 ml /¼ tsp ground ginger
75 g /3 oz ginger biscuits, crushed
50 g /2 oz coarsely chopped walnuts

1 Melt the butter in a heavy-based saucepan over a gentle heat. Add the syrup, the sugar and 30 ml /2 tbls water. Stir together until the sugar has dissolved.
2 Bring the mixture slowly to the boil, still stirring. Pour in the condensed milk and boil for 8 minutes.
3 The mixture is cooked when it reaches 115C /240F on a sugar thermometer; test that it sets into a soft ball in cold water.
4 Remove from the heat, stir in the vanilla essence and ginger and beat until the mixture thickens slightly (6–8 minutes).
5 Grease a shallow 23 × 12.5 cm /9 × 5 in tin. Add the crushed biscuits and walnuts to the cooled mixture, stirring to mix evenly.
6 Pour the mixture into the prepared tin, smoothing the top with a palette knife. Mark out 25 mm /1 in squares with the tip of a sharp knife, then leave to set.
7 Once the mixture has set completely, cut through the marked squares with a sharp knife. Wrap each square in coloured foil, then pack them in an airtight tin.

Peppermint creams

⏱🔪🔪 45 minutes, then 8 hours or more drying

Makes about 550 g /1¼ lb
1 medium-sized egg white
75 ml /3 fl oz thick cream
5 ml /1 tsp or more peppermint essence
about 550 g /1¼ lb icing sugar, sifted
a few drops of green food colouring
icing sugar, for dusting

1 Whisk the egg white in a bowl. Add the cream and peppermint essence. Mix well.
2 Gradually add the icing sugar, mixing until the paste is smooth and firm enough to handle. Taste and add a drop or two more peppermint essence if you prefer a stronger flavour. Work in enough green food colouring, a drop at a time, to tint the paste pale green. Knead until it is evenly coloured.
3 On a surface well dusted with icing sugar, roll out the paste to a thickness of about 5 mm /¼ in. Stamp it out into shapes using canapé cutters — plain rounds, fluted rounds, half moons, etc.
4 Put the sweets on cooking parchment and allow them to dry for 8 hours, turning once. Place them in paper sweet cases.

● These sweets will keep for up to 3 weeks in an airtight container.

Butterscotch

🔪🔪 30 minutes, plus cooling and wrapping

Makes about 350 g /12 oz
butter, for greasing
225 g /8 oz soft light brown sugar
30 ml /2 tbls golden syrup
2.5 ml /½ tsp salt
40 g /1½ oz butter
4 drops of vanilla essence

1 Grease a rectangular 20 × 15 cm /8 × 6 in tin or heatproof dish with butter.
2 In a heavy-based saucepan, combine the sugar, the golden syrup and the salt with 150 ml /5 fl oz water. Stir over a low heat until the sugar is dissolved.
3 When the sugar is completely dissolved, boil the syrup until it reaches 145C /290F on a sugar thermometer. Beat in the butter and remove the pan from the heat. Stir in the vanilla essence.
4 Pour the hot butterscotch mixture into the prepared tin or dish. Cool slightly, then mark it into squares with a sharp knife.
5 Allow the butterscotch to become quite cold and hard. Ease the slab out of the tin and break the butterscotch into neat squares.
6 Wrap each piece of butterscotch in a small piece of greaseproof paper and then gift-wrap in Cellophane.

● The only danger to guard against when making these sweets is crystallizing the syrup. To avoid this, use a damp pastry brush to brush back into the liquid any sugar crystals that begin to form on the sides of the saucepan. Any granules left will cause the syrup to turn cloudy and no amount of reboiling will make it clear again.

Butterscotch

Chocolate hazelnut truffles

⏱🔪🔪 15 minutes, 12–24 hours resting, then 30 minutes, plus packing

Makes about 40 truffles
225 g /8 oz unsweetened chocolate, coarsely grated
175 g /6 oz butter
60 ml /4 tbls thick cream
125 g /4 oz icing sugar, sifted
60 ml /4 tbls very finely chopped hazelnuts
To coat
175 g /6 oz chocolate vermicelli
120 ml /8 tbls cinnamon-flavoured cocoa
175 g /6 oz chopped hazelnuts
120 ml /8 tbls cocoa-flavoured powdered coffee

1 In a small saucepan combine the coarsely grated chocolate with the butter. Heat gently, stirring until melted, then remove from the heat and stir in the cream.
2 Gradually stir in the sifted icing sugar and very finely chopped hazelnuts. Stir until the mixture is free of lumps, then cover the saucepan and allow the mixture to rest in a cool, not cold, place for 12–24 hours.
3 Using a melon baller or your hands, make small balls of the chocolate mixture, about 15 mm /½ in in diameter. Finish each ball with your hands, so that the warmth of your hands causes the chocolate to melt slightly, allowing the final coating to adhere.
4 Roll each ball in one of the 4 coating ingredients to cover it evenly.
5 To pack, put each truffle in a paper sweet case and pack in small boxes. Keep them refrigerated until 2 hours before serving.

Festive Occasions

NEW YEAR'S EVE

Christmas is over but the celebrations continue, particularly in Scotland, with New Year's Eve festive fare. As an added bonus these unusual recipes will be welcomed at any time of the year.

New Year's Day has, at various times through the centuries, been commemorated on September 21st, December 21st, January 13th and March 25th; the last date was the one when the English celebrated their New Year from medieval times until 1752. The jollifications themselves have changed little over the years, however, particularly in Scotland and in some other parts of Europe, where these festivities overshadow even those of Christmas Day.

There are few who have not heard of haggis, perhaps the most traditional of dishes eaten at Hogmanay. It is also the centrepiece of the Burns's Night dinner (January 25th) when the haggis is 'addressed' with the poem that Robert Burns wrote in its honour. Yet there are few people outside Scotland who have eaten haggis — which is a large round sausage made of oatmeal and deer or sheep's liver. At Hogmanay, the haggis is usually brought in just after midnight as a 'gift to the New Year', accompanied by a kilted High-lander playing the bagpipes. It is then served with mashed swede and small glasses of neat whisky.

Since haggis never really tastes the same outside Scotland and is really best left to those expert at making it, it is probably better just to welcome the New Year with the bagpipes and the whisky — preferably malt whisky — while serving other traditional Scottish dishes for your party menu. Pink butter (see recipe) is a delicate and delicious combination of prawns and pounded smoked haddock — a tribute to the Scots' versatility of being able to produce a gourmet delicacy from simple ingredients. Where shrimps are unavailable, 'ham 'n' haddie' is another unusual combination which is equally delicious. Poached smoked haddock is coarsely flaked, then gently fried in butter with chunks of ham, then a little cream is poured on top and the dish browned under the grill. It is served, heaped upon pieces of fried bread with plenty of freshly ground black pepper.

Beef and venison, both home-produced, are popular as main courses. In years gone by, for a really big party in Scotland, a side of beef and a whole deer would be spit-roasted; and in some villages, particularly in the north of Scotland, the whole community would gather together round the fire — with much singing, dancing and drinking — while the meat was cooking.

Beef fillet with Scotch sauce

Fillet of beef with Scotch sauce (see recipe) is equally good hot or cold, and so is roast venison if served with cranberry sauce. In the remoter islands where beef or venison are more difficult to come by, salted roast duck or goose is the traditional dish and the vegetable accompaniment is always the same — Skirlie mirlie, which is a deliciously buttery combination of mashed turnips and floury potatoes.

On New Year's Day, perhaps to help modify the effects of those drams of whisky the night before, Black bun (see recipe) makes its appearance. A rich dark fruit cake baked in a huff paste, it was once served as a Twelfth Night cake. Through the centuries the serving of Black bun has been brought forward to help the New Year in, and often Black bun is made on New Year's Day to serve on New Year's Day the following year.

Pink butter

1½ hours,
then 4–5 hours chilling

Serves 12
700 g /1½ lb cooked unpeeled prawns
500 g /18 oz skinned filleted smoked haddock
6 anchovy fillets, mashed
2.5 ml /½ tsp freshly grated nutmeg
1.5 ml /¼ tsp cayenne pepper
2.5 ml /½ tsp lemon juice
15 ml /1 tbls tomato purée
175 g /6 oz butter
50 g /2 oz clarified butter
To serve
toast fingers
melted butter
finely chopped fresh parsley

1 Shell the prawns and put the shells into a large shallow pan with just enough water to cover them (about 700 ml /1¼ pt). Bring it to the boil, then simmer for 20 minutes.
2 Meanwhile, chop the prawns finely and reserve them.
3 Drain the prawn shells and return the water to the pan along with the smoked haddock. Bring to the boil again and simmer very gently for 20 minutes.
4 Remove the haddock from the pan with a slotted spoon. Strain the stock, reserve 45 ml / 3 tbls and keep the rest for soup. Put the haddock into a large bowl with the reserved stock and mash to a fine paste with the anchovy fillets, nutmeg, cayenne pepper, lemon juice and tomato purée.
5 Beat in the butter, mixing it to a smooth cream, and then add the prawns, stirring well to distribute them evenly. Put the mixture into a saucepan and heat it very gently for 5 minutes, stirring carefully to mix it, but not to cook it.
6 Press the mixture into a soufflé dish 18 cm /7 in in diameter and let it cool.
7 Melt the clarified butter gently and then pour it over the fish mixture. Refrigerate for several hours.
8 To serve, dip the toast fingers into melted butter to a depth of 25 mm /1 in, then dip the buttered ends into finely chopped parsley. Arrange them on a serving platter around the potted fish.

slices and serve immediately with the sauce handed separately.

9 If serving the beef cold, let the meat cool, cover it with foil and leave it until it is completely cold. Just before serving, carve it into slices about 15 mm /½ in thick. Arrange them on a serving platter in a circular pattern and serve with the sauce which should be heated to just below boiling point.

Black bun

 2½–3 hours

Serves 12
225 g /8 oz flour, plus extra for dusting
125 g /4 oz butter
2.5 ml /½ tsp baking powder
1 small egg, beaten
For the filling
125 g /4 oz flour
1.5 ml /¼ tsp salt
2.5 ml /½ tsp freshly grated nutmeg
2.5 ml /½ tsp mixed spice
5 ml /1 tsp ground cinnamon
10 ml /2 tsp ground allspice
5 ml /1 tsp ground ginger
1.5 ml /¼ tsp freshly ground black pepper
125 g /4 oz soft dark brown sugar
225 g /8 oz sultanas
350 g /12 oz raisins
50 g /2 oz almonds, freshly ground
freshly grated zest of 1 lemon
1 egg, beaten
90 ml /6 tbls whisky
30 ml /2 tbls black treacle

1 Prepare the tin. Rub the flour and butter together till they resemble fine breadcrumbs; stir in the baking powder. Mix to a paste with about 60 ml /4 tbls cold water.
2 Flour a board and a rolling pin and thinly roll out the pastry. Cut off one-third and use the rest to line a 1.7 L /3 pt loaf tin. Keep the remaining pastry for the lid.
3 Sift the flour, salt and spices together into a large bowl, then add the sugar, sultanas, raisins, ground almonds, lemon zest and stir well.
4 Bind the mixture with the beaten egg, whisky and black treacle and stir for 4–5 minutes to make sure everything is evenly mixed. Heat the oven to 150C /300F /gas 2.
5 Spoon the mixture into the casing, pushing it down and smoothing the top.
6 Brush the edges of the pastry with a little cold water and press on the lid, pushing down firmly to seal it well. Brush the top with the beaten egg, prick it all over with a fork and make 4 holes with a skewer right down to the bottom of the mixture.
7 Bake in the centre of the top shelf of the oven for 2–2½ hours until a skewer inserted into the centre comes out clean. Cover the top with foil, if necessary, after 1 hour to prevent the pastry burning.
8 Remove the cake from the oven and cool it for 5 minutes, then turn it out of the tin very carefully onto a flat plate or a board and let it cool completely. Store the bun for at least 2 weeks which will give it time for the flavour to mature. However, it will keep well in an airtight tin for up to 1 year.

Beef fillet with Scotch sauce

 1½–2 hours

Serves 12
2.3 kg /5 lb fillet of beef, all fat removed
1.5 ml /¼ tsp ground coriander
2.5 ml /½ tsp freshly ground black pepper
50 g /2 oz melted butter
juice of 2 medium-sized oranges
a parsley sprig, to garnish
orange slices, to garnish
For the sauce
3 large onions, chopped
40 g /1½ oz butter
15 g /1 tbls flour
5 ml /1 tsp strong Dijon mustard
275 ml /10 fl oz beef consommé
30 ml /2 tbls Scotch whisky
salt and freshly ground black pepper

1 Heat the oven to 230C /450F /gas 8.
2 Mix together the coriander and pepper and rub it over the beef. Tie the thin end of the fillet underneath so that the meat is all one thickness. Put it in a roasting pan.

Black bun

3 Brush the meat with the melted butter, turning it over and brushing underneath, then cook for 17–22 minutes per kg /8–10 minutes per lb for very rare meat, 30 minutes per kg /14 minutes per lb for medium rare and 46–48 minutes per kg /21–22 minutes per lb for well done meat, basting every 20 minutes. Add the orange juice after the first basting.
4 Meanwhile, put the chopped onions into a heavy-bottomed saucepan with the butter over a gentle heat and stir until the butter has melted. Cook until the onions are very soft and a golden colour — they must not be browned at all.
5 Stir in the flour and cook for 4–5 minutes, then stir in the mustard, mixing it in well.
6 Gradually add the consommé, stirring constantly, and then add the whisky. Simmer the mixture for 20 minutes, covered and stirring occasionally.
7 When the meat is cooked, transfer it to a warmed serving platter (if serving hot). Skim the fat off the pan juices, then add them to the sauce. Taste and season with salt and pepper as necessary.
8 If serving the beef hot, carve it into thin

CHINESE NEW YEAR

Chinese New Year is the time to enjoy some of the most delightful and delicious Chinese recipes. Try all of these traditional recipes and get the New Year off to an unusual start.

Around the world, the Chinese celebrate their New Year with great enthusiasm. The celebrations traditionally last from two to four weeks, with festivals, fireworks, dragon parades and feasts of even more delicious food than usual. The Chinese believe that the more dishes of rich food a person eats, the greater number of blessings he or she will receive from Heaven. As New Year is their most important festival, it is a time when large groups of family and friends gather together to mark the festivities with banquets and communal meals.

The Chinese calendar is based on a cycle of twelve lunar months rather than the solar months of the Western calendar. The years are named for twelve symbolic animals: the rat, the ox, the tiger, the hare, the dragon, the snake, the horse, the sheep, the monkey, the cock, the dog and the pig; so there is the Year of the pig, the Year of the rat, the Year of the snake and so on.

The Chinese New Year always falls during January or February and this is guaranteed because every few years in the Chinese calendar there is a 'leap month' when a whole month is repeated and then the Chinese year catches up with the Western year.

While there is no direct equivalent to the Western Christmas turkey dinner, special emphasis is attached to certain foods and dishes during the New Year celebrations. There are also certain everyday dishes which take on a special significance when they are served during the New Year's festivities. Eggs symbolize sons, and dishes such as Tea eggs (see recipe) therefore represent family strength and prosperity. Because chicken represents that mythical bird, the phoenix (which is the Chinese symbol of imperial majesty or royalty), chicken is preferred for banqueting and entertaining rather than the more usual pork dishes. Soy-glazed chicken (see recipe), which contains the haunting flavour of star anise, is especially suitable, as the glaze is red and red is a lucky, jubilant colour for the Chinese.

New Year food in northern and southern China differs somewhat. Filled dumplings are especially popular in the north. These usually contain fish, meat or vegetables and are then boiled, steamed or fried. Two of the most famous ones are included in this chapter, Sautéed northern dumplings (see recipe) and Shanghai sweet dumplings (see recipe). Northern families get together to make such dumplings, which are served with tea or rice wine. Another New Year's speciality is Peking's Silver thread buns, its name being a figurative description of the bun's centre.

Eight treasure rice pudding is a northern New Year's speciality. Made of glutinous rice, it sticks together and thus symbolizes a family staying together. The eight ingredients used in the pudding also symbolize the eight Buddhist treasures or blessings of this life.

Southerners eat less heartily, but they do enjoy a greater variety of New Year's fare. Many of their dishes are deep-fried titbits such as thinly sliced taro, yam or sweet potatoes, with salt sprinkled over them. These are served with tea or drinks. There is also a delicious sweet deep-fried dumpling made of glutinous rice flour, stuffed with red bean paste, coconut and sesame.

The Chinese make sweets almost as often as they buy them and during the New Year celebrations this is no exception. Chinese families spend several hours making their version of *nin go*, which can be translated as 'getting taller every year.' This is made of glutinous rice flour and of sugar and is very hard until it has been steamed or deep-fried. Then it expands, hence its name, and as it becomes much softer it also becomes extremely sticky.

Tea eggs

When shelled these aromatic eggs appear crazed, like old Chinese porcelain.

 2¼ hours

Serves 6
30 ml /2 tbls tea leaves, either Oolong,
Keemun, Orange Pekoe or Iron Goddess
of Mercy
12 small eggs
spring onion flower, to garnish
For the sauce
30 ml /2 tbls thick soy sauce
4 ml /¾ tsp salt
7.5 ml /1½ tsp sugar (optional)
15 ml /1 tbls medium-dry sherry
1 whole or 8 segments of star anise
25 mm /1 in cinnamon stick

1 Boil the tea leaves in 275 ml /10 fl oz water for 5 minutes. Strain the tea, discard the leaves and reserve the liquid.
2 Wash the eggs carefully. Pierce each one on its rounded end with a pin, to prevent it cracking.
3 Put the eggs into a large saucepan, cover them with plenty of cold water, then gently bring them to the boil and continue to boil them gently for 10 minutes.
4 Drain the eggs, then submerge them in cold running water for 5 minutes.

5 Gently crack the egg shells by tapping them with the back of a spoon or by rolling the eggs on a flat surface.
6 Put the sauce ingredients and the eggs into a large saucepan. Pour in the tea and add water to cover the eggs. Bring them to the boil, then simmer, covered, for 1½ hours.
7 Check the sauce occasionally and, if necessary, add more water. There should be about 150 ml /5 fl oz of sauce left at the end.
8 Remove the eggs. Do not shell them until you are ready to serve them, then garnish and accompany them with the remaining sauce.

● These eggs will keep in a covered container in the refrigerator for up to 2 weeks.

Soy-glazed chicken

 1¼ hours

Serves 6
2 whole or 16 segments of star anise
5 ml /1 tsp Szechuan peppercorns
45–60 ml /3–4 tbls corn or vegetable oil
6 large garlic cloves, peeled and bruised
6 chicken drumsticks
6 chicken wings
225 ml /8 fl oz thick soy sauce
75 ml /5 tbls soft brown sugar
30 ml /2 tbls Shaohsing wine or medium-dry
sherry
boiled rice, to serve

1 Put the star anise and the peppercorns in a small saucepan. Add about 350 ml /12 fl oz water; bring it to the boil. Reduce the heat and simmer for 15 minutes or until it has been reduced by one half. Strain and reserve the liquid.
2 Heat a wok over a high heat until very hot. Add 30 ml /2 tbls of the oil and swirl it around. Add 3 of the garlic cloves. When they sizzle and begin to colour, add the drumsticks and brown them for about 2 minutes, turning occasionally. Transfer them to a plate and reserve. Discard the garlic.
3 Add the remaining oil to the wok, swirl it around and then add the remaining garlic. Put in the chicken wings and brown them for 1 minute per side. Transfer them to the plate, and discard the garlic.
4 Lower the heat. Pour the spiced liquid into the wok, then add the soy sauce, sugar and wine or sherry. Bring the mixture slowly to the boil, stirring.
5 Return the drumsticks and wings to the wok and gradually bring the liquid to the boil. Spoon the hot sauce mixture over the chicken pieces for about 10 minutes.
6 Cover the wok and simmer for about 25 minutes or until the meat is cooked, turning the pieces over halfway through. Transfer the chicken pieces to a warm serving platter. Serve hot, accompanied by the remaining sauce and boiled rice.

Tea eggs, Shanghai sweet dumplings and
Soy-glazed chicken with boiled rice

Shanghai sweet dumplings

▐▐▐ 1 hour,
plus 10 minutes sautéeing (optional)

Makes 32 dumplings
225 g /8 oz canned red bean paste
225 /8 oz glutinous rice flour
corn or vegetable oil (optional)

1 Roll about 5 ml /1 tsp of the red bean paste between your palms until it is a ball slightly bigger than a marble. Repeat until all the bean paste is used.
2 Gradually stir 225 ml /8 fl oz cold water into the flour and work it into a smooth dough. There is no neccessity to knead.
3 Take a small piece of dough about the size of a chestnut and shape it into a round. Press a thumb into the round and insert a bean paste ball. Work the dough over the bean paste completely. Roll the dumpling between the palms to make it round and put it on a plate. Repeat until all the dough and bean paste have been used.
4 Bring 1.4 L /2½ pt of water to the boil in a large saucepan. Add about half of the dumplings, one by one, and let the water come back to the boil. Move the dumplings once or twice with a wooden spoon to prevent them from sticking to the pan.
5 Reduce the heat but continue to boil until the dough looks transparent.
6 Lift out the dumplings with a slotted spoon, drain them, and put them onto a

How to use chopsticks

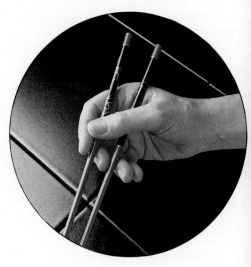

Hold one chopstick between your thumb and index finger and against your 3rd and 4th fingers. This chopstick supports the food.

Put the second chopstick against your index finger and support it with your thumb as though it were a pencil.

warmed serving plate. Cook the rest of the dumplings in the same way, draining and putting them on the serving plate.
7 Serve hot as they are or, if wished, when they are drained, fry them in a little oil over medium low heat, gently stirring, until they begin to brown; this gives the usually sticky dumplings a crisp outside.

Sautéed halibut

Sautéed halibut

▐▐ 45 minutes

Serves 4–6 with 3 or 4 other dishes
2×20 mm /¾ in thick halibut steaks (about 600 g /1¼ lb)
4 ml /¾ tsp salt
about 30 ml /2 tbls cornflour
75–90 ml /5–6 tbls corn or vegetable oil
2 slices of fresh root ginger, peeled
1 garlic clove, peeled and finely chopped
15 mm /½ in fresh root ginger, peeled and finely chopped
3 spring onions, cut across into small rounds
15 ml /1 tbls Shaohsing wine or medium-dry sherry
For the sauce
10 ml /2 tsp Worcestershire sauce
25 ml /1½ tbls thin soy sauce
1.5–2.5 ml /¼–½ tsp sugar
2.5 ml /½ tsp potato flour
75 ml /3 fl oz clear stock or water

1 Blot the steaks dry and rub them with salt on both sides. Using a fine sieve, lightly dust the cornflour over both sides of the fish.
2 Heat a wok over a high heat until it is very hot. Add 30 ml /2 tbls of oil, swirl it around and continue to heat it until the oil smokes. Add the ginger slices, let them brown, then discard them.
3 Add the fish steaks and shallow-fry them for about 3 minutes. Carefully slip a wok scoop or a metal spatula underneath and turn the steaks over to fry the other side for 3 minutes. Cook the fish on both sides again, lower the heat if necessary and add another 15 ml /1 tbls of oil if the fish looks dry. Cook until both sides are crisply browned but not burned. Transfer them to a warm serving plate and keep warm.
4 Discard the oil in the wok, then clean and dry it. In a small bowl, mix together the sauce ingredients and reserve.

5 Reheat the wok until it is very hot. Add the remaining oil, swirl it around, add the garlic, let it sizzle, then add the chopped ginger and spring onion rounds. Stir rapidly. Splash in the wine or the sherry. When the sizzling subsides, lower the heat.
6 Stir the sauce mixture, then pour it into the wok. Stir continuously until the liquid thickens, then pour it over the fish and serve, piping hot, immediately.

Sautéed northern dumplings

 3½ hours

Makes about 50 dumplings
275 g /10 oz flour
150 ml /5 fl oz boiling water
flour, for rolling
For the filling
30 ml /2 tbls dried shrimps, rinsed
5 ml /1 tsp Shaohsing wine or medium-dry sherry
275 g /10 oz Chinese cabbage
5 ml /1 tsp salt
225 g /8 oz boned pork loin with a little fat left on
6 spring onions, cut across into small rounds
30 ml /2 tbls sesame oil
For the marinade
4 ml /¾ tsp salt
10 ml /2 tsp thin soy sauce
a pinch of freshly ground black pepper
5 ml /1 tsp Shaohsing wine or medium-dry sherry
25 ml /1½ tbls corn or vegetable oil
For sautéeing
30 ml /2 tbls corn or vegetable oil
5 ml /1 tsp rice wine or white wine vinegar mixed with 10 ml /2 tsp corn or vegetable oil and 125 ml /4 fl oz hot water
20 ml /4 tsp flour blended with 125 ml /4 fl oz cold water

1 First prepare the dough by sifting the flour into a large bowl. Stirring with a pair of chopsticks or a wooden spoon, pour the boiling water gradually into the flour. Using one hand, work the flour and water together. Add 15 ml /1 tbls cold water and knead lightly for 1–2 minutes until it becomes a smooth dough. Do not overknead, the dough should be firm and pliable but not dry.
2 Cover the bowl with a dry towel and leave it in a cool room for at least 30 minutes.
3 Prepare the filling. Soak the shrimps in enough boiling water to cover them for 15–20 minutes. Drain them, reserving the soaking liquid. Chop the shrimps, place them in a bowl, add the wine or sherry, stir and reserve.
4 Discard any wilted or tough outer cabbage leaves. Cut out the hard core and shred the cabbage across as thinly as possible. Chop the shredded cabbage.
5 Put the cabbage into a bowl, mix in the salt and set it aside for about 30 minutes.
6 Meanwhile, finely chop the pork and put it into a large bowl.
7 Prepare the marinade by mixing together

the salt, soy sauce, pepper, wine or sherry and oil and then add it to the pork. Add 25 ml /1½ tbls of the reserved shrimp liquid and stir vigorously for 1 minute. Mix in the onion rounds and shrimps.
8 Squeeze out the excess water from the cabbage, a handful at a time, but leave it damp. Add the cabbage to the pork mixture. Stir in the sesame oil very thoroughly and refrigerate the mixture until the dumplings are ready to be filled.
9 Divide the dough in two pieces. Keep 1 piece covered with a cloth in the refrigerator. On a lightly floured surface, roll out the other piece into a long cylindrical roll, about 20 mm /¾ in in diameter. Cut the roll across into pieces each about 15 mm /½ in long and gently shape them into rounds.
10 Taking one piece of dough, flatten it gently with the base of your palm. Put the piece of flattened dough on a lightly floured surface and dust it with flour.
11 Roll out the flattened dough into a circle about 7.5 cm /3 in in diameter, with the centre slightly thicker than the edges. To do this, put the centre of the flattened dough between the thumb and the index and middle fingers of one hand. Rotate the dough in an anti-clockwise direction while, with the rolling pin in the other hand, gently roll down from the edge of the dough towards the centre.
12 Repeat until all the unrefrigerated dough is formed into rounds.
13 To wrap a dumpling with traditional decorative pleats, turn each round of dough, one at a time, over on its floured side and lift up the half of the dough farthest from you. Fold this into 6 straight pleats, each pleat

Sautéed northern dumplings

about 10 mm /⅓ in deep, forming a little pouch in the round.
14 Put about 10 ml /2 tsp of the filling into each pouch. Lift up the unpleated edge of the dough and pinch the 2 halves together to seal, making a crescent. Repeat until all the dumplings are formed.
15 Make more dumplings in the same way from the refrigerated batch of dough. The dumplings can be packed in an airtight container and frozen at this point, if wished. They will need to be defrosted before cooking.
16 Heat a heavy 20–25 cm /8–10 in frying-pan with a lid over a medium heat for 30 seconds or until hot. Add the oil and swirl it to cover the entire surface of the pan. Lower the heat and put in 12–15 dumplings, pleated-sides up and just touching. Cover the pan and cook for 5 minutes.
17 Pour the rice wine or vinegar mixture carefully into the pan, cover and continue to cook over a higher heat for about 7 minutes. The liquid should be absorbed by then and the bottoms of the dumplings should have become golden.
18 Pour ¼ of the flour and water mixture into the pan. Cover and cook for 1–2 minutes. The flour forms a crisp film linking the dumplings.
19 With a fish slice or metal spatula, remove as many dumplings as possible in a row and turn them over, brown side up, onto a warm serving plate. Serve these immediately while you continue cooking the other dumplings, or keep them all warm until you finish cooking the rest.

MOTHER'S DAY

A carefully prepared breakfast, beautifully arranged, is an excellent way of showing Mother how much she is appreciated. So make the most of this occasion — and breakfasts in general — with my tips and tantalizing recipes.

Begin this very special day with a treat for Mother: a splendid breakfast-on-a-tray which she is sure to appreciate.

The menu I have chosen is quick and simple to prepare: citrus-based Fresh fruit salad is a refreshing start, followed by Shirred eggs with crisp bacon garnished with a distinctive green pepper ring. Tangy Orange breakfast popovers, served hot with maple syrup or honey, are a little out of the ordinary — perfect for this occasion (the quantity I give will make enough for all the family, so no one need miss out!) It's a convenient dish to make as the batter can be prepared the night before and refrigerated; but do remember that on the day the popovers will need 30 minutes in the oven. Fresh coffee or tea completes this lovely menu.

There are other equally delicious alternatives for a special Mother's Day breakfast, and I give you recipes for some of them in this chapter. Fresh fruit and meat dishes, such as Cold ham and spiced peaches, and Ham and fruit breakfast appetizer, lend an exotic touch to your meal. If omelettes are your choice, why not try something different? Flat omelette of artichoke hearts, sprinkled with grated Parmesan and Gruyère cheese and then grilled, is ideal. For something sweeter, try my Raisin Brioches, served warm with preserves.

Whatever you choose, your carefully prepared Mother's Day breakfast will set a happy tone for the rest of the day.

Late breakfasts

In general, breakfasts are often hurried affairs with no time for the trimmings. But when the pace is more leisurely — at the weekend or during the holidays — then it is fun to relax and enjoy a late breakfast or brunch. This style of meal is a particularly good idea if you have guests staying. When you are planning a big dinner for the evening, a brunch (combining breakfast and lunch) is just the thing to sustain guests or family through the day, and it means that you are not permanently working in the kitchen. The traditional English breakfast of cereals, eggs, grilled meats or fish and toast is the

Fresh fruit salad, Orange breakfast popovers and Shirred eggs with crisp bacon

perfect menu here, and you can make your own imaginative variations.

Don't make life difficult for yourself by spending a long time in the kitchen before breakfast preparing complicated dishes. Instead, choose a selection of food, some of which is quick and easy to prepare and some of which can be cooked ahead and reheated at the last moment. If you have the energy, lay the table the night before.

Breakfast drinks

Jugs of lightly chilled fruit juice are a most welcome sight on the table: grapefruit, orange, tomato and apple juice are always popular. Mixed fruit juices also taste good — try orange and pineapple or grapefruit and pineapple. For special occasions, mix orange juice in equal quantities with sparkling dry white wine or champagne to make Bucks Fizz. You might like to offer both tea and freshly made coffee — the inviting aroma will entice even the laziest people out of bed!

Cereals

Muesli is one of the most nutritious of the cold breakfast starters. Basically consisting of one or more cereals, fruit, nuts and usually some sweetening, muesli can be varied to suit your family's taste. Try varying the ingredients, choosing from the following:
● Cereals: rolled oats or oatflakes and wheat flakes make the base of a muesli, with added wheatgerm or bran.
● Fruit: dried chopped apricots, prunes, chopped dates, sultanas or raisins can be mixed with fresh orange slices, apples and pears sliced and dipped in lemon juice, grapes or sliced bananas.
● Nuts: try chopped walnuts, hazelnuts or almonds.
● Sweetening: you may prefer to eat your muesli without sugar, but for those with a sweet tooth, offer brown sugar or honey.

Serve your muesli either with milk, thin cream, natural yoghurt or, if you prefer, evaporated milk. Natural yoghurt mixed with low-fat soft cheese or sieved curd cheese turns muesli into an even more substantial, energy-giving dish.

Porridge is the perfect starter for those with hearty appetites. The traditional Scottish way of serving porridge is with salt. These days, however, it is often served with brown sugar or honey and perhaps a little ground cinnamon or mixed spice. Add chopped nuts to give it 'crunch', or fresh, puréed or stewed fruit. Top it with cream or yoghurt.

The main course

If the family are not used to cooking breakfast, suggest that they grill the bacon, sausages and tomatoes first, keep them hot in the oven and then prepare the eggs. Poached eggs can be cooked and then kept in a bowl of warm, not hot, water for a short while, but fried or scrambled eggs need serving immediately as they quickly become rubbery.

Tasty fillers

Toast, fresh rolls and Breakfast oatcakes (see recipe) are really good served with butter and traditional English marmalade, home-made jam, lemon curd or honey.

Fresh fruit salad

10–15 minutes, plus chilling

Serves 1
2 small oranges
1 medium-sized grapefruit
1 small banana
½ small red dessert apple
a small cluster of green grapes
sprig of mint
½ lemon
caster sugar, to serve (optional)

1 Extract the juice from 1 orange and place the juice in a serving bowl. Peel the second orange and divide the flesh into segments, removing the membranes and pips. Add the orange segments to the bowl.
2 Halve the grapefruit from top to bottom. Peel one half and divide the flesh into segments, removing the membranes and pips. Squeeze the juice from the other half. Add the segments and juice to the bowl.
3 Slice the banana. Quarter and core the apple, then cut each quarter across into slices. Add these to the bowl and mix well.
4 Place the grapes on top, with the sprig of mint. Squeeze the juice of ½ lemon over the fruit salad. Chill until required.
5 Serve the fresh fruit salad chilled, accompanied by caster sugar if wished.

Shirred eggs with crisp bacon

10 minutes

Serves 1
3 slices streaky bacon
3 eggs
salt and freshly ground black pepper
15 ml /1 tbls thick cream or water
15 g /½ oz butter
15 ml /1 tbls grated Gruyère cheese
1 thinly sliced green pepper ring

1 Heat the grill to high. Grill the bacon slices until they are crisp, then drain them on absorbent paper.
2 Meanwhile, break the eggs into a bowl. Add salt and freshly ground black pepper and stir well with a fork until the yolks and whites are thoroughly mixed. Stir in the thick cream or water.
3 Select a heavy frying-pan or saucepan. Add the butter and heat it until it is sizzling but not coloured, then swirl the butter around so that the bottom and sides of the pan are well coated with it.
4 Pour in all the egg at once; set the pan over a low heat and start stirring immediately with a large wooden spoon. Keep stirring, making sure that the spoon reaches every part of the saucepan and keeping the whole mass of liquid egg on the move, until the eggs are creamy and almost ready.
5 Remove the pan from the heat and stir in the grated cheese. Adjust the seasoning. Spoon the mixture onto a hot plate.

6 Place the green pepper ring on top of the egg. Cut the crisply grilled bacon into thin strips and arrange them attractively inside the green pepper ring. Serve immediately.

Orange breakfast popovers

45 minutes

Makes 12
2 eggs
1 egg yolk
125 ml /4 fl oz milk
125 ml /4 fl oz orange juice (1 large orange)
15 ml /1 tbls melted butter
125 g /4 oz flour
1.5 ml /¼ tsp salt
grated zest of 1 orange
vegetable oil, for greasing
maple syrup or honey, to serve

1 Heat the oven to 230C /450F /gas 8.
2 In a large bowl, beat the whole eggs with the egg yolk. Blend in the milk, orange juice and melted butter.
3 Sift in the flour and salt and beat well until smooth. Strain the mixture into a jug and stir in the orange zest, then chill in the refrigerator for 5 minutes or until required.
4 Meanwhile, lightly oil a 12-bun tray and place it in the oven for 2–3 minutes to heat the oil. Remove it from the oven.
5 Three-quarters fill the hollows of the tin with the batter mixture. Bake in the oven for 15 minutes, then reduce the oven temperature to 200C /400F /gas 6 and bake the popovers for a further 15 minutes, or until they are crisp and well risen.
6 Serve the popovers hot, with maple syrup or honey.

Cold ham and spiced peaches

Cold ham and spiced peaches

25 minutes, plus cooling

Serves 2
2 firm ripe peaches
300 ml /10 fl oz dry white wine
30 ml /2 tbls white wine vinegar
1.5 ml /¼ tsp ground cinnamon
12 black peppercorns
6 cloves
60 ml /4 tbls sugar
2 thin slices of cooked ham

1 Put the peaches in a bowl, pour boiling water over them to cover and leave them for 30 seconds. Drain the peaches, then carefully peel off the skins. Halve them and remove the stones.
2 In a saucepan, combine the dry white wine, white wine vinegar, cinnamon, peppercorns, cloves and sugar. Heat gently, stirring until the sugar has dissolved completely. Bring to the boil, then reduce the heat so that the syrup simmers.
3 Add the halved peaches to the pan (they should be just covered by the syrup — if they are not, add a little more dry white wine). Simmer for 10–12 minutes, or until the peaches are tender but not soft. Remove the pan from the heat and allow the peaches to cool in the syrup.
4 Remove the cold peach halves from the syrup and drain them on absorbent paper. Slice them carefully.
5 To serve, roll up the ham slices and arrange each roll on an individual plate. Garnish with the sliced, spiced peaches.

Flat omelette of artichoke hearts

 20–25 minutes

Serves 1
15 ml /1 tbls olive oil
30 ml /2 tbls finely chopped onion
½ small garlic clove, finely chopped (optional)
2–3 canned artichoke hearts, drained and
*   thinly sliced*
3 eggs
salt and freshly ground black pepper
15 ml /1 tbls grated fresh Parmesan cheese
45 ml /3 tbls grated Gruyère cheese
flat-leaved parsley, to garnish

1 Heat the grill to high.
2 Heat the olive oil in a heavy 15 cm /6 in omelette pan. Add the finely chopped onion and garlic, if using, and sauté for 8–10 minutes until soft and translucent but not coloured.
3 Add the thinly sliced artichoke hearts and sauté them gently until they are heated through.
4 Break the eggs into a bowl and add 15 ml /1 tbls water, salt and freshly ground black pepper to taste. Stir vigorously with a fork or wire whisk for about 30 seconds.
5 Pour the egg mixture onto the vegetables in the pan and stir quickly for a second or two. As the egg starts to set, lift the edge in several places and tilt the pan so that the liquid egg runs underneath. Keep shaking the pan to prevent the omelette from sticking.
6 When the underneath of the omelette is set but the top is still very creamy, remove the pan from the heat. Sprinkle the grated Parmesan and Gruyère cheeses over it and place under the hot grill for 2 minutes, until the omelette is set on top and the cheese is browned. Serve immediately, garnished with flat-leaved parsley.

Raisin brioches

 about 1 hour, plus rising and overnight chilling

Makes 12
175 g /6 oz seedless raisins
350 g /12 oz strong flour
15 g /½ oz fresh yeast
350 g /12 oz strong flour
22.5 ml /1½ tbls sugar
2.5 ml /½ tsp ground cinnamon
2.5 ml /½ tsp salt
3 eggs, lightly beaten
100 g /4 oz butter
flour, for kneading
melted butter, for greasing
1 egg yolk, beaten with 10 ml /2 tsp
*   water, to glaze*
preserves, to serve

1 In a bowl, cover the raisins with boiling water and leave them to soak until they are well plumped up. Drain them and dry them thoroughly with absorbent paper and then

toss well in 15 ml /1 tbls of the strong flour.
2 In a medium-sized bowl, cream the fresh yeast with 60 ml /4 tbls lukewarm water. Sift in 65 g /2½ oz flour and mix well. Cover the bowl with cling film and leave the mixture to rise until it has doubled in bulk — about 20 minutes.
3 Sift the remaining flour into a large bowl with the sugar, cinnamon and salt. Make a well in the centre, add the yeast mixture and the beaten eggs and gradually incorporate them into the flour, beating vigorously with one hand.
4 Soften the butter to the point of melting. When the dough is smooth, add the butter and the floured raisins and beat by hand until they are thoroughly incorporated. The dough should be soft and shiny.
5 Cover the bowl with cling film and leave the dough in a warm place to rise until it has doubled in bulk — about 1½ hours. Place in the refrigerator to chill overnight.
6 When you are ready to start to shape the brioches, thoroughly grease 12 individual brioche moulds with melted butter. Gather the dough up out of the bowl and place it on a floured surface. With floured hands, knead the dough lightly until it is smooth.
7 Weigh the dough and cut off a quarter. Divide each portion into 12 so that you have

Raisin brioches

12 large pieces and 12 tiny pieces. Form each piece into a ball. Place a large ball in each mould and cut the top in a cross with a sharp knife. Place a smaller ball in the cross. Put the moulds on a baking sheet and cover them loosely with cling film. Leave them in a warm place to rise for 30 minutes, or until they have doubled in bulk. Meanwhile, heat the oven to 200C /400F /gas 6.
8 Brush the brioches lightly with the egg glaze and bake them in the oven for 10 minutes. Reduce the oven temperature to 190C /375F /gas 5 and bake for a further 10 minutes, or until the brioches are well risen and a rich golden brown colour.
9 Remove the baking sheet from the oven and turn the brioches out of their moulds onto a wire rack to cool.
10 Serve the brioches warm, with home-made preserves.

Ham and fruit breakfast appetizer

 10–15 minutes

Serves 1

1 thin slice of Parma ham
1 thin slice of cooked ham
1 small ripe avocado
lemon juice
1 ripe fig
25 g /1 oz wedge of Honeydew melon
1 ripe Comice pear
whole black peppercorns
whole coriander seeds

1 Lay the slice of Parma ham and the slice of cooked ham neatly on a flat plate.
2 Halve, stone and then peel the avocado. Cut off 2 slices. Arrange these opposite each other on the plate and brush them with lemon juice to prevent them from discolouring. Brush the remaining avocado all over with lemon juice, wrap it in cling film and reserve it for use in another recipe.
3 Cut the fig into 6 thin slices and place 3 slices on each avocado slice, filling the holes.
4 Remove the skin from the wedge of melon. Cut lengthways through the centre of the wedge, to three-quarters of the length. Lay the wedge on its side on the plate and open it out slightly.
5 Peel, halve and core the pear. Cut 5 thin neat slices and arrange them together on the melon. Brush them with lemon juice, to stop discoloration.
6 Serve the appetizer with the peppercorns in a pepper mill and the coriander seeds in a spice mill. Alternatively, sprinkle freshly ground pepper and coriander all over the appetizer just before serving.

Stuffed mushrooms

These mushrooms can be filled in advance and baked just before serving.

35 minutes

Serves 4

8 large flat mushrooms
15 g /½ oz butter, plus extra for greasing
1 medium-sized onion, finely chopped
75 g /3 oz smoked, rinded, streaky bacon slices or smoked ham, finely chopped
30 ml /2 tbls fresh brown breadcrumbs
1 medium-sized tomato, blanched, skinned and chopped
30 ml /2 tbls freshly chopped parsley
salt and freshly ground black pepper
30 ml /2 tlbs oil, for baking
parsley sprigs, to garnish

1 Heat the oven to 180C / 350F /gas 4 and lightly butter a large, flat ovenproof dish. Wipe the mushrooms. Remove and chop the stalks.
2 Heat the butter in a frying-pan and fry the onion until it is soft and transparent. Add the chopped bacon or ham and mushroom stalks to the onion and cook them for about 3–4 minutes until they are beginning to colour. Remove them from the heat.
3 Stir in the fresh brown breadcrumbs, the blanched, skinned and chopped tomato and the parsley. Season to taste with salt and

Flat omelette of artichoke hearts

freshly ground black pepper and mix well.
4 Place the mushroom caps, undersides uppermost, on the buttered ovenproof dish and divide the filling among them, spreading it out so that the mushroom caps are completely covered.
5 Pour a little oil over each of the filled mushrooms and bake them for 25 minutes. Serve them immediately, garnished with fresh parsley sprigs.

Devilled kidneys

The 'devil' sauce will mature and improve if it is made in advance.

15 minutes

Serves 4

8 lambs' kidneys
10 ml /2 tsp Worcestershire sauce
15 ml /1 tbls tomato purée
15 ml /1 tbls lemon juice
15 ml /1 tbls French mustard
a pinch of cayenne pepper
salt and freshly ground black pepper
30 ml /2 tbls oil or 25 g /1 oz butter
15 ml /1 tbls finely chopped fresh parsley, to garnish

1 Remove the skin from the kidneys, cut them in half and cut away the cores.
2 Mix together the Worcestershire sauce, tomato purée, lemon juice, mustard, cayenne pepper and salt and freshly ground black pepper to taste, and reserve.
3 Heat the oil or butter in a frying-pan over a moderate heat and then cook the kidneys

for approximately 3 minutes on each side.
4 Pour the devil sauce over the kidneys, then quickly stir them so that they are evenly coated.
5 Garnish with chopped parsley and serve.

Breakfast oatcakes

Oatcakes make a delicious change from toast, served with marmalade, honey or jam. Store them in an airtight container.

40 minutes

Makes about 16

175 g /6 oz medium oatmeal
50 g /2 oz flour
5 ml /1 tsp baking powder
a pinch of salt
5 ml /1 tsp sugar
40 g /1½ oz lard, melted
oatmeal, for sprinkling
lard, for greasing

1 Heat the oven to 180C /350F /gas 4. Put the oatmeal, flour, baking powder, salt and sugar in a mixing bowl. Mix them together, then make a well in the centre.
2 Pour the melted lard into the dry ingredients and mix with a fork. Add sufficient water to make a stiff dough.
3 Sprinkle a board with oatmeal and thinly roll out the dough on this. Next, cut it into circles with a floured 7.5 cm /3 in cutter, or cut it into triangles with a floured knife.
4 Place the shapes on a greased baking sheet and bake for 30 minutes. Leave them to cool on a wire rack. Serve warm or cold.

Kedgeree

Kedgeree is a traditional English breakfast dish — the version I give here is particularly convenient as it can be prepared the day before it is needed and simply reheated just before serving.

45 minutes, then
35 minutes reheating

Serves 4
500 g /1 lb smoked haddock
salt
125 g /4 oz long-grain rice
2 eggs, hard-boiled
30 ml /2 tbls lemon juice
cayenne pepper
freshly grated nutmeg
freshly ground black pepper
150 ml /5 fl oz thin or soured cream
50 g /2 oz butter
30 ml /2 tbls freshly chopped parsley
For the garnish
2–3 slices bread
parsley sprigs

1 Poach the haddock in 600 ml /1 pt salted water for about 15 minutes until it is tender, then skin, bone and roughly flake the fish. Meanwhile, put the rice in a saucepan with twice its volume of water and 5 ml /1 tsp salt. Bring the water to the boil, cover it with a lid and then simmer for about 15 minutes until the rice is tender and the water has been absorbed.

2 Peel and chop the hard-boiled eggs and carefully mix them together with the flaked haddock, rice and lemon juice. Add the cayenne, nutmeg and freshly ground black pepper to taste and stir in the cream. Turn the mixture into a buttered ovenproof dish and dot with butter. Cover it with foil and leave in the refrigerator overnight if wished.

3 Heat the oven to 180C /350F /gas 4. Uncover the kedgeree and bake it for 30 minutes, stirring once.

4 Meanwhile, toast the bread and cut it into triangles.

5 Stir the freshly chopped parsley into the kedgeree, arrange the toast triangles around the edge of the dish and place a few down the centre. Garnish the kedgeree with parsley sprigs and serve immediately.

Scrambled eggs with bacon

Easy-to-prepare, creamy scrambled eggs make a perfect breakfast dish. They must be cooked slowly — a safe way is to cook them in a bowl over a pan of hot water.

20 minutes

Muesli, Breakfast oatcakes, Devilled kidneys and Scrambled eggs with bacon

Serves 4
4 slices back bacon
25 g /1 oz butter
8 eggs
salt and freshly ground black pepper
Worcestershire sauce
60 ml /4 tbls thin cream
buttered toast, to serve

1 Grill the bacon until it is cooked through but not crispy. Drain on absorbent paper, then dice it and keep it warm.

2 Place the butter in a heatproof bowl and place the bowl over a pan of simmering water. When the butter has melted, remove the bowl from the pan and break in the eggs.

3 Season the eggs with salt, pepper and Worcestershire sauce to taste, then stir with a fork to mix well. Stir in the cream and return the bowl to the pan.

4 Stir the eggs with a wooden spoon until they are thick and creamy and almost set. Remove them from the heat immediately, stir in the diced bacon and serve the eggs on buttered toast.

● Replace the bacon with diced continental sausage, or cut continental sausage into strips and arrange them over the scrambled egg.
● Replace the bacon with diced tomatoes or, if you prefer, use green peppers.

PASSOVER

The food prepared throughout this important Jewish celebration has a symbolic meaning. It is also very tasty, so if you haven't tried this kind of cuisine before, let these recipes be your appetizing introduction.

Passover (or *Pesach*, in Hebrew) is the Jewish festival of freedom. It usually occurs in April, and lasts for eight days. It begins, on the eve of the first day, with a meal called a Seder (pronounced Sayder) which celebrates the Exodus of the Jews from Egypt during the rule of the Pharaohs. God had previously sent plagues to the Egyptians, to compel them to release the Israelites from bondage. The name Passover refers to the final plague when God killed the first-born sons of the Egyptians but passed over Jewish homes, thus sparing their children.

No leavened bread or other products made from ordinary flour may be eaten or even kept in the house during Passover. This recalls the hurried departure of the Jewish slaves — their dough did not have time to rise, so they cooked it as flat cakes. Preparations for the festival begin weeks beforehand. The whole house is thoroughly cleaned, and every crumb of bread is removed. On the day before the Seder, the head of the household makes a symbolic search for leavened bread or *chametz*. Instead of bread, matzot — thin flat wafers made of special flour and water — are eaten. Matzah meal, made from finely ground matzot, or

potato flour are used instead of ordinary flour. Leavening agents are banned, so eggs are beaten full of air to make cakes rise.

All packaged foods must be manufactured expressly for Passover. In the kitchen, special pots and pans are used and the table is set with crockery reserved for the festival.

The Seder

This is a happy meal, with the family and guests eating, drinking, and singing as they tell the story of the Exodus from a book called the Haggadah. The table is set with a white cloth, candlesticks and the best silver. Everyone has a wine glass, which is filled four times during the course of the evening, and there is an extra one set out for the prophet Elijah — tradition has it that he may visit any Jewish home on this night.

The focal point of the table is the Seder plate, which is divided into sections for each of the symbolic foods: a roasted lamb shankbone, a roasted hard-boiled egg, parsley dipped in salt water, bitter herbs (usually horseradish) and a paste-like mixture of fruit and nuts called Charoset (see recipe). There are also three matzot. All these foods have a special significance, for example, the salt

water symbolizes the tears of the slaves, and the Charoset the mortar they used in building cities for the Pharaohs. These foods are sampled before the main meal begins.

First everyone is served a hard-boiled egg, eaten with salt water, possibly followed by gefilte fish. Chicken soup with *knaidlach*, feather-light dumplings made from matzah meal, is traditionally served (see recipe).

The main course is likely to be a roast dish such as Roast chicken with mushroom sauce (see recipe) or roast lamb. Alternatively, a cold fish dish may be served — sole, plaice or haddock coated with matzah meal and beaten egg and fried, or halibut cooked in an egg and lemon sauce.

To accompany the main course, *tzimmes* might be served; this is a traditional dish eaten on the Sabbath and at holiday meals, made from carrots, swedes or potatoes. Tzimmes is sweetened with sugar and perhaps fruit and cooked slowly, sometimes with the addition of meat. Courgettes in fresh tomato sauce (see recipe) might also be served as part of the meal.

A light sponge cake is the customary dessert. This is made with finely ground matzah meal instead of flour, and may contain ground almonds, hazelnuts or walnuts. Bowls of cooked apricots, apples or fresh fruit may accompany the cake. Or, combine cake and fruit in Coconut lattice cake (see recipe). Black coffee or lemon tea (milk and meat may not be eaten at the same meal, according to Jewish dietary laws) follow, with biscuits.

A traditional Seder plate

Roast chicken with mushroom sauce

⏸⏸ 1¾ hours

Serves 4–6
1.8 kg /4 lb chicken, at room temperature
salt and freshly ground black pepper
chicken fat or oil, for greasing
3 ice cubes
150 ml /5 fl oz dry white wine
225 g /8 oz button mushrooms, sliced
2 large ripe tomatoes, blanched, skinned,
    seeded and chopped

1 Heat the oven to 220C /425F /gas 7. Using a damp cloth or absorbent paper, wipe the chicken clean both inside and out, then pat it dry. Season inside the cavity with salt and pepper.
2 Truss the chicken and season the outside.
3 Lightly grease a small roasting tin and place the chicken in it. Roast it for about 1¼ hours, turning it over after about 45 minutes. When you turn it, pour into a small bowl any fat and juices that run from the chicken; reserve these for the sauce.
4 Test that the chicken is cooked by inserting a skewer into the thickest part of the inside leg; the juices should run quite clear. Lower the heat to 150C /300F /gas 2. Remove the trussing skewer and strings from the chicken and place the chicken on a heated serving platter. Keep it warm in the oven while you make the sauce.
5 Add any fat and juices in the tin to those in the bowl. Drop in the ice cubes and stir for a few moments, until the fat hardens and rises to the surface. Lift off the fat and discard the ice cubes. Reserve juices and fat.
6 Add the wine to the roasting tin and boil over a high heat, stirring, to remove the sediment from the base of the tin. Reserve.
7 Put 15 ml /1 tbls of the reserved chicken fat into a frying-pan over a moderate heat. Sauté the mushrooms until they are golden, then add the tomatoes, the chicken juices and the wine. Season with salt and pepper, boil the sauce quickly until it becomes slightly syrupy, then pour it over the chicken.

● This dish can be made in advance and reheated — cut the chicken into serving pieces, cover them with sauce and then with foil. Reheat the chicken at 170C /325F /gas 3 for about 20 minutes.

Courgettes in fresh tomato sauce

Leeks, French beans and broccoli are all good cooked in this way and served either as a cold starter or hot with meat or fish. However, the Ashkenazim (Jews from central and Eastern Europe) do not eat certain vegetables at Passover, including beans, sweetcorn and peas.

⏸⏸ 30 minutes,
   plus optional cooling

Serves 4–6
30 ml /2 tbls oil
225 g /8 oz onions, chopped
450 g /1 lb ripe tomatoes, blanched, skinned,
    seeded and chopped
5 ml /1 tsp sugar
salt and freshly ground black pepper
450 g /1 lb courgettes, thickly sliced

1 Heat the oil in a saucepan. Add the onions and sauté them until they are soft, then add the tomatoes, sugar, salt and pepper. Cook over a low heat for 10 minutes.
2 Meanwhile, add the sliced courgettes to a pan of lightly salted boiling water and simmer for about 7 minutes, or until they are just tender. Drain them well and place them in a shallow serving dish.
3 Strain the tomato sauce over the top, pushing it through the sieve with a spoon. Serve at once or leave to cool.

Chicken soup with matzah balls

🕐⏸⏸ 3½ hours,
      plus chilling

Serves 4–6
2 kg /4½ lb boiling chicken
2 small onions, sliced
2 carrots, sliced
5 celery stalks, sliced
salt and freshly ground black pepper
For the matzah balls
2 matzot
30 ml /2 tbls chicken fat or oil
1 medium-sized onion, finely chopped
15 ml /1 tbls freshly chopped parsley
2 medium-sized eggs, beaten
salt and freshly ground black pepper
a pinch of ground ginger
30–60 ml /2–4 tbls medium-ground
    matzah meal

1 Place the chicken in a large deep saucepan. Add 1.7 L /3 pt cold water and bring it to the boil. Skim the froth from the surface, then add the vegetables and salt and pepper. Simmer very gently for 3 hours.
2 Remove the chicken and reserve it for another recipe. Strain the soup into a bowl. Allow it to cool, then place it in the freezer for several hours or refrigerate it overnight.
3 While the soup is chilling, make the matzah balls. Soak the matzot in cold water for 5 minutes, then drain and squeeze them dry.
4 Heat the fat or oil in a frying-pan. Cook the onion slowly until it is golden brown.
5 In a bowl, mash the drained matzot with a fork. Stir in the onion, parsley and eggs. Season generously with salt and pepper. Add the ginger and 15 ml /1 tbls matzah meal and mix well.
6 Dip your hands in matzah meal and roll the mixture into 25 mm /1 in balls. Chill them in the refrigerator for 1 hour or more.
7 When ready to cook, remove the layer of fat from the surface of the soup; bring the soup to the boil. Carefully lower the matzah balls into the soup and simmer gently for 20 minutes. Taste and adjust the seasoning. Serve 2–3 matzah balls in each bowl of soup.

Charoset

If you prefer a crunchier texture, chop the almonds and apples more coarsely. You can eat charoset spread on matzot.

 20 minutes

Serves 4–6
75 g /3 oz almonds, blanched
2 small dessert apples, peeled and cored
5–10 ml /1–2 tsp ground cinnamon
30 ml /2 tbls sweet red wine

1 Chop the almonds and the apples very finely. Add cinnamon to taste, and the wine.
2 Place the mixture in a small serving bowl and serve it on the Seder plate.

Coconut lattice cake

 1¼ hours,
plus cooling

Serves 6–8
oil, for greasing
4 medium-sized eggs, separated
100 g /4 oz caster sugar
75 g /3 oz fine matzah meal
For the topping
225 g /8 oz dried peaches or apricots
3 medium-sized egg whites
175 g /6 oz caster sugar
175 g /6 oz desiccated coconut

1 Heat the oven to 180C /350F /gas 4. Select an 18 cm /7 in cake tin about 5 cm / 2 in deep with a loose base; grease it and line it with greaseproof paper.
2 In a bowl, cover the peaches or apricots with boiling water and leave them to soak while you prepare the cake.
3 In a clean dry bowl, whisk the egg whites until they are frothy. Slowly add 25 g / 1 oz sugar and continue whisking until the egg whites are stiff.
4 In another bowl, whisk the egg yolks with the remainder of the sugar until they are pale yellow and very thick.
5 Carefully fold the 2 mixtures together, folding in the matzah meal at the same time. Spoon it into the prepared tin and bake for about 45 minutes.
6 While the cake is baking, prepare the topping. Whisk the egg whites until they are stiff. Fold in the sugar, a little at a time, then fold in the desiccated coconut. Drain the fruit well and chop it roughly.
7 When the cake is cooked, take it out of the oven and gently spread the fruit over the top. Put the meringue mixture in a piping bag with a large star nozzle and pipe around the outside of the cake and across the top in a lattice pattern.
8 Return the cake to the oven and cook it for a further 15 minutes, or until the meringue is tipped with brown. Cool on a wire rack, then remove the cake very carefully from the tin.

Roast chicken with mushroom sauce and Courgettes in fresh tomato sauce

EASTER

The first holiday weekend of the year helps us look forward to lighter, brighter and more cheerful summer days — the recipes in this chapter reflect these feelings.

Easter is the holiest festival in the Christian calendar. Even for those who do not fast during Lent, the Easter dishes are something to look forward to. Many of them are pagan in origin — gifts of eggs, for example, were exchanged as a token of renewed life — but others celebrate what is best in spring — lamb, fish and fresh vegetables.

Good Friday

The Easter holiday begins, particularly for those in Roman Catholic countries, on Good Friday. Although traditionally no meat is eaten on this day, elaborate fish dishes are prepared. Salt cod is a favourite ingredient: in the south of France it is pounded into a delicious paste and flavoured with garlic. In Venice and Spain it is treated in an almost identical way. In other parts of Italy the salt cod is stewed with onions in milk and then garnished with fried polenta, which is a maize meal porridge.

The Genoese make a very elaborate fish salad with potatoes, carrots, artichoke hearts, anchovies, olives, sea bass, salt cod and other varieties of seafood. This is topped with a rich, garlicky mayonnaise flavoured with parsley, fennel, capers and anchovies. The Holy Week pie (see recipe) uses many of the same ingredients and is then topped with beaten eggs and baked in the oven to make a rich, spicy omelette-style pie. Traditionally this was only eaten once a year — on Good Friday — and the custom was to cook a pie and give it to a neighbour who in turn would give you the pie she had cooked! A good idea, as long as you were sure that your neighbour was a good cook.

Although Hot cross buns (see recipe) are now always associated with Good Friday, the origin of them is thought to date back to wheat cakes made in honour of Astarte, a Phoenician fertility goddess. The cross on the top of the buns came much later when Christians began to celebrate Easter. Easter Saturday has little special food associated with it, rather it is the day to prepare for the Sunday feast. Most countries have their own version of an Easter cake and the baking of this would have to be started on Saturday. In Russia they make a yeast cake called *Kulitsch* which is wrapped in a spotless white napkin and taken to the church to be blessed by the priest; in Italy a similar cake is called *Columba*. In Poland the entire Easter meal is blessed by the priest, with pride of place going to the Pascal Lamb which is moulded out of butter or white sugar.

Simnel cake (see recipe) which is the traditional British Easter cake, was originally made by girls in service for Mothering Sunday (the one day during Lent when fasting rules were relaxed and girls were allowed to return home to visit their families). However, over the years it has gradually become part of the Easter fare.

Easter Sunday

Children will love to decorate their own eggs for their Easter breakfast and the simplest way is to hard-boil eggs in water with a few drops of food colouring — red, blue, green or yellow. (Adding 2.5 ml /½ tsp vinegar to the water helps the colour to 'take' better.) More complicated designs can be made by covering the eggs with strips of masking tape, in geometric patterns, before you boil them. The tape is then stripped off to reveal the patterns. This can be taken a stage further by boiling the eggs several times in different coloured waters, moving the masking tape around the egg each time it is boiled. Onion skins, wrapped around the egg with brown cotton will give an orangy, marbled effect. Flower petals of different colours placed underneath the onion skin will result in a multi-coloured mottled effect. The flower petals and onion skins are removed after boiling.

Stars, moons and other shapes can be stuck on the eggs before boiling; take them off afterwards and the eggs will have white patterns on a coloured background. Designs can also be added to the eggs, either previously boiled, or blown if you want to keep them, with wax crayons, vegetable dyes, water colours or even oil paints.

The Ukraine is famous for its highly complex designs, resembling tiny mosaic patterns, on eggs. Most of the egg is masked with bees' wax or tape and a tiny area is decorated at a time.

Another treat for children at Easter is chocolate eggs. While you can buy beautiful ones, it is fun to make your own by filling blown eggs with chocolate (see recipe). It is not difficult to do and is much cheaper and easier than buying egg moulds and moulding chocolate around the outside.

In some countries the eggs are hidden in the house or garden and the children go on a hunt to find them. Make Marzipan animals and Sugar mice (see recipe) and use them as pointers or clues; it will keep the youngsters busy until lunch time.

Spring lamb (symbolizing the innocence of Christ) has long formed the main course for a traditional Easter lunch. In Italy a leg of baby lamb is just about large enough to feed two people and is simply roasted with a few rosemary leaves and a little white wine, while in Rome baby kid is the famous Easter speciality. Saddle of lamb is popular in Great Britain and makes a beautiful centrepiece. Get the butcher to bone the lamb, and then stuff it with onions, oranges and watercress, and glaze it with a delicious mixture of redcurrant jelly and port (see recipe). These days many families choose to have a turkey instead, so for a change try Roast turkey with orange gravy (see recipe).

Before the lamb, it is usual to serve either a fish or egg starter. Sole fillets with coriander

sauce (see recipe) make an unusual and fresh-tasting dish; for a richer, smokier flavour substitute smoked cod for sole. Savoury eggs with green mayonnaise (see recipe) are simple to prepare and always popular. For a novel presentation, blow raw eggs and then fill the egg shells with Consommé egg pâté with chives (see recipe). Serve them in egg cups

Brightly decorated Easter eggs

with half the shell peeled carefully away; they make a really pretty dish — very much in keeping with Easter customs.

There are many desserts traditionally associated with Easter. The Russian Easter pudding, *Pashka* (see recipe) is similar to a cheesecake but lighter and it is decorated with the letters 'XB', the initials of the Russian words for 'Christ is risen'. You could make one in a rabbit mould for the children if you have a large party and they are eating separately. In parts of Spain an ice cream cake is traditional; a Pineapple ice cream cake (see recipe) gives a pleasant, tangy variation to the end of the meal and will appeal to both children and adults alike.

Solid chocolate eggs

 1½ hours

Makes 6 eggs
6 medium-sized eggs
500 g /1 lb plain or milk cooking chocolate
small sugar flower cake decorations
angelica leaves
sugar mimosa balls

1 Very carefully pierce a small hole in each end of the egg shell and blow out the contents of the egg. Enlarge one hole to 5 mm / ¼ in wide. Wash the shells carefully under cold running water and leave them to drain.
2 Ensure that the outside of the shell is dry, then with sticky tape attach a small piece of foil over the smaller hole. Repeat with all the remaining shells.
3 Put the chocolate into a bowl over a pan of hot water and allow it to melt. Spoon the chocolate into the egg shells, making sure that there are no air holes. Refrigerate the eggs until the chocolate is set.
4 Very carefully crack the egg shells and peel away the shell. Re-melt any remaining chocolate to stick the flowers, angelica leaves and mimosa balls onto the eggs in decorative patterns.

Sugar mice

 45 minutes, plus drying

Makes about 20
350–500 g /12 oz–1 lb icing sugar, sifted
1 medium-sized egg white
50 g /2 oz golden syrup, warmed
red colouring
cornflour
silver balls
thin string

1 Put ¾ of the sifted icing sugar into a bowl. Add the egg white and golden syrup and mix until the mixture is smooth. Knead to a dough, adding a little more icing sugar if necessary.
2 Divide the mixture in half and add a few drops of red colouring to one half to make it pale pink. Keep a little of the mixture on one side to make the ears and then dust your hands with cornflour and form the remainder into little mice (see picture).
3 To make the ears: make small balls, flatten and curve them and make one side of each ear slightly pointed. Press the pointed side of the ears into position on the heads. Use silver balls as eyes. Cut the string into as many pieces as you have mice. Knot the pieces of string and put the knotted ends into the mice to form their tails. Leave the mice to dry on a wire rack in a cool place.

Nutty apricot eggs

 30 minutes

Makes 25–30
125 g /4 oz dried apricots, very finely chopped
50 g /2 oz mixed nuts, finely chopped
50 g /2 oz ground almonds
250 g /8 oz marzipan
icing sugar
25 g /1 oz dessicated coconut
red food colouring
a small amount of melted chocolate

1 Mix the apricots, nuts and ground almonds into the marzipan until thoroughly blended. Sprinkle a little icing sugar onto your hands and form 25–30 egg shapes.
2 Divide the coconut in half and colour one half pale pink with the food colouring. Roll some of the eggs in white coconut and the rest in pink. Drizzle a little melted chocolate over each egg.

Easter bunnies

 1¼ hours

Makes about 10 bunnies
125 g /4 oz butter or margarine
125 g /4 oz caster sugar
1 medium-sized egg yolk
250 g / 8 oz flour
milk
silver balls and cake decorations
For the filling
50 g /2 oz butter
125 g /4 oz icing sugar
juice of ½ lemon or orange
For the icing
125 g /4 oz icing sugar
yellow or orange food colouring

1 Cream the butter and sugar together until light and fluffy. Gradually beat in the egg yolk, then fold in the flour. Add a little milk to make a stiff dough. Chill it for 30 minutes. Heat the oven to 200C /400F /gas 6.
2 Roll out the dough on a floured board to 5 mm /¼ in thick. Using a rabbit cutter, stamp out rabbit shapes and place them on a baking sheet. Bake for 12–15 minutes until they are golden. Cool.
3 To make the filling, cream all the ingredients together until the mixture is smooth. Sandwich the biscuits together carefully in pairs with the filling.
4 To make the icing, put the icing sugar in a bowl and mix in 15–30 ml /1–2 tbls water to give a smooth glossy icing which will coat the back of a wooden spoon. Add a drop or two of yellow or orange food colouring and mix thoroughly.
5 Spread the icing over one side of the biscuits. Use the silver balls to make eyes and the other decorations for buttons.

Chocolate raisin and marzipan eggs

 1 hour

Makes 24 eggs
250 g /8 oz plain chocolate
125 g /4 oz seedless raisins
15 ml /1 tbls rum (optional)
250 g /8 oz marzipan
5 ml /1 tsp coffee essence
drinking chocolate powder
chocolate vermicelli

1   Melt 175 g /6 oz chocolate in a bowl over a pan of hot water. Stir in the raisins and rum, if you are using it, and mix well. When firm enough, form the mixture into 24 small balls and chill thoroughly.
2   Knead the marzipan until pliable and work in the coffee essence. Roll out to about 3 mm /⅛ in thick and stamp out 24 rounds using a 5 cm /2 in plain cutter. Wrap the marzipan rounds around the chocolate and raisin balls, pressing the edges together to seal them, to form little eggs.
3   Melt the remaining chocolate in a small bowl over a pan of hot water. Dip each ball in the chocolate, drain off the excess, then coat half the balls in the drinking chocolate powder and half in the chocolate vermicelli. Allow the chocolate to dry completely before you serve the eggs.

Marzipan animals

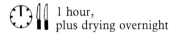 1 hour, plus drying overnight

Makes 4 chicks and 4 ducks
yellow colouring
450 g /1 lb marzipan (Almond paste — page 99)
silver balls
4 pipe cleaners
4 yellow feathers
green food colouring
almonds

1   Add yellow food colouring to half the marzipan and knead until it is pliable, then divide it into 4. Roll each piece into a ball.
2   For the chicks, pull ⅓ off one of the balls; mould the larger piece into a chick's body. Roll the smaller piece into a ball and shape a piece for the beak. Press in silver balls for eyes and press the head onto the body.
3   Cut the pipe cleaners into 5 cm /2 in lengths and bend them in half, pulling out the ends to form feet. Push the bent end of the pipe cleaners into the body to make 2 legs and feet. Push a feather into the tail of the chick. Make three more chicks, then leave them to dry overnight.
4   For 4 ducks, tint the rest of the marzipan green and divide it into 4 balls. Shape ¾ of each into a body, pulling out a tail. Shape the remaining piece into a head. Form beaks

Solid chocolate eggs, Marzipan animals, Sugar mice and Nutty apricot eggs

with almonds and press the head onto the body. Score wings with the back of a knife.
5   Repeat with the remaining marzipan balls, then leave the ducks to dry overnight before serving.

● Cats, mice and other animals can also be made using marzipan. Instead of using silver balls for the eyes, you could use small dots of Royal icing (page 26), with dark chocolate for the pupils. Also, partially dip the animals in chocolate for added flavour.

Spicy hot cross buns

The cross on these buns represents the Crucifixion and the spices symbolize the oils used to anoint the body of Christ.

 2½ hours, including rising

Makes 16
450 g /1 lb flour, plus extra for dusting
15 ml /1 tbls dried yeast
5 ml /1 tsp sugar
150 ml /5 fl oz tepid milk
5 ml /1 tsp ground cinnamon
5 ml /1 tsp freshly grated nutmeg
5 ml /1 tsp ground allspice
5 ml /1 tsp salt
50 g /2 oz caster sugar
50 g /2 oz candied mixed peel
50 g /2 oz currants
50 g /2 oz butter, melted
1 egg, beaten
butter, for greasing
40 g /1½ oz caster sugar, to glaze

1   Sift half the flour into a large bowl and make a well in the centre.
2   Mix the yeast in another bowl with the sugar and blend in the milk and 50 ml /2 fl oz warm water. Leave the mixture to stand for 5 minutes until it is frothy.
3   Pour the liquid into the well in the flour and stir, then cover and leave the mixture to rise for 30 minutes.
4   Sift the remaining flour into another bowl, add the cinnamon, nutmeg, allspice and salt. Add the caster sugar, candied peel and currants.
5   When the first mixture has doubled in size, add it to the second and stir in the melted butter and beaten egg. Mix it really well with your hands and then knead until the dough is very smooth. Cover it and leave for 1 hour.
6   Turn out the dough onto a lightly floured surface and pat it out. Divide it into 16 pieces and shape these into rounds.
7   Heat the oven to 220C /425F /gas 7.
8   Grease and flour a baking sheet and put the rounds on it, not too closely together. With the tip of a knife, mark each round with a cross on the top, then leave the buns in a warm place for 15 minutes until they are well risen.
9   Bake for 15 minutes or until golden.
10   Dissolve the sugar for the glaze in 30 ml / 2 tbls warm water. As soon as you take the buns out of the oven, brush them with the glaze and then leave them to cool slightly. They should be served warm.

Holy Week pie

Salt cod has been eaten on Good Friday in many European countries for hundreds of years. In this recipe it is combined with other seafood, topped with a layer of egg and baked to make a superb pie.

 soaking the salt cod, then 2 hours

Serves 6–8
350 g /12 oz salt cod
75 ml /3 fl oz olive oil, plus extra for greasing
1 large onion, grated
½ small chilli (optional)
1 garlic clove, crushed
2.5 ml /½ tsp salt
2 large tomatoes, blanched, skinned and coarsely chopped
90 ml /6 tbls finely chopped fresh parsley
10 ml /2 tsp coriander seeds, crushed
5 ml /1 tsp ground cumin seeds
3 cloves
225 g /8 oz peeled and boiled prawns
450 g /1 lb white crabmeat
12 medium-sized clams, opened and juices reserved
juice of 1 large lemon
225 g /8 oz canned palm or artichoke hearts, drained and coarsely chopped
freshly ground black pepper
6 eggs, beaten
1 large onion, finely sliced, to garnish
12 black olives, stoned and halved, to garnish
To serve
green salad
lemon wedges

1   Soak the salt cod in a large bowl of water for 24 hours, changing the water every 2 hours or so.
2   Drain the fish, then skin it and carefully bone it. Reserve.
3   Heat the oil in a large, heavy-based saucepan over a moderate heat. Add the onion, chilli (if using), garlic and salt. Stir it and add the tomatoes, parsley, coriander, cumin and cloves. Cover the pan and cook for 10–15 minutes, stirring occasionally.
4   Add the salt cod, prawns, crabmeat and drained clams to the pan. Cook for 30 minutes over a medium heat, stirring it occasionally so that the mixture doesn't stick to the base of the saucepan.
5   Turn off the heat, sprinkle the dish with the lemon juice and leave it to stand for 10 minutes.
6   Add the clam juices and palm or artichoke hearts. Stir them into the mixture and season with freshly ground black pepper and a little more salt if necessary.
7   Heat the oven to 190C /375F /gas 5.
8   Grease a large ovenproof casserole with a little olive oil and transfer the fish mixture to it. Pour the beaten eggs over the mixture, then arrange the sliced onion and halved black olives on top.
9   Bake in the oven on the centre shelf for 30–40 minutes, or until the eggs are quite dry and browned on top.
10   Serve the pie, cut into wedges, either hot, warm or cold with a green salad and lemon wedges.

Consommé egg pâté with chives

🕐 ⫲⫲⫲ 45 minutes, plus 24 hours

Serves 6
12 eggs
12 hard-boiled eggs
175 ml /6 fl oz mayonnaise (page 90)
175 ml /6 fl oz beef consommé
4 ml /¾ tsp curry powder
2.5 ml /½ tsp ground white pepper
180 ml /12 tbls very finely snipped fresh chives
toast, to serve

1 With a pin make a small hole at one end of each raw egg, then make a larger hole at the other end. You can gently break the egg shell with the point of the pin to enlarge the hole to about 3 mm /⅛ in.
2 Holding the egg over a bowl, blow through the small hole to push out the egg white and yolk. Keep the eggs for another recipe. Gently run cold water through the empty egg shells and then leave the shells upright to dry.
3 Halve the hard-boiled eggs and scoop out the yolks into a bowl. Use the whites in another recipe.
4 Mash the yolks with the mayonnaise until smooth. Gradually add the consommé, stirring thoroughly to mix well.
5 Season this mixture with the curry powder and the ground white pepper, then beat in the finely snipped chives so they are evenly distributed through the mixture.
6 Cover the small hole in each empty shell with a piece of foil and sticky tape, then pour in the consommé egg mixture through a tiny funnel or a 3 mm /⅛ in piping nozzle. Stand the eggs upright in the refrigerator to set for 12 hours. Put the remaining mixture in a cool place.
7 After 12 hours the mixture in the egg shells will have settled, so top them up with the rest of the mixture. If it has set in the

Stuffed saddle of lamb

Savoury eggs with green mayonnaise

bowl, warm it slightly over a pan of simmering water, but be careful not to let the mixture get so hot that the eggs cook. Leave for a further 12 hours in the refrigerator.
8 Just before serving, peel away the shell. Stand the eggs in egg cups and serve with fingers of hot toast.

Savoury eggs with green mayonnaise

⫲⫲ hard-boiling the eggs, then 45 minutes

Serves 4
4 eggs, hard-boiled, plunged in
  cold water and left until cold
40 g /1½ oz frozen prawns, defrosted
1.5 ml /¼ tsp lemon juice
a pinch of cayenne pepper
7.5 ml /½–1 tbls finely chopped mixed
  fresh parsley, watercress and tarragon

For the green mayonnaise
15 g /½ oz fresh parsley sprigs
15 g /½ oz fresh watercress sprigs
225 ml /8 fl oz mayonnaise (page 90)
7.5 ml /½ tbls each finely chopped fresh
  parsley, watercress and tarragon
freshly ground black pepper
1.5–2.5 ml /¼–½ tsp lemon juice or wine
  vinegar (optional)

1 First make the green mayonnaise: carefully wash the parsley and watercress sprigs. Bring 300 ml /10 fl oz salted water to the boil, plunge in the washed herbs and simmer for 6 minutes. Drain well, then pat the herbs as dry as possible on absorbent paper. Put them in a mortar and crush them finely, then press them through a sieve to make them finer still.
2 Reserve 60 ml /4 tbls of the mayonnaise for later use. Blend the remaining mayonnaise with the sieved herbs, stir in the finely chopped parsley, watercress and tarragon and season to taste with freshly ground black pepper, and a little lemon juice or wine vinegar, if wished. Chill in the refrigerator until ready to use.
3 Prepare the stuffed eggs just before serving as the filling tends to discolour if it is left exposed to the air for too long. Pound the prawns to a smooth paste in a mortar. Shell the hard-boiled eggs, cut them in half lengthways and scoop out the yolks, taking care not to break the whites.
4 Rub the egg yolks through a fine nylon sieve, then mix them well with the pounded prawns. Bind the mixture with the reserved 60 ml /4 tbls mayonnaise and season with the lemon juice and cayenne pepper.
5 Cut a thin slice from the rounded side of each egg white half, if necessary, so that it will stand firmly. Fill each egg white with the prawn mixture, piling it up and smoothing it over.
6 Spread the green mayonnaise in a shallow rectangular serving dish large enough to take the stuffed eggs side by side. Arrange the eggs on the layer of mayonnaise and sprinkle them with the finely chopped mixed green herbs. Serve these as a first course.

Stuffed saddle of lamb

 1¾–2¼ hours

Serves 6

1.1 kg /2½ lb small saddle of lamb, boned
* weight*
50 g /2 oz butter
3 large onions, very finely chopped
2 bunches of watercress, finely chopped
1 large orange, peeled and chopped
2.5 ml /½ tsp powdered bay leaves
2 sprigs of fresh rosemary
2 garlic cloves, peeled but left whole
30 ml /2 tbls redcurrant jelly
15 ml /1 tbls Dijon mustard
30 ml /2 tbls port
salt and freshly ground black pepper

1 Ask the butcher to bone the saddle for you but not to roll or tie it.
2 Melt the butter over a medium heat, add the onions, cover the pan with foil and cook very gently for 25 minutes until the onions are soft but not coloured.
3 Put the onions and their juices into a large bowl, add the watercress, chopped orange and powdered bay leaves. Stir well.
4 Turn the lamb on its back, skin side down, and open it out. Put one sprig of rosemary and one garlic clove on each side of the lamb and then arrange the watercress stuffing down both sides. Carefully fold over the outer flaps and then tie with string.
5 Turn the lamb skin side up and put it on a rack in a roasting tin. Heat the oven to 200C /400F /gas 6.
6 Put the redcurrant jelly into a small saucepan over a gentle heat and stir until it

Roast turkey with orange gravy

begins to melt. Take it off the heat and stir in the mustard and the port, mixing well.
7 Season the lamb with salt and freshly ground black pepper and paint the skin with the redcurrant jelly mixture. Cook in the oven for 1 hour 5 minutes for pink lamb, 1½ hours for well done, basting occasionally.
8 Transfer the lamb to a warmed serving dish and put it back in the turned-off oven.
9 Put the roasting tin over a moderate heat and add 30 ml /2 tbls water. Bring it to the boil and stir, scraping all the sediment from the tin. Pour the gravy into a warmed sauce-boat and serve with the lamb.

Roast turkey with orange gravy

 3½–4 hours

Serves 8

1 turkey, about 4.5 kg /10 lb dressed weight
30 ml /2 tbls olive oil
1.5 ml /¼ tsp dried oregano
1.5 ml /¼ tsp dried rosemary
salt and freshly ground black pepper
225 g /8 oz butter
150 ml /5 fl oz dry white wine
juice of 2 small oranges
1 garlic clove, finely chopped
1 chicken stock cube
For the orange gravy
25 g /1 oz butter
30 ml /2 tbls flour
turkey giblet stock
giblet meats
salt and freshly ground black pepper

1 Heat the oven to 220C /425F /gas 7. Prepare and truss the turkey.
2 Rub the turkey all over with olive oil and season with dried oregano and rosemary, salt

and freshly ground black pepper. Lay the bird in a roomy roasting tin breast side up.
3 Melt the butter in a heavy saucepan. Remove it from the heat before it starts to sizzle.
4 Cut a double-thickness piece of muslin large enough to cover the whole turkey. Rinse the muslin in cold water and wring it out. Soak it in melted butter and gently squeeze out the excess. Drape it over the turkey. Roast it on the lowest shelf of the oven for 15 minutes.
5 Add the dry white wine, orange juice and chopped garlic to the remaining melted butter. Crumble in the stock cube and stir.
6 Reduce the oven temperature to 180C / 350F /gas 4. Turn the bird on its breast for 15 minutes, then reverse it to its original position.
7 Baste the turkey with some of the butter mixture and then baste every 15 minutes, making sure that the muslin is completely moistened with the butter mixture or pan juices each time. After the turkey has been in the oven for about 2¾–3¼ hours, remove the muslin to allow the bird to brown for the last 45 minutes of the cooking time.
8 When the turkey is tender, remove the strings and skewers. Transfer the bird to a hot serving dish and keep it hot in the turned-off oven. Pour the juices and crusty bits from the roasting tin into a bowl. Leave it for 1 minute, then skim off the fat.
9 To make the orange gravy: melt the butter in a heavy saucepan; blend in the flour and stir over low heat for 2 minutes. Gradually add 275 ml /10 fl oz giblet stock and the skimmed pan juices, whisking vigorously with a balloon whisk. Bring to the boil and simmer, stirring, until the gravy has thickened (6–8 minutes). Chop the giblet meats finely, add to the sauce, and adjust the seasoning.
10 Serve the orange gravy in a hot sauce-boat, with the turkey.

Sole fillets with coriander sauce

🍴 40 minutes

Serves 6
12 small fillets or 6 large fillets of Dover sole
25 g /1 oz butter
2 shallots, finely chopped
1 sprig of fresh parsley
300 ml /10 fl oz dry white wine
salt
freshly ground black pepper
coriander leaves, to garnish
For the sauce
1 large bunch of fresh coriander leaves,
  trimmed of roots and stems, washed and
  coarsely chopped
3 anchovy fillets, chopped
15 ml /1 tbls Dijon mustard
2 egg yolks, beaten
75 ml /5 tbls thick cream

1 Melt the butter in a large heavy-based saucepan, add the shallots and cook gently for 10 minutes, stirring occasionally, until they are soft and translucent.
2 Put the sole fillets, in one layer, on top of the lightly cooked shallots, add the sprig of parsley, then cover with dry white wine and 150 ml /5 fl oz water. Season with salt and freshly ground black pepper and poach for 8–10 minutes.
3 Remove the fillets of Dover sole with a slotted spoon, then carefully roll them up into a curl shape and then keep them warm. Strain the poaching liquid into a smaller pan and boil it rapidly until it is reduced to 300 ml /10 fl oz.
4 Put the chopped coriander leaves, anchovy fillets and Dijon mustard into a blender and blend to a purée.
5 Add the purée to the reduced stock in the pan and turn the heat down to low.
6 Beat the egg yolks with the thick cream and add a little of the hot stock. Blend it well and pour the mixture into the pan. Stir constantly for 3–4 minutes until the sauce is slightly thickened. Check the seasoning — you are unlikely to need more salt because the anchovies are quite salty.
7 Divide the sauce among 6 individual warmed serving plates, put 2 rolled up sole fillets in the middle of the sauce on each plate and serve immediately garnished with coriander leaves.

Pineapple ice cream cake

🍴 45 minutes, plus 3–4 hours freezing, then 10 minutes

Serves 6–8
Basic party sponge mix (see page 75)
450 g /1 lb canned crushed pineapple
butter, for greasing
300 ml /10 fl oz thick cream
45 ml /3 tbls icing sugar
chocolate caraque, to garnish

1 Heat the oven to 180C /350F /gas 4.
2 Take one quarter of the canned crushed pineapple and drain it well in a sieve, reserving the juice.
3 Add the drained pineapple to the whisked sponge mixture and fold in well.
4 Grease two 19 cm /7½ in sandwich tins with butter, then line the bases with two circles of greaseproof paper and grease these as well. Divide the sponge mixture between the two tins and bake in the oven for 25–30 minutes until the cakes have shrunk away from the sides of the tins and are springy to the touch.
5 Remove the cakes from the oven, leave them for a few minutes to cool slightly, then invert them onto a cool cloth. Peel off the greaseproof paper, turn them the right way up on a wire rack and leave to cool.
6 Meanwhile, purée the remaining pineapple and reserved juice in a blender.
7 Whip the thick cream in a large bowl until soft peaks form, then fold in the sugar.
8 Combine the puréed pineapple with 175 ml /6 fl oz of the whipped cream, lightly folding together until thoroughly mixed.
9 Divide the mixture between two 19 cm / 7½ in sandwich tins and freeze for 1–1½ hours. Stir the ice cream with a fork then return it to the freezer for 2½–3 hours.
10 About 30 minutes before serving, take the ice cream out of the freezer and put it in the refrigerator to soften slightly.
11 Just before serving, wipe the bottom of the sandwich tins with a cloth wrung out in hot water. Put one layer of sponge on a serving plate and turn out one ice cream layer on top of it. Cover with a second sponge layer. Turn the second ice cream layer out onto a plate then gently slide it into

Pineapple ice cream cake

position on top of the other layers. Smooth the top with a palette knife, if necessary.
12 Spread the remaining whipped cream around the sides of the cake. Sprinkle the top of the cake with chocolate caraque and serve immediately.

Russian Easter pudding

Similar to a cheesecake, this simple sweet called *Pashka* by the Russians, is usually made in a deep clay flower-pot.

🕐 12 hours draining, plus 30 minutes, then 12 hours chilling

Serves 16
1.5 kg /3 lb 5 oz cottage or curd cheese
100 g /4 oz blanched almonds, chopped
100 g /4 oz candied mixed peel, chopped
200 g /7 oz seedless raisins, chopped
100 g /4 oz glacé cherries, chopped
250 g /9 oz butter, softened
3 medium-sized eggs
200 g /7 oz caster sugar
100 ml /3½ fl oz clotted, thick or soured cream
5 ml /1 tsp rose-water
For decoration
blanched almonds
glacé cherries
candied fruit
angelica

1 Drain the cottage or curd cheese by hanging it in a cheesecloth bag over the sink for at least 12 hours.
2 Rub the drained cheese through a sieve into a bowl. Mix the chopped almonds and candied peel, raisins and cherries with the

softened butter and mix them all thoroughly into the cheese.

3 Whisk the eggs with the sugar until they are pale yellow and frothy, then mix them into the cottage cheese mixture, whisking thoroughly. Whisk in the clotted, thick or soured cream and rose-water and continue mixing until it is completely smooth.

4 Line a flower-pot, which is large enough to hold the pudding, with two layers of cheesecloth. Put the pudding into the flower-pot, fold the ends of the cloth over the top and cover it with a small plate, weighted to press down the contents. Stand the pot upright in a bowl to catch the whey and place it all in the refrigerator for at least 12 hours.

5 When ready to serve, unfold the cheesecloth and carefully turn the pudding out onto a flat serving dish. Decorate the pudding with almonds, glacé cherries, candied fruit and angelica.

Easter babka

Most *babka* recipes are based on 10 or more egg yolks, so this is a relatively economical version. Cakes made with yeast do not keep well, so eat them within a few days.

 4 hours

Makes 1 tall cake
500 g /18 oz strong white flour
25 g /1 oz fresh yeast or 15 ml /1 tbls dried yeast
30 ml /2 tbls vodka or rum
a pinch of powdered saffron (optional)
7.5 ml /1½ tsps finely grated lemon zest
250 ml /9 fl oz tepid milk
2 medium-sized egg whites
a pinch of salt
4 medium-sized egg yolks
100 g /3½ oz vanilla sugar or caster sugar, plus a few drops of vanilla essence
75 g /3 oz butter
50 g /2 oz raisins
15 g /½ oz candied peel, finely chopped
25 g /1 oz chopped almonds (optional)
For the icing
250 g /9 oz icing sugar
15 ml /1 tbls lemon juice
candied orange peel, to garnish (optional)

1 Put the vodka or rum into a wineglass, add the powdered saffron, if using, and the grated lemon zest.

2 Pour the tepid milk into a large bowl and crumble in the fresh yeast or sprinkle the dried yeast over the surface. Leave for 5 minutes, then stir in 25 g /1 oz of the sugar. Cover the bowl with a damp cloth and leave the mixture in a warm place for 15 minutes, or until the yeast is foaming.

3 Sift 250 g /9 oz of the flour into the yeast mixture and stir thoroughly with a wooden spoon to remove any lumps. Cover the bowl with a damp cloth and leave it in a warm place to double in bulk (this usually takes about 1 hour).

4 Beat the egg whites and a pinch of salt until firm enough for stiff peaks to form. Beat the eggs yolks with the rest of the vanilla sugar or sugar and essence and the

Russian Easter pudding

vodka or rum, saffron and grated lemon zest in the wineglass.

5 Stir the egg yolk mixture into the yeast mixture. Sift in all but 25 g /1 oz of the remaining flour and fold in the egg whites. Use a wooden spoon to mix the dough, then knead it with your hands for 20–30 minutes until it is no longer sticky but has become smooth, elastic and no longer sticks to your hands or to the sides of the bowl. Grease the bowl with butter and leave the dough in it, covered with a damp cloth, in a warm place for about 30 minutes.

6 Thoroughly butter a 17.5 cm /7 in brioche tin, or a 2 L /3½ pt loose-bottomed ring mould or a gugelhupf mould. Dust the buttered surfaces with the remaining flour and shake off the excess.

7 Melt the butter and let it cool. Pour it over the dough, add the raisins, the candied peel and the chopped almonds, if you are using them, and knead the dough again thoroughly, until it is smooth and elastic (about 10 minutes).

8 Arrange the dough in the tin or mould, making sure it does not more than half fill it. Cover the tin or mould with a damp cloth and leave it in a warm place for about 45 minutes for the dough to rise. Heat the oven to 180C /350F /gas 4.

9 Bake the babka for 50–60 minutes or until the top is light brown and a skewer inserted into the centre of the cake comes out clean. Remove it from the oven and cool on a wire rack. Stir the lemon juice and 30 ml / 2 tbls water into the icing sugar until it is smooth and then dribble it over the cake. Garnish with candied orange peel if wished and then serve.

Polish doughnuts

These doughnuts are a favourite at Easter in Poland. Sometimes 15 ml /1 tbls of rum is added to the dough with the soured cream.

 1 hour

Makes about 60
20 g /¾ oz butter
50 g /2 oz caster sugar
1 medium-sized egg, lightly beaten
250 g /9 oz flour, sifted
15 ml /1 tbls distilled vinegar
about 250 ml /9 fl oz soured cream or yoghurt
flour, for rolling
vegetable oil, for deep frying
icing sugar

1 Cream the butter and sugar together with the egg. Add the flour and vinegar and beat the mixture to a smooth paste, gradually adding enough of the soured cream or yoghurt to make a moist dough which is still stiff enough to roll out.

2 Take a third of the dough and thinly roll it out on a floured board. Cover the rest of the dough with cling film to keep it moist. Slice the rolled out dough into strips about 12.5 cm × 25 mm /5 × 1 in and make a slit in the middle of one strip about 5 cm /2 in long. Pass one end of the strip through the slit giving it a twist. Treat the remaining strips in the same way.

3 Heat the oil in a deep-fat frier to 180C / 350F. Add the strips a few at a time and fry them until they are golden brown. Drain the doughnuts on absorbent paper and sprinkle them with icing sugar.

Simnel cake

Traditionally this cake was made for Mothering Sunday (the 4th Sunday in Lent) when girls who were in service were allowed home to see their mothers. Nowadays, it is associated more with Easter, and the eleven marzipan balls are said to represent the eleven faithful Apostles.

⏰🍴 35 minutes, plus 7 hours baking, then maturing

Makes 1×25 cm /10 in square cake or 28 cm /11 in round cake
700 g /1½ lb flour
a large pinch of salt
10 ml /2 tsp mixed spice
10 ml /2 tsp cinnamon
225 g /8 oz glacé cherries
225 g /8 oz chopped mixed peel
700 g /1½ lb butter
700 g /1½ lb soft brown sugar
11 eggs
45 ml /3 tbls black treacle
finely grated zest and juice of 2 lemons and
  2 oranges
1.1 kg /2½ lb currants
450 g /1 lb sultanas
450 g /1 lb raisins
225 g /8 oz almonds, blanched and chopped
45 ml /3 tbls brandy or rum
800 g /1¾ lb marzipan
30–45 ml /2–3 tbls sieved apricot jam
beaten egg white
caster sugar
glacé icing (page 27)
yellow chicks and ribbon, to decorate

1 Line the inside of a 25 cm /10 in square or a 28 cm /11 in round cake tin with a double thickness of greased greaseproof paper. Heat the oven to 150C /300F /gas 2.
2 In a bowl sieve together the flour, salt and spices. Wash and dry the cherries. Cut them into quarters. Wash and dry the peel.

Easter biscuits

3 Cream the butter and sugar together until the mixture is light and fluffy. In a bowl beat together the eggs, black treacle and fruit juices. Gradually beat the egg mixture into the creamed mixture. Add a little of the flour with the last few additions of egg.
4 With a metal spoon, fold in the remaining flour, fruit zests, dried fruits and nuts, then add the brandy or rum. Fold them in until the cake mixture has a dropping consistency.
5 Reserve 100 g /4 oz of the marzipan. Divide the remaining marzipan in half and, reserving one piece, roll the other to a 25 cm /10 in square or 28 cm /11 in round.
6 Place half the prepared cake mixture in the lined and greased tin. Smooth the surface, then put the marzipan on top and cover it with the remaining cake mixture.
7 Tie a double thickness of thick brown paper around the outside of the tin. Place the tin on a pad of brown paper on the lowest shelf in the oven. Bake for 5 hours, then lower the heat to 140C /275F /gas 1 for 2 hours, but keep checking the cake when it is close to the end of the suggested cooking time. Cover the top of the cake with crumpled foil if it browns too quickly.
8 When a skewer is inserted in the centre and comes out clean, the cake is cooked. Cool it and remove the paper.
9 When the cake is cold, roll out another marzipan 25 cm /10 in square or 28 cm /11 in round. Brush the top of the cake with warm, sieved apricot jam and place the rolled-out marzipan on top. With a sharp knife cut the edge of the marzipan into a series of v-shapes.
10 Make 11 small balls from the reserved 100 g /4 oz marzipan. Place them around the edge of the cake pushing them down slightly to anchor them. Brush the surface and the balls with well-beaten egg white, sprinkle it with caster sugar and grill it until golden.
11 Leave the cake to cool before spreading

a little glacé icing in the centre. Tie a ribbon around the cake and place several fluffy yellow chicks on top of it.

Easter biscuits

🍴 40 minutes

Makes about 24
150 g /5 oz flour
a pinch of salt
5 ml /1 tsp mixed spice
75 g /3 oz softened butter or margarine
50 g /2 oz caster sugar
25 g /1 oz currants, washed
finely grated zest of ½ lemon
15 ml /1 tbls beaten egg

1 Heat the oven to 170C /325F /gas 3; lightly grease a baking sheet. Sift the flour, salt and mixed spice carefully onto a clean plate.
2 In a large bowl, cream together the butter or margarine and the sugar. Add the sifted flour and spice to the creamed mixture, together with the currants, lemon zest and egg. Mix all the ingredients to a smooth dough.
3 On a lightly floured board roll the dough out to a thickness of 5 mm /¼ in and cut it into round shapes using a 5 cm /2 in pastry cutter.
4 Place the biscuits on the prepared baking sheet and bake for 20–25 minutes, until they are a golden brown colour.
5 Carefully transfer the biscuits from the baking sheet to a wire rack and leave them to cool completely before storing them in an airtight tin or serving them.

Almond biscuits

These little biscuits, called *Tejas de almendras* in Spain, are traditionally eaten at Easter time. If there are any left over, they keep quite well in an airtight tin.

🍴 30 minutes

Serves 4
150 g /5 oz caster sugar
150 g /5 oz butter
50 g /2 oz almonds, blanched, lightly
  toasted and chopped
100 g /4 oz flour, sieved
25 g /1 oz ground almonds
a pinch of salt
grated zest of one lemon
4 egg whites

1 Heat the oven to 180C /350F /gas 4. Grease a baking sheet using butter. In a large bowl cream the sugar and the butter together until the mixture is light and fluffy. Stir in the almonds, flour and ground almonds, salt and lemon zest.
2 Lightly whisk the egg whites and fold them into the mixture. Drop teaspoons of the mixture onto a well-buttered baking sheet, spacing them out well. Bake for about 15–20 minutes until golden.

Children's Parties

PLANNING A PARTY

Children's parties need careful planning to ensure that everything runs smoothly on the day. If you follow my guidelines here, you will be off to a good start for a fun-filled occasion for the children *and* for yourself.

The best advice I can give you is to start your preparations well in advance. Study my Party countdown, and aim to do most of your food preparation the day before the party, leaving you free to join in the fun with the children.

What to serve
Children will not notice the difference between home-made ice creams and bought ones. Instead, concentrate your energy on making the birthday cake.

For toddlers: plan to have small, firm items of food which the under-fives can grasp without crumbling them to bits — cold cocktail sausages (or chipolatas twisted in the middle and split to make mini-sausages) served plain are ideal. Sandwich fillings should be firm, preferably pasty and easy to bite, such as mild processed cheese spread, curd cheese mixed with tomato ketchup, or ham or fish paste.

Serve small cakes and biscuits vividly iced but without gooey jam or messy cream. Cut

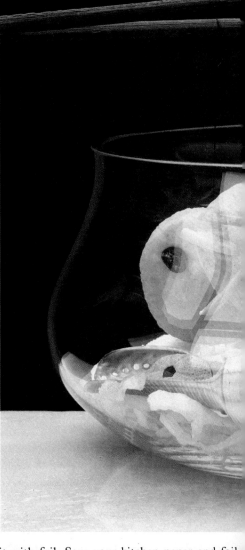

---

bought Madeira cake into small cubes or oblongs and coat with Glacé icing (see page 27). Pipe animal outlines in contrasting colours on top or decorate them with coloured chocolate buttons when the icing is half set. Brighten up plain round biscuits by piping funny icing faces on them. Jelly boats (see recipe) look spectacular and are sure to be appreciated.

For the five-to-eights: they like much the same food as the younger ones, though they are likely to eat more. As well as sausages and sandwiches, offer them pineapple and meat kebabs. Spear the drained canned pineapple chunks alternately with cubes of luncheon meat onto cocktail sticks. A Goldfish bowl or two will be very popular (see recipe), and plain crisps are a must.

For place cards, decorate sweet oblong biscuits with the children's names in piped icing. Serve bought chocolate biscuits individually wrapped in foil; bought biscuits iced and decorated with coloured sweets; bought cakes iced with glacé icing; and finish the tea with small tubs of bought ice cream and wafers.

For older children: eight- to eleven-year-olds will need a big spread of food to sustain them. Serve Bacon and apple skewers (see recipe), and bought sausage rolls or mini hot dogs: drain, steam and cool canned cocktail frankfurters, then place them in buttered bridge rolls. Make mock pizzas by buttering small round cheese biscuits, sprinkling them lightly with grated mild cheese and dabbing with tomato ketchup before putting them into the oven until the cheese melts. Don't forget to include potato sticks, different flavoured crisps, peanuts and popcorn. Jam tarts (bought or home-made) in lots of colours will always be popular, as will little iced cakes. Different coloured iced biscuits and foil-wrapped chocolate biscuits make the table even brighter. You might also like to serve ice-cream cones.

Scatter small dishes of varied, colourful sweets on the table for the children to help themselves. Team up Crumb fudge squares and Brownies (see recipes) with bought marshmallows for contrast.

Planning a theme
It is great fun to choose a theme, such as a Circus party (see page 62) or a Flower party (see page 58). Whatever the theme, the table will be the focal point of the room.

Space party: Create a 'module' by covering the walls of the room with crumpled foil strips, using non-marking adhesive. If you feel that this will cost too much, just concentrate on one corner of the room. Make panels of knobs and buttons by covering cardboard rectangles and ovals with foil and sticking on foil buttons and knobs. Attach the panels to walls on the crumpled foil.

Turn the table into a food machine. Cover

---

it with foil. Save your kitchen paper and foil cardboard rolls, cover them in foil and stick them to the sides of the table vertically. Napkins, plates and plastic mugs should be all white.

Use your imagination about costumes and make space helmets or hats. Guests could come in their own creations.

For going-home presents, buy small space rockets or mini-torches, or even foil-covered chocolate money.

Nursery rhyme party: Cover one wall (or even the whole room) with thick, light-coloured paper. Draw outlines of favourite story-book characters on the paper and get the children to colour them in. Supply a selection of coloured, thick felt-tip pens (water-based to avoid staining clothes). Or cut out and colour nursery rhyme figures and then hang the scenes from the ceiling, for example, a cardboard moon, cow, dog, dish, and spoon.

Create a toadstool table. Use a round table and cover it with red paper or a red cloth, gather it underneath the table in folds and secure it with tape. Make a large cardboard tube and cover it with brown paper, place it under the table to make a stalk. Cut out small white paper circles and attach them to the red cloth or paper on the table. Make 'grass' cushions for the children to sit on by covering a square of green crêpe paper with shredded green crêpe paper. If you have

Party countdown

About three weeks before the party
Write a guest list and send out invitations. If your party is to have a theme, mention this on the invitations.

One to two weeks before the party
Choose the menu. Plan games. Make a shopping list which includes paper plates, straws, candles, masks (for children over five — younger ones may be frightened), prizes and going-home presents. Buy paper goods and non-perishable food. Make pastries, cakes and ice creams which will freeze.

Two days before
Make any paper decorations needed for the table, hats, masks, etc.
Make templates for cakes, if needed.
Make fudge, if serving.

One day before
Make sponge cake, if needed; ice the cake.
Make other baked food: petits fours, jam tarts, biscuits, Brownies and Goldfish.
Cook sausages, drain and wrap. Make sandwiches and wrap them in cling film. Make pineapple and meat kebabs and prepare Bacon and apple skewers; cover and refrigerate. Prepare mock pizzas. Make jellies.

On birthday party day
Cover the floor under the party table with an old sheet or rug. Lay the table, arranging bowls of crisps, nuts and sweets.
Chill fizzy drinks, fruit juices and squashes.
Remove all wrappings and prepare the table.
Put finishing touches to the cake.
Finish Jelly boats and Goldfish bowl.

unaware that the crockery has been removed. Clinking plates and calls of 'oops! you almost broke a plate', add to the illusion as you guide the child along. After the blindfold is removed, each child stays in the room to watch the others do the same thing.

Dead lions is a calming game to end the party. Children lie still on the floor and pretend to be dead lions. Whoever lies the quietest for the longest time wins a prize.

Good luck — I hope it's not too exhausting!

Goldfish bowl

45 minutes,
plus chilling and cooling

Makes 24 goldfish
75 g /3 oz Double Gloucester or Red Leicester
  cheese, finely grated
75 g /3 oz softened butter, plus extra for
  greasing
175 g /6 oz flour, plus extra for flouring
salt
white pepper
a pinch of mustard powder
1–2 egg yolks
1.5 ml /¼ tsp paprika (if using Double
  Gloucester)
24 drained capers
48 almond slivers
1 medium-sized round lettuce, to serve
small seashells, to garnish (optional)

1 In a large bowl, work the cheese with the back of a spoon until pasty. Add the butter and cream well.
2 Sift together the flour and a pinch each of salt, pepper and mustard. Add them to the creamed mixture little by little, beating until just blended.
3 Beat 1 egg yolk in a small bowl. Add half to the cheese mixture, reserving the rest. If necessary, add a little cold water to the cheese mixture to make a firm dough. Scoop the pastry into 2 balls, wrap them in a polythene bag and chill until firm. Heat the oven to 190C /375F /gas 5.
4 Roll 1 of the pastry balls out on a floured surface until it is about 5 mm /¼ in thick, leaving the second ball, still in its polythene bag, in the refrigerator.
5 With a 5 cm /2 in round biscuit cutter, cut out 12 pastry circles. Pat them into fish shapes, slightly broader at one end than the other. Repeat the process using the second ball of pastry.
6 Place the pastry fish on a lightly greased and floured baking sheet. Mix the reserved half egg yolk with a few drops of water and brush it over the fish, using the second egg yolk if necessary. Sprinkle with a few grains of paprika if using Double Gloucester.
7 Press a caper into each fish near the broad end as an eye, and press 2 almond slivers in a V shape into the other end for a tail. Bake for 12 minutes or until they are golden brown, then leave them to cool.
8 To serve, shred the lettuce finely and place it in the bottom of 2 or more plain glass bowls or dishes. A few seashells around the sides enhance the effect. Make fishing rods and lines, attach one fish to each. Arrange these in the centre of each bowl.

Goldfish bowl

enough stools, completely cover them with 'grass' to make tuffets. Use red and white plates, mugs and napkins. Guests can come as their own favourite characters to complement the scene.

For going-home presents, buy some nursery rhyme or story-book novelties. For example, a plastic spider (Little Miss Muffet) or sugar mice (Hickory Dickory Dock).
Beach party: Two- to four-year-olds who are generally too young to play organized games will love being left to play with sand and water.

Ideally this is a fair-weather party to be held in the garden. You will need a paddling pool and a sand pit and as many water and sand toys as you can find. A rocking horse can masquerade as a donkey to give rides up and down the 'beach'. If you can get a keen enough adult, put on a Punch and Judy show. Hang out flags or bunting (made with triangles of coloured paper) and bunches of gaily coloured balloons.

You can still give a beach party in the winter months! Have a selection of small boats and other nautical toys for the children to play with on the floor. Cut out starfish, sea-horse, octopus and seaweed shapes and suspend them from the ceiling.

Cover the table with a deep blue tablecloth or paper. Cut out thin wavy lines from white cardboard, and glue or tape them to the sides of the cloth to resemble waves. Supply Neptune forks and crowns, and mermaid wigs, made from strips of yellow tissue or crêpe paper, for the children.

Going-home presents can include plastic buckets and spades; novelty 'fish' pens, blue notepaper, 'pebble' sweets or sticks of rock.

Party games
Pass the parcel, played to music, is an old favourite. Smaller children will enjoy the Secret colour game. A bowl of coloured chocolate buttons is placed on the table. One child leaves the room, and the rest choose a 'secret' colour. The other child returns and is allowed to eat chocolate buttons (without selecting the same colour twice) until he or she picks the secret colour. Chocolate squares is a very popular game. Each child is given a bar of chocolate and can eat as much as he likes — as long as only knives and forks are used — no fingers!

In the Memory game, objects on a tray are shown to the children for 30 seconds; a prize goes to whoever writes down the most objects that he or she can remember after the tray has been covered and taken away. Tiptoe through the china is great fun. The children watch you arrange 12 plates on the floor; then they are sent out of the room. One by one, they are brought back into the room, blindfolded, to walk between the plates,

Bacon and apple skewers

🍴 35–40 minutes

Serves 12
4 large cooking apples
100 g /4 oz Demerara sugar
24 slices back bacon
olive oil
12 small fingers of toast

1 Heat the oven to 180C /350F /gas 4.
2 Peel, core and cut up each apple into 6 segments. Place them in an ovenproof dish and sprinkle with Demerara sugar.
3 Bake in the oven for 15–20 minutes, or until the segments are soft but still hold their shape. Heat the grill to high.
4 Wrap a slice of bacon around each apple segment and spear 2 at a time on wooden cocktail sticks. Reserve the apple syrup.
5 Brush the grill grid with olive oil and

Jelly boats

place the bacon and apple skewers on the grid. Grill 7.5 cm /3 in away from the heat for 3 minutes each side, or until the bacon is golden all over.
6 Dip each finger of toast in the grill pan drippings and spear a slice on the end of each cocktail stick.
7 Before serving, brush the bacon with the syrup from the apples to glaze.

Jelly boats

🍴 45 minutes,
plus cooling and chilling

Serves 12
3 jelly tablets, 135 g /4¾ oz each, in different colours
6 medium-sized oranges
For the garnish
36 cocktail sticks
36 small squares of brightly coloured paper

1 Each jelly tablet is divided into 16 squares. Using scissors, cut off 6 squares of each colour, and reserve the rest for making another dessert.

2 Cut 1 of the jellies into squares and place them in a small saucepan with 125 ml /4 fl oz water. Heat gently, stirring constantly, until the jelly melts, then pour it into a chilled jug. Repeat twice, using the remaining jellies and pouring them into separate jugs. Let them cool.
3 While they are cooling, halve the oranges and scoop out all the flesh. Reserve the flesh for another recipe or see the recipe suggestion below. Stand the skins, hollow side up, on a plate and chill.
4 When the jellies are cold but not yet set, pour them into the skins. Chill for several hours or overnight, until set firmly.
5 With a sharp knife, cut each orange half into 3 equal sections. Chill until party time.
6 Stick each cocktail stick through a paper square, to represent a mast and sail. Stick the other end of the cocktail stick through the centre of each boat. Arrange the boats on a serving plate, alternating the colours.

● One by one make up, according to the instructions, the leftover jellies. Set them in stripes, with the reserved orange flesh, chopped, between the layers, allowing each colour to set before adding the next.

Brownies

Children will love these delicious chocolate squares which are ideal for a party — and there will be no messy fingers!

 1 hour, plus cooling

Makes 16
100 g /4 oz flour
5 ml /1 tsp baking powder
5 ml /1 tsp salt
150 g /5 oz plain chocolate
225 g /8 oz butter, softened, plus extra
for greasing
450 g /1 lb caster sugar
4 eggs
2.5 ml /½ tsp vanilla essence
100 g /4 oz walnuts, coarsely chopped

1 Heat the oven to 180C /350F /gas 4. Butter a 30×20 cm /12×8 in baking tin.
2 Sift the flour, baking powder and salt together 3 times into a bowl.
3 Break the chocolate into the top pan of a double boiler and place it over hot water until it has melted, stirring occasionally with a wooden spoon. Leave it until just cool.
4 In a large bowl, combine the softened butter and the caster sugar. Beat together for 5 minutes or until it is light and fluffy. Next, thoroughly beat in the eggs, 1 at a time.
5 Add the sifted flour mixture to the creamed mixture and beat well, then stir in the melted chocolate and the vanilla essence and beat until smooth. Stir in the walnuts.
6 Spread the mixture in the baking tin and bake in the oven for 35–40 minutes, or until the surface is firm to the touch.
7 Remove the tin from the oven and allow the brownies to cool in the tin for 5 minutes (it will settle a little as it cools). Cut it into squares.
8 Allow the brownies to cool completely before removing them from the baking tin.

Crumb fudge squares

This nutritious sweetmeat keeps excellently, so it can be made well in advance.

15 minutes,
plus 2 hours setting

Makes 36 squares
100 g /4 oz butter, plus extra for greasing
175 g /6 oz toasted bran breakfast cereal or
crustless wholemeal bread
30 ml /2 tbls clear honey
50 g /2 oz muscovado sugar
50 g /2 oz unsweetened cocoa powder, sifted
1.5 ml /¼ tsp vanilla essence
caster sugar, for sprinkling

1 Lightly grease an 18 cm /7 in square shallow baking tin. Reduce the cereal or bread to fine, even crumbs using a food processor if available.
2 Put the butter, honey and sugar into a small, heavy-bottomed saucepan. Place over a low heat and cook, stirring, until the butter melts. Add the cocoa powder and cook, stirring, for 2 minutes. The mixture should be fully blended and syrupy.
3 Remove the pan from the heat and thoroughly work in the crumbs and vanilla essence. Press the mixture evenly into the tin and mark into 36 squares. Cover with cling film and leave in a cool place for 2 hours.
4 Cut the fudge into squares along the marked lines and sprinkle generously with caster sugar. Store in an airtight tin.

A FLOWER PARTY

Delight your little girl by giving her a birthday celebration she'll love — a Flower party. It's a charming idea, featuring a rose-and-lily table centrepiece surrounded by delicious sweet and savoury treats, all with a floral theme.

It's very likely that your child's first real party will be a birthday party. Mine certainly was. I remember that it was based on a sailor theme, complete with paper sailor hats and miniature battleships on a sea-blue cake!

An overall theme for your child's party will help you plan the food and decor — and both are equally important to the success of the occasion. All small children will enjoy my Circus party (see page 62), with biscuit animals riding on a sandwich train, and a colourful merry-go-round cake.

Little girls in particular will love my Flower party here. On a pretty table, decorated to give the impression of a flower garden, it features flower-shaped sandwiches (see recipes) and a lovely Pink posy cake (see recipe), embellished with a delicate cluster of pink roses and set within a special Floral centrepiece (see instructions). Macaroon petals with cherry centres (see recipe) complete the charming scene.

I have kept the taste of the food simple, to suit children, but the flowery decoration is quite elaborate in order to make the theme really effective. Mention to the mothers of the other children what the theme is in

advance and suggest that the children come in fancy dress — you might like to award a prize for the most imaginative outfit. Flower-inspired costumes are easy enough to put together and need not be too expensive. They will help to make the occasion a great success and give your birthday girl and her friends a really memorable party.

Pink posy cake

This pretty cake is guaranteed to delight any girl on her birthday.

🔪🔪🔪 1 hour, cooling and setting, plus making the posy

Pink posy cake, surrounded by Floral table centrepiece, with flower sandwiches

MENU

Flower sandwiches

Macaroon petals

Pink posy cake

To decorate:
Floral table centrepiece

Party countdown

One week before the party
Make a complete shopping list and start the shopping.
Make the Floral table centrepiece.

Two days before the party
Make the Rose posy. Store in an airtight container.
Make the Macaroon petals. Store in an airtight container.
Cook the chicken for the sandwiches. Wrap in cling film and refrigerate.

The day before the party
Make the layers for the Pink posy cake.

Early on the day of the party
Make the frosting and assemble the Pink posy cake.
Prepare the flower sandwiches. Wrap in cling film and refrigerate.
Lay the table.

One hour before the party
Make the Macaroon petals.
Decorate the cake with the posy.
Put the flower sandwiches on the table.

Serves 8–12
melted butter and flour, for the tins
75 g /3 oz flour
75 g /3 oz cornflour
4 ml /¾ tsp baking powder
6 eggs, separated
175 g /6 oz caster sugar
red food colouring
To decorate
desiccated coconut
Rose posy (see recipe)
For the frosting
500 g /18 oz sugar
3 egg whites
a pinch of salt
red food colouring
2.5 ml /½ tsp vanilla essence

1 Brush 3 × 21.5 cm /8½ in round sandwich tins with melted butter. Cut 3 circles of greaseproof paper to fit the base of the tins. Line the tins and brush the paper with melted butter. Dust the tins with flour, shaking out any excess. Heat the oven to 200C /400F /gas 6.

2 Sift the flour, cornflour and baking powder together twice. Reserve.

3 In a large bowl combine the egg yolks and sugar. Whisk until thick and creamy.

4 In another bowl, whisk the egg whites until stiff but not dry. Fold the whisked egg whites into the yolk mixture, place the bowl over a saucepan of hot water and whisk until the mixture is very light and fluffy.

5 Transfer ⅓ of the mixture to another bowl; tint it pink with a little red food colouring.

6 Using a large metal spoon, fold ⅔ of the flour mixture into the plain batter. Fold the remaining mixture into the pink batter.

7 Pour the pink batter into one of the prepared tins. Divide the plain batter between the 2 other tins.

8 Bake the cakes for 15 minutes, or until well risen and springy to the touch. Turn out onto wire racks and leave to get cold.

9 Make the frosting. In a heavy-based saucepan, combine the sugar and 225 ml / 8 fl oz water. Stir over a low heat until the sugar is completely dissolved. Bring to the boil and boil without stirring to 115C /240F; at this temperature a sample dropped into cold water will form a soft ball.

10 Meanwhile, using an electric mixer, whisk the egg whites with a pinch of salt until stiff but not dry.

11 Remove the syrup from the heat and leave until the bubbles subside. Stir in a little red food colouring and the vanilla essence. Whisking continuously, pour the syrup onto the egg whites in a thin stream. Continue whisking until the frosting is cold and very thick.

12 Spread the cake layers with the frosting, then sandwich them together, putting the pink cake layer in the centre.

13 Swirl the remaining frosting over the top and sides of the cake, then press the desiccated coconut over the sides. Leave to dry. Just before serving, decorate with the Rose posy (see page 61).

Macaroon petals

 45 minutes

Makes 12
butter, for baking sheets (or rice paper)
125 g /4 oz ground almonds
75 g /3 oz caster sugar
2 drops almond essence
2 egg whites
6 glacé cherries, halved

1 Heat the oven to 150C /300F /gas 2. Line 2 or 3 baking sheets with greaseproof paper and lightly grease with butter (or line the sheets with rice paper).

2 In a large bowl sift together the ground almonds with the caster sugar and add the almond essence.

3 In a small bowl, whisk the egg whites until stiff but not dry. With a large metal spoon gently but thoroughly fold the egg whites into the almond mixture.

4 Fit a large piping bag with a 15 mm / ½ in star-shaped nozzle and spoon in the mixture. Pipe stars onto the prepared baking sheets, 5 cm /2 in apart. Decorate the centre of each macaroon with half a glacé cherry.

5 Bake the macaroons in the oven for 30 minutes, or until they are a pale golden colour. Turn the baking sheets occasionally during cooking. Remove from the oven and allow the macaroons to cool for 1–2 minutes before transferring them to a wire rack with a spatula. When cold store the macaroons in an airtight container.

Template for floral table centrepiece

1 Using scissors, cut out the lily, rose and leaf templates from a piece of card.

2 Make the lilies. Using the template, draw 5 lily shapes on pink tissue paper, then 5 shapes on blue tissue paper. Lay the shapes on top of each other, alternating the colours. Make 1 small stitch through the centre of the lily to hold the layers together, leaving long thread ends.

3 Pinch together the centre of the flower and tie the thread ends round it to secure the base of the lily.

4 Holding the base, pull down each petal to open the flower. Repeat to make 5 lilies.

5 To make the roses, proceed as above, using 10 pink tissue paper shapes. Repeat to make 5 roses. If you wish to make small roses to decorate the base of the stem of the cake stand, trim the rose template 25 mm / 1 in all round and proceed as above.

6 Prepare the leaf base. Draw a 40 cm /16 in circle on a piece of light green card. Using the template, draw 12 pairs of leaves spaced evenly apart around the outline of the circle. Cut out the shape.

7 Glue the roses and the lilies alternately around the circle, leaving the leaf shapes to make a fluted edge.

8 If you wish, stick the smaller roses around the base of the stem of the cake stand, using small adhesive pellets.

Rose posy

making the paste,
then 1 hour

Makes 12 roses
red and green food colouring
oil, for greasing
1 small egg white, lightly beaten (optional)
For 8 oz paste
100g /4 oz ground almonds
50 g /2 oz caster sugar
*50 g /2 oz icing sugar, sifted, plus extra for
    rolling*
1.5 ml /¼ tsp vanilla essence
2 drops almond essence
2.5 ml /½ tsp lemon juice
1 small egg, lightly beaten

1 Make the paste: combine the ground
almonds with the sugars in a large bowl. Mix
well. Add the vanilla and almond essences
and lemon juice. Knead thoroughly by hand,
gradually adding the lightly beaten egg until
the paste is smooth and pliable.
2 Tint 150 g /6 oz paste pale pink. Tint
50 g /2 oz paste pale green.
3 Divide the pink paste into 24 portions.
Keep covered until needed. Lightly oil a
board. Take a portion and roll it in your
hands into a ball. Place it on the oiled board
and press with your fingers into a circle.
With a small palette knife, smooth it over
repeatedly to flatten it gradually and thin the
edges. Cut it sharply down the centre into 2.
4 Lift one half off the board and roll it
tightly round to make the centre of the bud,
thick edge downwards. Take the other half,
curve it slightly round a finger, thick edge
downwards, and curl back the thin edges a
little. Shape this piece around the centre bud.
5 Repeat with portions of paste to make
outer petals, until you have a 'bloom'. If you
find the petals do not stick, use a little egg
white to stick them on.
6 Squeeze the bottom of the rose together
to make a stem and push a cocktail stick into
it. Stick into a grapefruit or apple and leave
to dry. Repeat to make 12 roses.
7 To serve, arrange the roses in a posy on
the cake (see picture), leaving 1 or 2 of the
flowers on cocktail sticks in the centre, to
give the posy height. Roll out the green paste
and cut out 14 leaf shapes, then make vein
markings on them with a small, sharp knife.
Arrange in position, using a little egg white
to stick them on if necessary.

● If you wish, you can vary the colour of
your roses by tinting half of the pale pink
paste a deeper pink. Use the deep pink paste
to make the tightly rolled bud and centre
petals.
● This quantity of almond paste is more
than is needed for your Posy cake — make the
extra roses and freeze them for future use.

Chicken almond
flower sandwiches

cooking the chicken and making the
mayonnaise, then 10 minutes

Makes 8
*75 g /3 oz cooked chicken, skinned and
    thinly sliced*
25 g /1 oz piece celery stick, thinly sliced
15 g /½ oz flaked almonds, toasted
15 ml /1 tbls Mayonnaise (see page 90)
salt and freshly ground black pepper
a pinch of cayenne pepper
4 thin slices day-old white bread
softened butter
fresh parsley or cress, to garnish

1 In a bowl, combine the chicken, celery
and almonds. Add the mayonnaise and stir
well, using a wooden spoon. Season with salt
and black pepper, and cayenne pepper.
2 Spread the bread with softened butter.
Divide the chicken almond mixture between
2 slices of bread and make 2 sandwiches.
3 Using a 5 cm /2 in flower-shaped biscuit
cutter, cut each sandwich into 4 flower
shapes. Wrap in cling film and keep chilled
until needed. Serve, garnished with fresh
parsley or cress.

Cheese and nut
flower sandwiches

10 minutes

Makes 12
100 g /4 oz cream cheese
25 g /1 oz peanuts, finely chopped
2.5 ml /½ tsp lemon juice
225 g /8 oz day-old fruit loaf (12 thin slices)
softened butter
fresh parsley or cress, to garnish

1 In a bowl combine the cream cheese,
peanuts and lemon juice. Beat well.
2 Spread the bread slices with the softened
butter. Divide the cheese mixture among 6
slices of fruit loaf, and make 6 sandwiches.

*Flower sandwiches: Chicken almond, Cheese
and nut and Egg and bacon*

3 Using a 5 cm /2 in flower-shaped biscuit
cutter, cut 2 flower shapes from each sandwich. Wrap in cling film and keep chilled
until needed. Serve, garnished with fresh
parsley or cress.

Egg and bacon
flower sandwiches

making the mayonnaise,
then 20 minutes, plus cooling

Makes 12
a small knob of butter
50 g /2 oz bacon, finely chopped
2 eggs
5 ml /1 tsp Mayonnaise (see page 90)
5 ml /1 tsp freshly chopped parsley
freshly ground black pepper
6 thin slices day-old wholemeal bread
softened butter
fresh parsley or cress, to garnish

1 In a small frying-pan, melt the butter.
Add the bacon and sauté until it is crisp,
stirring. Remove from the heat.
2 In a bowl, beat the eggs lightly with
15 ml /1 tbls water. Pour the mixture into
the frying-pan, return it to the heat and stir
until the eggs start to set. Turn the mixture
into a bowl and leave it to get cold.
3 Stir the mayonnaise and parsley into the
egg mixture and season with pepper to taste.
4 Spread the bread slices with softened
butter. Divide the egg mixture among 3
slices of bread, and make 3 sandwiches.
5 Using a 5 cm /2 in flower-shaped biscuit
cutter, cut 4 flower shapes from each sandwich. Wrap in cling film and keep chilled
until needed. Serve, garnished with fresh
parsley or cress.

CIRCUS TIME

If you are organizing a children's party, try using a Circus theme. Children love food made into animal shapes, so surprise them with my Merry-go-round cake or an Animal train.

Many children love going to the circus, so why not bring the circus to the home as the theme for a children's party. This subject gives you plenty of scope for originality and it is something the children will love to discuss and help you plan.

Send out special invitations decorated with circus pictures and ask your guests to come dressed-up as clowns or acrobats. Or, if you feel that this is not practical, you could make clown hats or exciting masks out of coloured cards.

If you are feeling more adventurous, make 2-layer net tutus and clown ruffs for the children. These could always be made out of crêpe or tissue paper, but then they will probably tear before the end of the fun and games. It's a marvellous idea if you provide face paints, laid out on a table with plenty of small mirrors, or one large mirror. Let the guests put on their own crazy make-up but do remember to supply lots of tissues to clean the resulting rainbow-coloured hands before they touch anything else.

To give the room in which the party is being held a circusy atmosphere, decorate it like a big top. To do this cut a large circle of cardboard and cover it with lots of different coloured strips of crêpe or tissue paper. To this circle, attach very long strips of brightly coloured paper. Stick 4 pieces of string to the circle then attach them to the ceiling (using non-marking adhesive) so that the circle is suspended. Next, take the long strips of paper and attach them to the walls of the room to give a tent effect. Large bunches of balloons in each corner of the room add colour, or you could have nets filled with balloons to let down at the end of the party.

To make the table look like a circus ring, use a circular table if you have one, or borrow one for the party. Cover it with a sand-coloured tablecloth or make one from crêpe paper. Line the edge of the table with coloured card so that it stands above the rim of the table and looks like the edge of a circus ring. Arrange all the food on coloured paper napkins cut into different shapes, such as balloons, placed around the table. Place a name tag in each child's place, or write the child's name in sugared letters around the edge of the plate.

Use something circular, like a cake tin, to make a centre-piece stand for the Merry-go-round cake. Attach a strip of card to it so that it has sloping sides and decorate this with strips of coloured paper to echo the big top theme.

For going home time, buy lots of small bags of sweets or make some extra animal biscuits and pipe the children's names on them. Buy some long, thin balloons and twist them into animal shapes or, if you don't feel up to this, buy plastic trumpets or any other instruments — they'll certainly ensure a noisy home-going.

Party countdown

One week before the party
Prepare a comprehensive shopping list and start the shopping.
Cut out the animal templates.

Two days before the party
Make the Animal biscuits. Keep them in an airtight container.
Make layers for the Merry-go-round cake. Keep them in an airtight container.

The day before the party
Prepare the parts of the Animal train. Wrap them in cling film and refrigerate.
Ice the Animal biscuits; return them to the airtight container.

Early on the day of the party
Make the filling for the Merry-go-round cake. Finish decorating the cake.

Up to one hour before the party
Assemble the Animal train on the table.

Merry-go-round cake

about 1½ hours, plus cooling, plus making the animal biscuits

Serves 12
melted butter and flour, for the tins
275 g /10 oz flour
90 ml /6 tbls cocoa powder
15 ml /1 tbls instant coffee granules
15 ml /1 tbls baking powder
7.5 ml /1½ tsp bicarbonate of soda
275 ml /10 fl oz milk
juice of ½ lemon
175 g /6 oz butter, softened
250 g /9 oz caster sugar
3 eggs, well beaten
1.5 ml /¼ tsp vanilla essence
juice of ½ orange
For the chocolate filling
100 g /4 oz plain chocolate
50 g /2 oz unsalted butter
100 g /4 oz icing sugar, sifted
1 egg yolk
To finish the cake
350 g /12 oz icing sugar
yellow food colouring
10 striped candy or barley sugar
* sticks, about 15 cm /6 in long*
tiny coloured sweets
Animal biscuits (see recipe)
½ × Butter cream (page 76), coloured
* orange*

1 Brush 3×22 cm /8½ in round sandwich tins with melted butter. Cut 3 circles of greaseproof paper to fit the base of the tins.

Line, butter and flour each tin. Heat the oven to 190C /375F /gas 5.
2 Into a bowl, sift together the flour, the cocoa powder, the coffee granules, the baking powder and the bicarbonate of soda. Repeat twice more.
3 Put the milk in a bowl and add the lemon juice, stirring them together until the milk curdles.
4 In a mixing bowl, combine the butter and the caster sugar, beating them together until they are fluffy. Beat in 15 ml /1 tbls of the flour mixture.
5 Add the beaten eggs, the flour mixture and the curdled milk to the creamed mixture, alternately and a little at a time, beating well after each addition. Stop adding the milk if the batter becomes too liquid, it should be soft but still hold its shape.
6 Beat in the vanilla essence.
7 Divide ¾ of the batter between 2 of the prepared tins and spread it evenly. Spread the remaining batter smoothly in the third tin.
8 Bake the cakes until they are well risen and shrink slightly from the sides of the tins. This will take 20 minutes for the thick layers, 15–17 minutes for the thinner one. Leave the cakes in the tins for 2–3 minutes, then turn them out onto a wire rack and leave them to get cold.
9 Meanwhile, make the filling for the cake. Break the chocolate into a small bowl and place it over a saucepan of hot water until melted. Leave to cool without letting the chocolate harden.
10 In a bowl, beat the butter until it is creamy. Gradually add the icing sugar, beating vigorously. Beat in the egg yolk until it is well blended. Gradually add the melted chocolate, beating the mixture until it is completely smooth.
11 When the layers are cold, prick the 2 thick ones all over with a fork. Sprinkle with the orange juice. Spread one layer with 105 ml /7 tbls chocolate filling and sandwich with the second layer.
12 Sift the icing sugar into a bowl. Add enough hot water to give a stiff but flowing consistency and tint with a little yellow food colouring. Spread the yellow icing evenly over the top and sides of the sandwiched layers with a palette knife, decorate the sides with rows of coloured sweets, then leave the cake to set.
13 To assemble the merry-go-round, place it on a board or flat plate. Push the candy or barley-sugar sticks firmly into the top of the cake to resemble poles.
14 Place the remaining layer of cake on a thin 20 cm (8 in) cake board and spread the top and sides smoothly with chocolate filling, using a spatula or palette knife. Decorate with coloured sweets.
15 Carefully place the last layer on top of the candy sticks, with the decorated side uppermost.
16 Stick an animal biscuit (see page 64) to each candy pole with a little dab of chocolate filling. Spoon the orange butter cream into a piping bag fitted with a star nozzle and pipe around the base of the cake. Decorate the board with more sweets if you wish.

Merry-go-round cake

Animal biscuits

Cardboard animal shapes can be used as guide lines. Helping you to draw and cut out the animals will be a way of involving the children in the preparations.

🍴🍴 30 minutes,
then setting

Makes 24 biscuits
350 g /12 oz flour
50 g /2 oz icing sugar
50 g /2 oz caster sugar
225 g /8 oz butter
flour, for rolling
For the icing
450 g /1 lb icing sugar
orange, blue, yellow and red food colouring

1 Heat the oven to 375F /190C /gas 5.
2 Sift the flour and the icing sugar into a bowl, then stir in the caster sugar.
3 Cut the butter into small pieces. Add it to the flour mixture, rubbing it in with your fingertips until the mixture has the texture of

Animal train

coarse breadcrumbs. Knead to a smooth, fairly stiff dough.
4 On a lightly floured board, roll out the dough to about 3 mm /⅛ in thick. Alternatively, roll between 2 sheets of cling film without extra flour. With a sharp knife and using a variety of animal-shaped cardboard cut-outs (see page 66) as guides, cut out 24 animal shapes. Or use animal-shaped biscuit cutters.
5 Lay the animal shapes on baking sheets and bake for 7–10 minutes, or until they are crisp.
6 Remove the biscuits from the sheets with a palette knife and lay them on wire racks to cool. Make sure the biscuits do not overlap, or they will bend.
7 Meanwhile, prepare a glacé icing. Sift the icing sugar into a bowl and add enough hot water to give a stiff but flowing consistency. Divide the icing equally among 4 small bowls and tint each with a few drops of a different food colouring.
8 Dip 6 animals into each bowl of icing. Remove and leave to set. To keep the remaining icing soft, place the bowls in a large pan and pour hot water to come halfway up the outsides of the bowls. When the icing on the animal biscuits has completely

set, you can pipe on features in contrasting colours for each animal. Leave to set.
9 Use 9 of the biscuits to finish the cake and serve the rest separately.

Animal train

The animal train consists of an old-fashioned steam engine, plus 3 cages on wheels. You will need 2×225 g /8 oz packets of pumpernickel slices, 1×225 g /8 oz packet of 4 cm /1½ in pumpernickel rounds and 2×5 cm /2 in rounds.

🔪🔪🔪 3 hours, including making the cages and the animals

Serves 8–12
1 large brown loaf, unsliced
65 g /2½ oz softened butter
100 g /4 oz liver sausage
salt and freshly ground black pepper
1 small white loaf, unsliced
1 slice pumpernickel
4×4 cm /1½ in pumpernickel rounds
2×5 cm /2 in pumpernickel rounds
skin of 1 medium-sized cucumber
1 small carrot

1 Make the engine. Cut all the crusts from the brown loaf. Discard. Cut a slice lengthways 15 mm /½ in thick and 7.5 cm /3 in wide. Trim the loaf to 16 cm /6½ in long, 6 cm /2 in wide, 5 cm /2 in thick. Reserve the remaining bread for the grizzly bears.

2 Lightly run a rolling pin over the slice of brown bread to make it less likely to crack. Spread the bread lightly with softened butter.

3 In a bowl, combine the remaining softened butter with the liver sausage, beating until well blended. Season to taste with salt and freshly ground black pepper. This mixture will be used to stick together the different parts of the engine.

4 Reserving 75 ml /5 tbls liver sausage mixture, spread the remainder evenly over the brown bread slice, using a spatula or palette knife. Roll this up tightly starting from a short side. Wrap it up in cling film and chill.

5 Meanwhile, make the cab. Cut and discard the crusts from the white loaf, then trim it into a 9 cm /3½ in high rectangle, 6.5 cm /2½ in wide and thick.

6 Remove the chilled roll from the refrigerator. Fill any cracks that may have appeared with the liver sausage mixture and spread a little liver sausage along the seam

and over one end of the roll. Press the roll firmly on top of the brown bread rectangle, keeping it to one end.

7 Spread the base of the white bread rectangle with liver sausage and place it against the end of the roll, to make the cab. Spread the top with a little liver sausage.

8 Trim the slice of pumpernickel to fit over the top of the cab and place on the liver sausage.

9 Using the pumpernickel trimmings, cut 2 window shapes. Spread one side of each with a little liver sausage mixture and stick to the sides of the cab. Reserve the remaining trimmings for the animals.

10 Make the wheels. Using the liver sausage mixture, stick the 4 smaller pumpernickel rounds to the front of the engine, 2 on each side. Stick the 2 larger rounds either side of the rear of the engine. (If you wish, decorate the wheels as for the cages, step 7.)

11 Make the fender. Cut narrow, even-sized strips of cucumber peel. Using the liver sausage mixture, attach them vertically to the front of the engine in parallel lines. Cut 2 more strips, one for the top and one for the bottom. Attach as above.

12 Stick 2 carrot cylinders to the top of the engine body with the reserved liver sausage.

The cages

225 g /8 oz cottage cheese
200 g /7 oz Roquefort cheese, or another
* creamy blue cheese*
75 g /3 oz softened butter
150 ml /5 fl oz thick cream, whipped
15 ml /1 tbls finely chopped fresh parsley
freshly ground black pepper
275 g /10 oz cream cheese
1.5 ml /¼ tsp green food colouring
12 slices pumpernickel
42 small wooden skewers, cut to about
* 11.5 cm /3¾ in*
42 striped drinking straws, cut to
* 9.5 cm /3¾ in*
9 stuffed olives, thinly sliced
12×4 cm /1½ in pumpernickel rounds

1 Sieve the cottage cheese into a bowl. Crumble in the Roquefort cheese or other blue cheese and add the softened butter. Mix until they are well blended.

2 Fold in the whipped cream and the chopped parsley. Season to taste with freshly ground black pepper.

3 In another bowl, combine the cream cheese with a little green food colouring, beating together until smooth. Reserve.

4 To make the base of a cage, spread 2 slices of pumpernickel with a little cottage cheese mixture and sandwich them together.

5 Make the bars. Pierce the edge of the base at regular intervals with 14 skewers. Slip a straw over each skewer. Place an animal inside the cage.

6 Sandwich two more slices of pumpernickel with the cottage cheese mixture to make the roof of the cage. Stud the sides with stuffed olive slices. Carefully place the roof on top of the bars, pressing it down to secure it. Repeat steps 4, 5 and 6 to make 2 more cages.

7 Prepare the wheels. Fit a piping bag with a small plain nozzle and spoon in the coloured cream cheese. Pipe a spiral to decorate one side of each pumpernickel round. Stick the wheels in place on the cages with a little more cream cheese.

The leopards, lions and grizzly bears

For the leopards
1 slice pumpernickel
2 pumpernickel rounds
40 ml /8 tsp cream cheese
2 slices processed yellow Cheddar cheese
1 black olive, stoned
a small piece canned pimento
chives

For the grizzly bears
5 slices brown bread, crusts removed
20 ml /4 tsp cream cheese
pumpernickel trimmings

For the lions
2 slices pumpernickel
40 ml /8 tsp cream cheese
3 slices processed orange Cheddar cheese
1 black olive, stoned
a small piece canned pimento
1 slice processed yellow Cheddar cheese

Animal templates

1 Make 2 leopards. Either use the animal templates (see left-hand side of the page) to cut around, or you can cut 2 hump shapes from the slice of pumpernickel to make the bodies. Reserve the trimmings. Cut 2 heads from the pumpernickel rounds, reserving the trimmings. Lightly spread both sides of the bodies and heads with cream cheese, using a palette knife. Cover both sides with the processed Cheddar cheese, trimming the slices of cheese to fit exactly over the bodies and heads. The cheese will help the heads to stick to the bodies.

2 Cut eyes and spots out of the black olive and stick them in place with a little cream cheese. Cut the nose and ears out of the canned pimento and stick them in place. Cut the chives to make whiskers and then stick them in place with cream cheese.

3 Make 2 grizzly bears. Using a gingerbread man biscuit cutter no more than 9 cm / 3½ in high, cut 4 shapes from the brown bread slices. Next spread the slices with cream cheese and sandwich them together. Trim the sandwiched slices to make the bears.

4 Cut 8 paws, 2 noses and 4 ears from the pumpernickel trimmings. Stick them in place with cream cheese.

5 Make 2 lions. Using the templates cut 2 lions, lying down, out of the pumpernickel slices. Spread both sides of each lion shape lightly with cream cheese and then cover with processed cheese, trimmed to fit.

6 Cut 4 eyes out of the black olive and 2 noses out of the pimento or olive. Stick in place with cream cheese. To make the manes, shred the processed yellow cheese and stick the shreds carefully in place with a little cream cheese. Alternatively, cut 2 comb shapes out of the processed yellow cheese and stick them in place with cream cheese.

● Try making monkeys, or zebras and tigers with stripes of black olive slivers.

To assemble the train
To assemble the train, cover a large strip of cardboard with foil or a brightly coloured napkin. Cut pumpernickel trimmings to make some couplings, if you wish. Place the engine

Leopards, lions and grizzly bears in the cages of the Animal train

in front on the prepared 'track', then the 3 cages linked together by the pumpernickel couplings, if you are using them. Arrange some of the animals outside their cages. To eat, remove the bars and slice the base and the roof of the cages.

Do-it-yourself sundaes

⏱ 1 hour

Serves 12
*a selection of colourful ice creams, such as
    vanilla, chocolate and strawberry*
For the butterscotch sauce
50 g /2 oz butter
75 g /3 oz sugar
65 g /2½ oz Demerara sugar
175 ml /6 fl oz golden syrup
a pinch of salt
100 ml /4 fl oz thick cream
For the raspberry sauce
*450 g /1 lb raspberries, fresh or frozen and
    defrosted*
100 g /4 oz icing sugar, sifted
For the chocolate sauce
125 g /4½ oz plain chocolate
40 g /1½ oz butter
75 ml /3 fl oz thick cream
75 ml /3 fl oz thin cream
To decorate
275 ml /10 fl oz thick cream, whipped
90 ml /6 tbls toasted flaked almonds

1 Make the butterscotch sauce. In a saucepan, combine the butter, the sugar, the Demerara sugar, the golden syrup and a pinch of salt. Stir over a low heat until the sugar has dissolved.
2 Bring to the boil, then simmer for 20 minutes, stirring occasionally. Add the cream and beat until smooth. Chill.
3 Make the raspberry sauce. Press the raspberries through a fine sieve into a bowl, and beat in the icing sugar. Reserve.
4 Make the chocolate sauce. In the top pan of a double boiler, combine the chocolate and the butter. Place over simmering water and stir with a wooden spoon until it has melted.

5 Gradually beat in the thick and thin cream. Bring to the boil and simmer for 2–3 minutes, stirring. Leave until lukewarm.
6 Meanwhile, transfer the ice creams to the main part of the refrigerator to soften slightly. Spoon the whipped cream into a piping bag fitted with a star nozzle.

A Do-it-yourself sundae

7 To serve, let the children choose their own combinations of ice cream and sauce. Layer them up in tall sundae glasses. Pipe a whirl of whipped cream on top and scatter with flaked almonds.

A TEA PARTY

Children love asking their friends home to tea, and birthday tea parties are always popular. Other days can also be made into special occasions by providing tea after a school event or a holiday outing.

A tea party can be a lot of fun for children. The selection of food described here will be most suitable for 5- to 8-year-olds, but younger children will also enjoy these colourful dishes. The recipes are deliberately simple, so that the children themselves can help to make them.

Use paper cloths, plates and napkins for mopping up. They help to give the party atmosphere, besides making the clearing up easier. If you are planning to have any games after the tea party, they will be much more successful if they are organized in advance. Make sure you have the equipment you need and it is advisable to remove anything breakable from the room!

Food and drink

There is a vast choice of bought foods that children adore, so buy a supply of crisps and savoury snacks and nuts, plus chocolate biscuits. Keep the food in bite-size portions. Do not make too many sandwiches but try to provide savouries as well as sweet cakes: sausages on sticks for dunking into a sauce, or mini hot dogs, with relishes.

Savoury pinwheels can be made by spreading buttered slices of white and brown bread (with the crusts cut off) with yeast extract or peanut butter, rolling them up firmly and cutting them into rounds. These can be prepared in advance, covered with cling-film and refrigerated until they are needed, then cut them through just before serving. Animal sandwiches are also popular and easy to make: use animal cutters to shape the slices of brown or white bread, spread with peanut butter, mashed banana or creamed egg and cress. Make eyes with currants and decorate the bodies with chopped walnuts.

Ideas for novelty cakes are shown on pages 74–79. For small cakes use the basic Victoria sponge recipe on page 78. Bake the mixture in pretty paper cases and then finish them with different coloured icings and decorate with chocolate buttons or hundreds and thousands.

Ice cream is always a big success: you can either buy and fill cones, or decorate scoops of ice cream with chocolate or strawberry sauce, small sweets or wafers.

Serve home-made lemonade in the summer, fizz up squashes with soda water or make a fruit punch and garnish it with fruit. To make milk shakes, buy flavoured packets of shake mixture and mix with milk in a blender, or make your own delicious fresh Strawberry shakes or Banana malt shakes from the recipes on pages 80 and 81.

Gingerbread men are an all-time winner with children of any age. The recipe given here is richly-flavoured and very delicious.

Not only at Christmas time but also for a birthday party, the gingerbread men can be made with holes in the top of their heads so that they can be hung up as attractive and edible decorations!

Sausage-pastry twizzlers

 50 minutes

Serves 8
200 g /7 oz frozen puff pastry, defrosted
8 pork sausages
1 medium-sized egg, beaten
tomato ketchup and cucumber relish, to serve

1 Heat the oven to 220C /425F /gas 7.
2 Roll out the pastry into a rectangle 30×20 cm /12×8 in and then cut it into eight 30 cm /12 in long strips.
3 Moisten one edge of each strip with water and roll around each sausage, overlapping the moistened edge of each strip very slightly; leave the sausage ends uncovered.
4 Place on a baking sheet and brush the pastry with the beaten egg. Bake for 20–25 minutes until the pastry is golden brown.
5 Spear with lollipop sticks if wished. Serve immediately, with tomato ketchup and cucumber relish.

Starry mincemeat pies

 40 minutes

Serves 12
175 g /6 oz flour, plus extra for dusting
salt
40 g /1½ oz vegetable fat
40 g /1½ oz margarine
225 g /8 oz mincemeat
icing sugar, to dust

1 Heat the oven to 200C /400F /gas 6.
2 Sieve the flour with a pinch of salt, then rub in the fats until the mixture resembles fine breadcrumbs.
3 Add 30–37.5 ml /2–2½ tbls cold or iced water to the mixture and mix to a firm dough. Knead the pastry, then put it in the refrigerator for 10 minutes to chill.
4 On a floured surface roll out the pastry to 3 mm /⅛ in thick. Using a 7.5 cm /3 in cutter, cut out 12 rounds of pastry and fit them into a greased 12-hole bun tin.
5 Knead together the pastry trimmings, re-roll and cut out 12 stars, using a star-shaped cutter.
6 Spoon 10 ml /2 tsp mincemeat into each pie case, and place a pastry star on top of the mincemeat.
7 Bake in the oven for 15–20 minutes. Cool them on a wire tray, then lightly dust with icing sugar to serve.

Sausage-pastry twizzlers, Funny face biscuits and Traffic light jellies; colourful paper napkins and plates add to a cheerful tea party spread that children will love

Traffic light jellies

 15 minutes,
plus setting

Serves 8
100 g /4 oz tablet lime jelly
100 g /4 oz tablet orange jelly
100 g /4 oz tablet raspberry jelly

1 Dissolve the lime jelly in 150 ml /5 fl oz hot water, cool it quickly with a few ice cubes and then add cold water to make the jelly up to 600 ml /1 pt.
2 Divide the liquid among 8 deep glasses, approximately 225 ml /8 fl oz in capacity. Put the glasses in the refrigerator for 1–2 hours to set.
3 When the lime jelly has set, dissolve the orange jelly in the same way, allow it to cool slightly, then divide this among the glasses and return them to the refrigerator to set.
4 Repeat the procedure with the raspberry jelly.
5 About 20 minutes before you are ready to serve them, take the glasses out of the refrigerator to allow the jellies to come to room temperature.

Peanut butter cookies

10 minutes,
then 30–35 minutes baking

Makes 18
100 g /4 oz butter, plus extra for greasing
100 g /4 oz crunchy peanut butter
100 g /4 oz soft brown sugar
175 g /6 oz wholemeal flour, plus extra for flouring
2.5 ml /½ tsp bicarbonate of soda
1 egg
50 g /2 oz unsalted peanuts, skinned

1 Heat the oven to 180C /325F /gas 3. Grease a large baking sheet.
2 In a large bowl, cream together the butter, peanut butter and sugar.
3 In a separate bowl, sift together the flour and bicarbonate of soda.
4 Add the egg to the creamed mixture, then stir in the flour and bicarbonate of soda until well mixed. Alternatively, mix in a food processor.
5 Shape the mixture into a ball. Break off small even-sized pieces and roll them into balls, using floured hands.
6 Place the balls on the prepared baking sheet and flatten them slightly with the palm of your hand. Sprinkle each with a few unsalted, skinned peanuts.
7 Bake for 30–35 minutes, or until cooked through and browned. Transfer to a wire rack with a palette knife and leave the cookies to get cold before serving.

Crunchy clusters

10 minutes, then setting

Makes 15
100 g /4 oz soft margarine
60 ml /4 tbls clear honey
15 ml /1 tbls cocoa powder
225 g /8 oz muesli

1 In a saucepan, combine the margarine, honey and cocoa powder. Heat them until they bubble, stirring continuously with a wooden spoon.
2 Remove the pan from the heat. Stir in the muesli until well blended. Leave to cool.
3 Spoon the mixture into small paper cases and leave them to get cold and harden.

● These Crunchy clusters will keep for several days in an airtight container.

Gingerbread men

Funny face biscuits

 45 minutes

Makes 16 biscuits
175 g /6 oz margarine, softened, plus extra for greasing
75 g /3 oz caster sugar
1 small lemon
175 g /6 oz flour, sifted
225 g /8 oz icing sugar, sieved
1 packet dolly mixture sweets
16 diamond-shaped cake decorations
1 glacé cherry
4 mint rings

1 Heat the oven to 170C /325F /gas 3.
2 In a bowl, cream together the margarine and sugar until light and fluffy.
3 Finely grate the zest from the lemon and squeeze the juice from one half. Add the zest and juice to the creamed mixture; gradually work in the sifted flour to form a dough.

Knead until the dough is smooth. Chill in the refrigerator for 10 minutes.
4 On a lightly floured surface roll out the dough to 5 mm /¼ in thick. Using a 6.5 cm / 2½ in cutter, cut into rounds and place them on a greased baking sheet.
5 Bake them in the oven for about 15–20 minutes or until the biscuits are a golden brown. Remove them from the baking sheet and cool them on a wire rack.
6 Squeeze the juice from the remaining half of the lemon, strain it into the icing sugar and blend it to make a thick glacé icing, adding a little cold water if necessary.
7 Spread the icing evenly over the biscuits, stopping just short of the edges.
8 Before the icing sets, decorate the biscuits. Use the dolly mixture sweets for half of them, making eyes with the round 2-tone sweets cut in half, noses with the jelly sweets and mouths with the square 2-tone sweets cut into 3. On the remaining biscuits use the diamond-shaped cake decorations for eyes, a small piece of glacé cherry for the nose and half a mint ring for each smile.

Gingerbread men

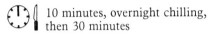 10 minutes, overnight chilling,
then 30 minutes

Makes 16
350 g /12 oz flour
5 ml /1 tsp ground allspice
5 ml /1 tsp ground ginger
5 ml /1 tsp ground cinnamon
a pinch of salt
2.5 ml /½ tsp bicarbonate of soda
175 g /6 oz butter
60 ml /4 tbls soft light brown sugar
120 ml /8 tbls golden syrup
90 ml /6 tbls milk
butter, for greasing
flour, for cutters
currants, for decoration
glacé cherries, finely sliced, for decoration

1 Sift the flour, allspice, ginger, cinnamon, salt and bicarbonate of soda into a bowl.
2 In another large bowl, whisk the butter until soft. Add the sugar and golden syrup and whisk continuously until light and fluffy.
3 With a large metal spoon, fold the flour mixture alternately with the milk into the butter mixture. Once blended, bring the mixture together with the palm of your hand and knead it until smooth. Wrap the dough in foil or cling film, and chill overnight in the refrigerator.
4 Heat the oven to 190C /375F /gas 5. Lightly grease 2 or 3 baking sheets.
5 Roll out the dough to about 3 mm /⅛ in thickness. With a floured gingerbread-man cutter cut out 16 shapes.
6 Arrange the gingerbread men on the prepared baking sheets. Decorate with currants and finely sliced glacé cherries and bake in the oven for 10–15 minutes, or until lightly golden and firm to the touch. Turn the baking sheets occasionally during cooking. Transfer the gingerbread men to a wire rack with a palette knife and allow them to cool. When they are cold they can be stored in an airtight container or individually frozen.

HALLOWE'EN

The bewitching time when you can conjure up these positively ghoulish delicacies for a spine-chilling party that is enormous fun — and definitely not for the faint-hearted!

Cat's eyes cakes and Strawberry shakes

On All Hallows' eve — the eve of All Saints' day, the last night of October — witches and free spirits roam at will, as do imaginative youngsters, draped in ghostly white, uttering loud blood-curdling cries. With such strong mythical and magical connections, it's a wonderful excuse for a party. Make it a fancy dress party, complete with ghosts, witches, devils and cats. Set the scene with candles and night-lights eerily contained in hollowed-out pumpkins. Put the flesh to good use by making tasty Pumpkin pie and Hallowe'en bites (see recipes).

Put aside one room of the house completely for the occasion — remove all breakables, valuables and small pieces of furniture that may get knocked over.

Your offspring will probably have plenty of ideas for decor. As long as these are not too outlandish, let them have a hand in the decoration so that they feel the party is really theirs.

Replacing ordinary light bulbs with red ones will give the room a cavernous atmosphere. You can cover the food table with a plastic cloth to protect it, then shroud it with a large, old white sheet.

Paper masks on the walls will add to the general air of horror; you could even have one as a table centrepiece lit from behind with a torch (not a candle in this instance — it would be too dangerous). Novelty shops have glow-in-the-dark masks, paper skeletons, skeletons printed on black balloons and other

items that will add the right creepy note.

Invitations should be spooky too, and should indicate that suitably macabre dress will be required.

Choose food that can be cooked in advance and kept warm if necessary. Skeletons, skulls, bones and blood-coloured sauces are suitably horrific and can be concocted out of quite ordinary ingredients. Skeleton spare ribs (see recipe) make a good grim centrepiece for the ghouls' table, served with a bowl of spicy tomato ketchup as 'blood sauce'. The spare ribs can be kept hot in a very low oven for about 30 minutes if you don't wish to serve them immediately.

Baked potatoes are easy and always popular and they can be turned into gruesome faces (see recipe). A block of butter can be shaped into a skull to serve with them.

Cakes and biscuits to nibble between party games can be decorated appropriately or cut into suitable shapes. For instance, small chocolate cakes can be iced with owl or cat faces (see recipe). These can be given to any children in the neighbourhood who come knocking on the door for the increasingly popular 'trick or treat' — the trick may be a gruesome prank, but a treat will protect you.

All this excitement is thirsty work, so make sure you have some witches' brew on hand. Serve the drinks in large, dark-coloured 'cauldron' pots and float a few small apples

or oranges spiked with cloves on the top.

Ginger beer can be coloured with a few drops of red food colouring to make a suitably blood-curdling drink. Tingly and refreshing Orange spine-chillers (see recipe) and mouthwatering strawberry milkshakes (see page 80) are sure to be popular.

Children will love the novelty of garishly coloured ice-cubes: simply add food colouring to the water before you freeze it into cubes or other shapes.

Have a bucket of water with apples floating on top; leave the stalks on and let the children bob for them — they must extract the apples from the water using only their teeth — no hands allowed!

Toffee apples (see recipe) are decorative and will satisfy the sweet-toothed. Devil's delight sweets (see recipe), piled into witches' hat cones, make delicious and appropriate going-home presents. To make witches' hat cones, cut 15 cm /6 in squares from black matt paper. Roll into cones and twist the bottoms. Fill them with the sweets and turn over the tops to keep the surprises hidden from sight.

Skeleton spareribs with 'blood' sauce

 1¼ hours

Serves 6–8
90 ml /6 tbls peanut oil
1 large onion, finely chopped
1.8 kg /4 lb pork spareribs, separated
salt
30 ml /2 tbls soy sauce
60 ml /4 tbls treacle
7.5 ml /1½ tsp ground ginger
15 ml /1 tbls tomato purée
850 ml /1½ pt chicken stock, home-made or from a cube
tomato ketchup, to serve
6 spring onions, finely chopped, to serve (optional)

1 Heat the oil in a large, heavy-based frying-pan over a medium heat, then add the onion and sauté for 5 minutes. Remove and reserve the onion, leaving as much oil as possible in the pan.
2 Sprinkle the spareribs all over with salt. Add them to the pan in batches and brown them quickly on both sides. Remove them from the pan.
3 Return the onion to the pan. Add the soy sauce, treacle, ground ginger and tomato purée and stir them together for 2–3 minutes, then gradually add the chicken stock, stirring well.
4 Return the ribs to the pan and simmer for 20 minutes.
5 Turn the ribs over so that they are thoroughly coated with sauce, cover and simmer for a further 20 minutes. Meanwhile, heat the oven to 200C /400F /gas 6.
6 Transfer the ribs to a roasting tin, pour any sauce left in the pan over them and put the tin in the centre of the oven for 30 minutes or until the ribs are crispy and have absorbed most of the sauce, turning once.

7 Arrange the ribs on a large oval platter in the shape of a skeleton. Use the long spare ribs for the arms and legs, keeping the shorter ones for the ribs. Place any remaining ribs on another serving plate.
8 Pour the remaining sauce into a small bowl, top up with tomato ketchup, stirring well; stir in the spring onions, if wished.
9 Put the bowl of sauce on the oval platter at the top of the skeleton, where the head should be, and serve.

● The spare ribs can be kept hot in a very low oven for about 30 minutes if you don't wish to serve them immediately.

Hallowe'en bites

1 hour,
plus 30 minutes chilling

Makes 8 pies
350 g /12 oz flour
a pinch of salt
2.5 ml /½ tsp ground cinnamon
2.5 ml /½ tsp ground ginger
175 g /6 oz butter
2 medium-sized egg yolks
flour, for rolling
For the filling
350 g /12 oz pumpkin purée (canned, or made from 450 g /1 lb pumpkin flesh, steamed and puréed)
100 g /4 oz soft light brown sugar
3 medium-sized eggs, beaten
salt
60 ml /4 tbls milk
150 ml /5 fl oz thin cream
5 ml /1 tsp ground cinnamon
a pinch of ground cloves
2.5 ml /½ tsp ground ginger
30 ml /2 tbls pumpkin seeds

1 Heat the oven to 190C /375F /gas 5.
2 To make the pastry, sift together the flour, salt and spices and rub in the butter with your fingertips until it resembles fine crumbs. Beat the egg yolks with 30 ml /2 tbls water and stir them into the mixture to make a firm dough. Wrap in cling film or foil and chill for 30 minutes.
3 To make the filling, beat together the pumpkin purée, sugar, eggs, salt, milk, cream and spices, until well blended.
4 Roll out the pastry on a lightly floured surface. Cut it into 11.5 cm /4½ in rounds and then line 8 greased individual Yorkshire pudding tins. Prick the pastry bases with a fork. Re-roll any trimmings and cut them into 8 wedge shapes about 25 mm /1 in long. Dampen the pastry rims and press a wedge onto each one to make the stalks.
5 Pour the filling into the cases and scatter the pumpkin seeds over the centre. Bake in the oven for 30–35 minutes until the filling is set. Leave in the tins to cool.

Potato mouths with 'skull' butter

1¼ hours

Serves 6
6 potatoes, washed but unpeeled
salt
225 g /8 oz butter in one block, softened
4 spring onions
3 slices of pressed ox tongue, halved

1 Heat the oven to 200C /400F /gas 6.
2 Prick the potatoes all over with a fork and make a slit lengthwise along one side of each potato, not quite from end to end.
3 Rub the potatoes all over with salt and bake for 1 hour or until they are soft in the centre when pierced with a fork.
4 Meanwhile, shape the butter into a skull, pushing some of the butter up to one end and rounding it with a palette knife (see picture). With the handle of a knife, draw an oblong to represent the mouth cavity, sketching in 2 rows of teeth. Refrigerate the butter.
5 Cut the white part of the spring onions into 12 × 25 mm /1 in lengths and cut out 12 very thin rounds from the firm green part. Reserve the white and green parts separately.
6 Remove the cooked potatoes from the oven and make another cut along the slit in each. Insert 2 pieces of white spring onion into either end of each slit to represent long teeth (see picture).
7 Take a half slice of tongue and fold the sides over so they overlap in the middle. Insert it into the middle of a slit with the rounded edge hanging out. Repeat with the remaining half slices of tongue.
8 Make 2 small round holes with an apple corer above the slits and insert a green spring onion round into each hole to make eyes. Serve the potatoes hot, accompanied by the 'skull' butter.

Pumpkin pie

If you are going to use fresh pumpkin, buy 1 kg /2 lb and stew it over a low heat until virtually all the liquid has evaporated.

making the pastry case,
then 1 hour

Serves 8
2 eggs
100 g /4 oz sugar
15 ml /1 tbls molasses
1.5 ml /¼ tsp ground ginger
2.5 ml /½ tsp freshly grated nutmeg
5 ml /1 tsp ground cinnamon
a pinch of ground cloves
2.5 ml /½ tsp salt
450 g /1 lb canned or stewed pumpkin
375 ml /13 fl oz milk
25 cm /10 in unbaked pastry case
275 ml /10 fl oz thick cream, whipped

1 Heat the oven to 200C /400F /gas 6. Combine the eggs with the sugar, molasses, spices and salt; blend well. Add the pumpkin and milk, mix well and check the spices. Pour into the pastry case.
2 Bake in the centre of the oven for 40 minutes or until set. Serve warm or cold with sweetened whipped cream, if desired.

● You can usually buy a wedge of fresh pumpkin from the greengrocer but make sure it has been wrapped in cling film as exposure to air causes rapid drying out.

Pumpkin pie

Coffin cake

This is a suitably macabre — yet delicious — addition to your ghoulish table; a funereal black ribbon tied around the cake enhances the dramatic effect.

🕐 🍴 making the sponge, overnight cooling, plus 30 minutes

Serves 6–8
100 g /4 oz flour
100 g /4 oz self-raising flour
2.5 ml /½ tsp salt
40 g /1½ oz butter, softened
100 g /4 oz margarine, softened
115 g /4½ oz caster sugar
2 eggs, beaten
5 ml /1 tsp vanilla essence
30 ml /2 tbls evaporated milk
50 g /2 oz cocoa powder
90 ml /6 tbls raspberry jam
For the icing
350 g /12 oz icing sugar
7.5 ml /1½ tsp coffee essence
5 ml /1 tsp chocolate essence
about 60 cm /2 ft black ribbon, to decorate
(optional)

1　Heat the oven to 180C /350F /gas 4.
2　Make the sponge mixture: sift the flour and salt together. In a large mixing bowl cream the butter and margarine together with a wooden spoon until pale. Beat in the sugar until the mixture is smooth, fluffy and light.
3　Gradually beat in the eggs, taking care to beat very well after each addition to prevent curdling. Beat in the vanilla essence.
4　Using a metal spoon, gradually fold in the flour and lightly mix until it is evenly incorporated.
5　Pour the evaporated milk over the mixture, then sift over the cocoa powder. Gently fold them in until evenly blended.
6　Pour the sponge mixture into a prepared 850 ml /1½ pt loaf tin, smooth the surface and bake on the top shelf of the oven for 30–40 minutes, or until the cake feels springy to the touch and a skewer inserted comes out clean.
7　Remove the cake from the oven, cool it in the tin for 10 minutes, then turn it out onto a wire rack and cool it overnight.
8　To make the icing, sift the icing sugar into a large bowl and add 55 ml /3½ tbls warm water. Stir until the icing is very smooth. Reserve 60 ml /4 tbls of the icing and stir the coffee essence into the rest.
9　To make the coffin shape, cut the 2 corners off one end of the cake, measuring 25 mm /1 in from each edge on the end and 4 cm /1½ in down each side. Taper the sides so the foot of the coffin measures 5 cm /2 in. Cut the coffin-shaped cake horizontally through the middle.
10　Make slits the length of the bottom half of the sponge, not cutting quite through to the bottom, to let the jam trickle through.
11　Put the jam into a small saucepan and heat gently until it is just beginning to melt. Pour it over the bottom half of the sponge, then cover with the top layer.
12　Stir the coffee-flavoured icing with a palette knife dipped in hot water. Spread the

Coffin cake, Skeleton spareribs with 'blood' sauce, Potato mouths with 'skull' butter, and Orange spine-chillers

icing smoothly over the entire surface of the sponge cake.
13　Mix the chocolate essence into the reserved icing, make a greaseproof paper icing bag and fit it with a 15 mm /½ in plain nozzle. Spoon in the chocolate icing.
14　Pipe the shape of a skull, starting just above the widest part of the cake. Make the eyes, a nose and a mouth. Pipe crossed bones.
15　Tie a black ribbon around the sides of the cake, if wished; keep the cake in a cool place until ready to serve.

Cat's eyes cakes

🍴 50 minutes, plus cooling

Makes 16–18 cakes
100 g /4 oz flour
25 g /1 oz cocoa powder
2.5 ml /½ tsp baking powder
100 g /4 oz caster sugar
100 g /4 oz butter, softened
2 medium-sized eggs
2.5 ml /½ tsp vanilla essence
75 g /3 oz small chocolate drops
about 30 ml /2 tbls milk

For the decoration
75 g /3 oz plain chocolate
40 g /1½ oz butter
salt
225 g /8 oz icing sugar, sifted
2–3 drops green food, colouring

1　Heat the oven to 190C /375F /gas 5.
2　In a mixing bowl, sift together the flour, cocoa and baking powder. In another bowl, beat the sugar and butter together until the mixture is light and fluffy, then gradually beat in the eggs. Add the vanilla essence, then stir in the sifted ingredients a little at a time.
3　Stir in the chocolate drops and beat in enough milk to give the mixture a soft dropping consistency.
4　Put 16–18 paper baking cases on a baking sheet and half-fill them with the mixture. Bake the cakes for 20 minutes or until they are well risen and firm. Remove from the oven and cool on a wire rack.
5　Decorate the cakes. Melt the chocolate and butter in the top pan of a double boiler over simmering water.
6　Remove it from the heat and beat well. Beat in 45 ml /3 tbls hot water and a pinch of salt. Gradually add 175 g /6 oz of the icing sugar and beat until the mixture is smooth. Leave to cool, then spread the icing over the cakes and leave it to set.
7　Mix the remaining icing sugar with just enough cold water to make a piping

Devil's delight

Delight your young guests with these tasty sweets, presented in 'witches hats' (see introduction).

30 minutes, plus 4 hours setting

Makes 450 g /1 lb
450 g /1 lb lump sugar
25 g /1 oz powdered gelatine
50 g /2 oz chopped walnuts
a few drops red food colouring
a few drops strawberry flavouring
flavourless oil, for greasing
50 g /2 oz icing sugar
25 g /1 oz cornflour

1   Put the lump sugar into a saucepan with 150 ml/5 fl oz water and stir over a low heat to dissolve the sugar. Increase the heat and bring it to the boil.
2   Sprinkle the gelatine over 60 ml /4 tbls cold water in a small bowl and set the bowl in a pan of barely simmering water until the gelatine dissolves. Increase the heat and allow the simmering water to come to the boil so that the gelatine mixture becomes hot. Keep it warm.
3   Boil the syrup until it reaches 115C / 240F; at this temperature a small amount dropped into cold water forms a firm but pliable ball. Remove the pan from the heat, immediately.
4   Stir in the warm gelatine solution, the nuts, colouring and flavouring. Pour at once into a greased 18×12.5 cm /7×5 in tin and leave for at least 4 hours to set.
5   Sift the icing sugar and cornflour together onto greaseproof paper. Turn the confection out and cut it into squares, then toss it in the sugar mixture to coat. Store in an airtight container.

Orange spine-chillers

10 minutes, plus 2–3 hours freezing

Makes 6 drinks
6 large oranges
350 ml /12 fl oz fizzy lemonade

1   Cut off the top 20 mm /³⁄₄ in of the oranges, then scrape out the flesh inside with a grapefruit knife, being careful not to break the skins. Reserve the flesh.
2   Put the hollow orange shells into the freezer for 2–3 hours to freeze solid.
3   Meanwhile, put the orange flesh into a blender or food processor and blend or process it, then strain it through a nylon sieve and reserve the juice.
4   Mix the orange juice with the fizzy lemonade and chill it in the refrigerator.
5   About 30 minutes before serving, take the orange cups from the freezer and fill them to within 15 mm /¹⁄₂ in of the top with the orange-lemonade.
6   Put the orange cups back in the refrigerator until ready to serve. Serve the orange spine-chillers with drinking straws.

consistency. Using a greaseproof paper piping bag fitted with a small plain nozzle, pipe eyebrows and long white whiskers on each face. Colour the remaining icing green with food colouring, fill another piping bag and pipe on the eyes.

Trick or treat toffee apples

20 minutes

Makes 8 toffee apples
8 small dessert apples, stalks removed
225 g /8 oz soft dark brown sugar
25 g /1 oz unsalted butter
15 ml /1 tbls golden syrup
5 ml /1 tsp malt vinegar

1   Push a wooden skewer through the centre of each apple, and lightly grease a baking tray.
2   Put the sugar, butter, syrup, vinegar and 75 ml /5 tbls water into a saucepan and stir over a low heat until the sugar has dissolved. Bring it to the boil and cook until the temperature of the toffee reaches 143C / 290F; at this temperature a small amount of the mixture dripped into cold water separates into threads and becomes hard.
3   Remove the pan from the heat and

quickly dip each apple into the toffee, turning it to coat it completely. Then place it in a bowl of cold water so that the toffee sets hard.
4   Lay the apples on their sides on the baking tray until the toffee cools. Wrap them in cling film until ready to serve.

Trick or treat toffee apples

NOVELTY CAKES

Children are delighted with gaily decorated, colourful cakes, and novelty ones have even more appeal. With a little effort and following my suggestions you can create an eye-catching centrepiece for the party table.

The birthday cake is the star at a children's party. You can get by making a simple one, decorated with sweets, but an unusually-shaped birthday cake will add sparkle and magic to a children's party. All children love to be surprised and the unveiling of a novelty cake will meet with shouts of delight and be the highlight of the party. Here are several ideas for novelty cakes.

Party cake tips

Very fresh cake is difficult to trim and ice neatly, so bake the cake the day before you want to decorate it. It is often much more convenient to ice and decorate it the evening before the party — choose the time you are least likely to be interrupted. Alternatively, bake the cake in advance and freeze it. Defrost, cut, assemble and ice the cake the day before the party.

Buy a cake board of the appropriate shape and size for the cake or use a chopping board covered with foil for a very large cake. Have food colourings, piping nozzles and paint brushes handy, as well as a box of assorted liquorice sweets, as these are extremely useful in providing little extras. Cake trimmings can be used to make trifles or other desserts and any left-over icing can be piped onto small cakes or biscuits.

Apply the decorations while the icing is still soft and use a clean pair of tweezers to handle silver balls (dragées), small sweets and so on. Chocolate decorations are best added as close to the serving time as possible since they tend to soften. Do not put sugar-coated chocolate buttons on the cake too far in advance or their colouring will run. (Reserve a little icing or use jam to stick such last-minute decorations in place.)

Most of the cakes described here are based on the simple Basic party sponge cake mixture which is easily adapted to different cake tins and produces a light, open-textured cake. You can flavour the batter with a few drops of vanilla or almond essence, or a little finely grated orange or lemon zest, or colour it with a few drops of edible food colouring. When baking a deep cake, cover it with greaseproof paper after 30–40 minutes cooking to prevent it browning too much. The methods of making Apricot glaze and Butter cream are included in this chapter and I have given a selection of delicious variations on the basic butter cream recipe — so you can choose your flavours and colours.

Protect your decorated cake with an in-verted large tin or rigid container, and keep it in a cool place. Do not store a glacé iced cake for more than 2 days or the icing will dry out and crack.

These days it is quite easy to buy ready-made fondant icing, and it is often well worth doing so when you are making novelty cakes.

Maypole cake

This is because it can be easily modelled and also because it gives a smooth result. Store the fondant icing in an airtight container.

Ideas for round cakes

Clock cake: use 1½ × Basic party sponge cake mix (see recipe) and bake as for the Maypole cake (see recipe). When cold, sand-wich the cakes together with 45–60 ml /3–4 tbls apricot jam. Brush the sides with Apricot glaze (see note, page 77), then roll it in coloured sugar strands or hundreds and thousands until it is completely coated. Trans-fer it to a 23 cm /9 in cake board or serving plate. Secure a greaseproof paper collar around the cake to prevent the icing dripping down the sides. Blend 100 g /4 oz sifted icing sugar with 15 ml /1 tbls warm water and pour over the top of the cake. Leave the icing until set, then remove the paper collar.

Put 25 g /1 oz melted chocolate into a piping bag fitted with a writing nozzle and pipe the numerals 1–12 on the top of the cake, about 5 cm /2 in from the edge. Pipe the hands of the clock, 'setting' them to the child's age. Place a ring of chocolate buttons or sugar flowers around the top edge of the cake to finish it off neatly.

Drum cake: use 2 × Basic party sponge cake mix (see recipe) and bake in two deep, 18 cm /7 in round tins for about 1¼ hours. When cold cut each cake horizontally in half and layer together with seedless raspberry jam. Melt 5 ml /3 tbls more jam with 5 ml /1 tsp water and brush over the sides of the cake.

Roll out 225 g /8 oz marzipan or Almond paste (see page 99) to a rectangle, about 53 cm × 11.5 cm /21 in × 4½ in; press around the sides of the cake and seal the join. Transfer to a 23 cm /9 in cake board or serving plate. Secure a greaseproof paper collar around the cake. Blend 100 g /4 oz sifted icing sugar with 15 ml /1 tbls warm water and pour over the top of the cake; leave until set, then remove the paper collar.

Put 25 g /1 oz melted chocolate into a piping bag fitted with a writing nozzle and pipe diagonal lines of chocolate around the sides of the cake, from the top to bottom

edges. Allow these to set, then pipe another series of diagonal lines across the first set, to make a diamond pattern. Use the remaining chocolate to pipe birthday greetings and the child's name on the top of the cake.

Put 75 g /3 oz Butter cream (see recipe) into a piping bag fitted with a star nozzle and pipe a border around the bottom and top edges of the cake. Stick a gold dragée in the centre of each diamond shape with jam. To finish, place 2 red lollipop sweets on the top of the cake to represent the drum sticks.

Marshmallow topped cake: use 1½ × Basic party sponge cake mix (see recipe) and bake in a loose-bottomed deep, 18 cm /7 in round tin for about 1¼ hours. As soon as you remove the cake from the oven, cover the hot surface with 100 g /4´ oz halved marshmallows. Pack them tightly and press them firmly, cut side down, onto the cake. (The heat of the cake causes the marshmallows to melt slightly and stick to the cake). Let the cake cool for 30 minutes, then remove from the tin and peel off the lining paper. Decorate the edge of the cake with a paper cake frill.

Ideas for using square cakes
Shaggy dog cake: use 1½ × Basic party sponge cake mix (see recipe) and bake in a

deep, 16.5 cm /6½ in square tin for about 1¼ hours. When cold, cut the cake horizontally in half and sandwich back together with 45 ml /3 tbls apricot jam. Brush the top and sides with Apricot glaze (see note page 77). Blend 175 g /6 oz sifted icing sugar with 20–25 ml /4–5 tsp warm water to give a thick coating consistency. Reserve 7.5 ml /½ tbls icing and use the rest to coat the cake. Tint some desiccated coconut green with a few drops of edible food colouring and sprinkle it over the top while the icing is still soft, to represent grass.

Spread the reserved icing over one end of a Swiss roll. Place the roll on the top of the cake and spread with 75 g /3 oz Chocolate butter cream (see recipe). Mark the butter cream with a fork to suggest a dog's coat. Press small sweets on to the iced end of the roll to mark the eyes, nose and tongue. Scatter a few sugar flowers over the 'grass'.

Treasure chest: use 1½ × Basic party sponge cake mix (see recipe) and bake in a 1.7 L /3 pt loaf tin for about 55 minutes. Cut off the top third of the cake when cold, and reserve as a lid. With a spoon, scoop out a thin layer of crumbs from the remaining piece of cake, to within 15 mm /½ in of the edges, to make a shallow cavity. Place this piece of cake on

a rectangular cake board or serving plate.

Make 175 g /6 oz Chocolate butter cream (see recipe) and use this butter cream to ice the base and the lid, leaving the cavity in the base and the underside of the lid plain. Fill the cavity with foil-covered chocolate 'coins', sweet 'necklaces' and other 'jewellery'. Replace the lid at a slight angle so that the coins and jewellery show through. To finish, decorate with jelly diamonds or sugar-coated chocolate buttons.

Humpty Dumpty cake: use 1½ × Basic party sponge cake mix (see recipe) and bake in a 1.7 L /3 pt loaf tin for about 55 minutes. When it is cold, trim the top of the cake level and place it, trimmed side down, on a wire rack. Brush the top and sides with 45 ml / 3 tbls Apricot glaze (see note, page 77), then spread with 100 g /4 oz melted chocolate. Leave until it is set, then transfer the cake to a rectangular cake board or serving plate.

Mould 65 g /2½ oz marzipan or Almond paste (see page 99) into an egg shape. Using a fine paintbrush and edible food colourings, paint eyes, eyebrows and a mouth on the egg. Roll out a little more almond paste into 4 thin sausage shapes for the arms and legs and attach to the egg with apricot glaze. Work a little cocoa powder into a small ball of almond paste, then fashion it into a hat and secure it to the top of the egg with apricot glaze. Using coloured Glacé icing (see page 27) pipe flowers around the sides of the cake. Sit Humpty on top of the cake, so that his legs dangle over the edge.

Basic party sponge mix

🕐 35 minutes, plus cooling

Makes 2 × 19 cm /7½ in cakes
melted butter and flour, for sandwich tins
100 g /4 oz self-raising flour
5 ml /1 tsp baking powder
100 g /4 oz soft margarine
100 g /4 oz caster sugar
2 eggs
a few drops of vanilla essence

1 Heat the oven to 170C /325F /gas 3.
2 Brush the bases and sides of 2 × 19 cm / 7½ in sandwich tins with melted butter. Line the base of each tin with a neat circle of greaseproof paper and brush that with melted butter as well. Lightly dust the bases and sides of the tins with flour.
3 Sift the flour with the baking powder into the mixing bowl of your electric mixer and add the remaining ingredients. Whisk until well mixed (1–2 minutes). Divide the mixture between the prepared sandwich tins. Place them in the hot oven and bake for 25–30 minutes. The cakes are cooked when they slightly shrink away from the sides of the tins and spring back into shape when pressed lightly with a finger.
4 Remove the cakes from the oven and leave for 1–2 minutes to settle. Next, turn them out onto a clean tea-towel. Peel off the greaseproof paper and invert the cakes onto a wire rack to cool right side up.

Making a Butterfly cake

Use 2 × Basic party sponge cake mix (see recipe). Grease a deep 23 cm /9 in square cake tin and line it with greased greaseproof paper. Pour the sponge mixture into the tin and level the surface, then make a slight hollow in the centre. Bake for about an hour and five minutes, until the top of the cake is golden and springy to the touch.

Cool the cake in the tin for 5 minutes, then turn it out onto a wire rack and peel off the lining paper. Leave the cake upside down to cool completely.

Trim the cake to level it off. Slice the cake in half horizontally and sandwich it together with 60 ml /4 tbls of apricot jam. Cut the cake in half diagonally to make 2 triangles, then trim off the triangle tips opposite the cut edge.

Sieve 90 ml /6 tbls of apricot jam into a small, heavy-based saucepan, add 30 ml / 2 tbls water, and stir over a low heat until the mixture has melted. Brush the sides of the cakes, except the trimmed corners, with some of the melted jam. Spread 50 g /2 oz desiccated coconut on a large plate. Press the jam-coated sides of the cake into the coconut one at a time until they are evenly coated.

Brush the trimmed corner of each cake with melted jam. Place the 2 pieces of cake on a 30 cm /12 in silver cake-board, with the trimmed corners almost touching, to make a butterfly shape. Place 3 flaky chocolate bars in the gap, one on top of another, then push the 2 'wings' together.

Sift 225 g /8 oz icing sugar into a bowl, then beat in 30–45 ml /2–3 tbls warm water to give a thick coating consistency. Put 30 ml / 2 tbls of icing into a small bowl. Add sufficient cocoa powder to make a fairly dark

brown icing, then spoon this icing into a small piping bag fitted with a writing nozzle.

Brush the top of the cakes with the remaining melted jam. Spread the white icing smoothly and evenly over the top with a knife. Immediately pipe parallel lines of brown icing down the 'wings'. Draw a skewer through the brown lines to give a 'feather' effect (see picture below).

Neaten the edges, removing any surplus icing, then leave the cake to set.

Two hours before you serve the cake, empty out the contents of 3 small packets of sugar-coated chocolate buttons. Melt 15 ml / 1 tbls apricot jam, and brush a little jam on each chocolate button. Stick the buttons around the edges of the cake.

Finally, curl the tops of 2 liquorice sticks and arrange them to form the 'antennae'.

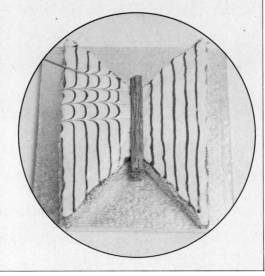

Butter cream

In its basic form, butter cream icing is stiff enough for piping. If egg yolks are added the consistency becomes very similar to crème au beurre.

🕐 15 minutes

Fills and covers a 22 cm /8½ in sandwich cake
100 g /4 oz butter, softened
225 g /8 oz icing sugar, sifted
1–2 egg yolks (optional)
flavouring (see below)
colouring (optional)

1 Beat the butter with a wooden spoon or whisk it with an electric mixer until it is light and fluffy.
2 Gradually beat in the sifted icing sugar, a few spoonfuls at a time.
3 For a richer, smoother-textured cream, beat in the egg yolks (if you are using liquid flavouring, use only 1 egg yolk).
4 Add the flavouring and the colouring, choosing from the selection given below.

Flavourings for Butter cream
Vanilla: use 5–10 ml /1–2 tsp vanilla essence to taste.
Lemon: use 5 ml /1 tsp grated lemon zest and 30–45 ml /2–3 tbls lemon juice.
Orange: use 5 ml /1 tsp grated orange zest and 30–45 ml /2–3 tbls orange juice. Add orange colouring, if you wish.
Chocolate: use 100 g /4 oz plain chocolate, melted and cooled slightly, or 60 ml /4 tbls cocoa, sifted.
Coffee: use 30 ml /2 tbls instant coffee dissolved in 15 ml /1 tbls boiling water, cooled.
Strawberry, raspberry and blackcurrant: use 125 ml /4 fl oz fruit purée, made from 225 g / 8 oz fresh fruit, sieved.
Liqueur: use 30 ml /2 tbls liqueur; add colouring if you wish. Liqueurs can also be used with dry flavourings, for instance, use Cointreau to replace orange juice in orange-flavoured butter cream.
Peppermint: use 5–10 ml /1–2 tsp peppermint essence. Add green food colouring.
Honey and nut: use 25 g /1 oz chopped walnuts and 125 ml /4 fl oz clear honey.

● If you wish to make the butter cream in advance, keep it in the refrigerator and remember to bring it out to allow it to soften before use.

Maypole cake

Most children love this colour scheme but you can, of course, change it if you prefer. Thin gift-wrap ribbons are best; wind them tightly around a pencil if you want them to spiral down from the candy maypole. Do remember to remove the decorative ribbons before you attempt to light the candles.

🕐🕐 50 minutes, plus cooling, then 45 minutes decorating

Makes 12 slices

*1½ × Basic party sponge mix (see recipe)
 baked in 2 × 19 cm /7½ in round tins
 each 4 cm /1½ in deep*
45–60 ml /3–4 tbls apricot jam
45 ml /3 tbls apricot glaze (see note below)
*orange Butter cream based on 175 g /6 oz icing
 sugar (see recipe)*

To finish
red, green and gold decorative balls (dragées)
red, pink and yellow sugar flowers
striped candy stick
red, green and yellow jelly babies
candles and candle holders
thin red, green and gold ribbons

1 Sandwich the cold cake together with the jam and place on a 23 cm /9 in cake board or serving plate. Brush the cake with apricot glaze, then spread with orange butter cream. Stud the top and sides (if wished) with dragées and sugar flowers.

2 Push the candy stick firmly into the centre of the cake. Arrange the jelly babies and candles on top of the cake, then tape the ribbons to the top of the maypole. You can top the maypole with a small fresh flower.

● Apricot glaze is not an icing in itself, but it is used to glaze the cake underneath many icings to prevent crumbs spoiling the smooth finish.

To cover a 20 cm /8 in cake, sieve 45 ml / 3 tbls apricot jam into a small saucepan, add 15 ml /1 tbls water and heat gently, stirring. When the jam is melted, remove the pan from the heat and leave the glaze to cool slightly before using.

Castle cake

2 hours, plus cooling the cakes, then 1 hour decorating

Makes 12–14 slices

*3 × Basic party sponge cake mix (see recipe),
 ½ coloured with green food colouring and
 ½ coloured with pink food colouring and
 baked in two deep, 16 cm /6½ in square tins*
90 ml /6 tbls red jam
200 g /7 oz chocolate hazelnut spread
8 chocolate-covered mini Swiss rolls

To finish
2 lime jelly tablets
3 chocolate-covered wafer fingers
jelly diamond cake decorations
coloured dragées
3 × 50 g /2 oz triangular milk chocolate bars
toy knights, to decorate

1 Trim the cakes, if it is necessary, and cut each in half horizontally. Sandwich them together with jam, then neatly trim off each corner. Place the cake on a 30 cm /12 in cake board.

2 Use most of the chocolate hazelnut spread to cover the cake. Press 1 mini roll against each of the trimmed corners. Trim one end of the remaining rolls level, if necessary, and spread with a little chocolate hazelnut spread. Place on top of the first set of rolls to make 4 turrets. (Fill in any gaps with chocolate hazelnut spread).

3 Make up the lime jellies according to the manufacturer's instructions, pour them into shallow trays and then leave them until they are set.

4 Put chocolate hazelnut spread on the underside and on one end of the wafer fingers; place them on the cake board, in the centre of the base of the front side of the cake, to represent the drawbridge. Use jelly diamonds to make the portcullis, then use dragées to mark a gateway around the portcullis.

5 Make the battlements on the top edges of the cake, between the turrets, by using the triangular chocolate bars. Trim the bars to size (use the trimmings on the back edge).

6 Arrange jelly diamonds around the sides of the cake to represent windows, then stick 3 more down the front of each turret with chocolate hazelnut spread. Put a little hazelnut spread on the top of each turret and decorate with a ring of dragées.

7 Just before serving, break up the jelly with a fork and spoon it around the castle to represent the moat. Place the knights in position, on and around the castle.

Castle cake

Hedgehog

This rich-tasting creation will add a touch of luxury — and charm — to your party table.

🕐 🍴🍴🍴 soaking the prunes overnight, 45 minutes, plus cooling and chilling

Serves 8–12

2 × Basic party sponge cake mix (see recipe), baked in 2 × 1.1 L /2 pt oval pie dishes

For the maraschino syrup

200 g /7 oz sugar
30 ml /2 tbls syrup from bottle of maraschino cherries

For the praline

100 g /4 oz sugar
5 ml /1 tsp lemon juice
100 g /4 oz blanched almonds, toasted
vegetable oil, for greasing

For the filling and decoration

100 g /4 oz unsalted butter, softened
75 g /3 oz caster sugar
2 egg yolks
175 g /6 oz bottled maraschino cherries, halved
300 ml /10 fl oz thick cream, whipped
100 g /4 oz blanched almonds, halved and toasted
3 prunes, soaked overnight, drained and stoned

1 Make the cakes and then leave them to cool completely on a wire rack.

2 To make the maraschino syrup, combine the sugar with 300 ml /10 fl oz water in a heavy saucepan. Bring to the boil, stirring, and simmer for 15 minutes. Cool and flavour with the maraschino syrup.

3 To make the praline, dissolve the sugar in a heavy saucepan with the lemon juice and 30 ml /2 tbls water over a gentle heat, then boil it to a light caramel. Add the toasted almonds, mix well and pour onto lightly oiled foil on a cold surface. Allow to harden, then break it up and pound finely with a mortar or in a blender.

4 To make the filling, beat the unsalted butter until fluffy and then beat in the sugar. Beat in the egg yolks and 120 ml /8 tbls powdered praline until smooth. Fold the remaining praline and halved cherries into the whipped cream.

5 When cold, cut each cake in two horizontally. Cut one large layer into strips. Moisten the layers and soak the strips with the maraschino syrup.

6 Put the largest layer on an oval plate. Spread it with half the whipped cream. Add the next layer and heap the strips in the centre, trimming and patting them to form a hedgehog shape, with the remaining whipped cream. Press on the last layer. Trim one end to a point.

7 Spread the praline butter cream over the top and sides of the cake. Then spike it all

Hedgehog

over with the toasted almonds (see picture)

8 Cut up one prune and use the pieces for the mouth, nose and eyes. Halve the remaining 2 prunes and sculpt for the feet. Chill the cake until ready to serve.

Spaceship cake

Assembled correctly, my Spaceship cake is sure to be a stunning, popular centrepiece. A model spaceman or alien monster sitting at the base of the 'ramp' adds to the extra-terrestrial effect!

🕐 🍴🍴🍴 making cakes and butter creams, then 1½–2 hours assembling

Serves 6–8

Chocolate Victoria sandwich sponge

melted butter and flour, for can and bowls
225 g /8 oz softened butter
225 g /8 oz caster sugar
2.5 ml /½ tsp vanilla essence
2.5 ml /½ tsp finely grated lemon zest
4 eggs
200 g /7 oz flour
10 ml /2 tsp baking powder
25 g /1 oz cocoa powder

To assemble

225 g /8 oz chocolate Butter cream (see recipe)
100 g /4 oz green Butter cream (see recipe)
100–150 g /4–5 oz icing sugar
4 chocolate discs, about 25 mm /1 in across
8 long mint-flavoured chocolate sticks
1 ice cream cone
1 packet oblong ice cream wafers
coloured chocolate buttons
spearmint sweets, quartered
1 mint-chocolate wafer
1 model alien monster or spaceman, to decorate

1 Heat the oven to 170C /325F /gas 3. Butter and flour a 400 g /14 oz size empty can and 2 × 1 L /1¾ pt ovenproof bowls.

2 In a large mixing bowl, combine the butter with the caster sugar, vanilla essence and finely grated lemon zest. Cream them together with a whisk until light and fluffy.

3 In another bowl, whisk the eggs until light and frothy.

4 Whisk the egg mixture, a few spoonfuls at a time, into the creamed butter and sugar mixture. Do not add the eggs too quickly, as this might make the mixture curdle.

5 Sift the flour, baking powder and cocoa powder over the creamed mixture a little at a time, folding it in lightly but thoroughly with a large metal spoon.

6 Divide the batter between the can, which should be a quarter full, and the two bowls. Bake the can for 30–35 minutes and the bowls for 1–1¼ hours. Cool the cakes for 10 minutes before turning them out onto a wire rack. Leave the cakes until cold, preferably 24 hours.

7 Sandwich the bowl cakes together with some of the chocolate butter cream to make a globe.

8 Cut the rounded top off the cake from the can, ice its cut surface and stick it on top of the globe to form a dome.

9 Cover the dome and the rest of the cake from the can with the chocolate butter cream, smoothing it evenly with a palette knife.

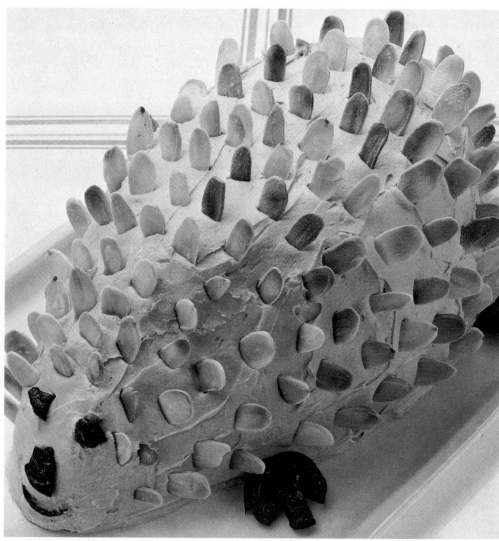

10 Stand the 'can' cake on a cake board and put the body of the spaceship on top. Position the 4 chocolate discs around the edge of the board and prop up the spaceship with 2 mint chocolate sticks, resting the bottoms of the sticks on the chocolate discs.
11 Cut the middle section out of the ice cream cone and stand it inside the base of the cone. Put the pointed end on top, attaching it with green butter cream.
12 Cut 6 'fins' from the oblong wafers. Make 6 cuts in the base of the cone with a sharp knife and insert the fins. Stand this on top of the spaceship.
13 Cut enough 25 mm × 15 mm /1 in × ½ in strips of wafer to stick in the icing around the body of the cake to form a ledge about halfway down. Cut more fins from other wafers and insert them vertically beneath the ledge at each intersection.
14 Put a second ledge of wafers 25 mm /1 in below the base of the cone on top of the cake.
15 Arrange coloured chocolate buttons around the cake below the cone and at the top of the 'can' cake. Arrange the spearmint sweets around the cake above and below the middle ledge to resemble lights. Edge the wafers with green butter cream.
16 Surround the base with unsifted icing sugar 'snow'.
17 Position the mint-chocolate wafer to form a ramp. Stand a model of an alien monster or a spaceman next to the ramp.

Tanker lorry

It's well worth the care and effort to make this wonderfully realistic tanker lorry cake. Red butter cream provides the brilliantly coloured finish.

 making the cake and butter cream, then 1 hour

Serves 6–8
Chocolate Victoria sandwich sponge mixture
  (see previous recipe)
butter and flour, for the tins
225 g /8 oz red Butter cream (see recipe)
90 ml /6 tbls apricot jam
6 liquorice wheels
100 g /4 oz sugar
vegetable oil, for greasing
coloured chocolate buttons
small edible silver balls
liquorice strips
175 g /6 oz ready-made bought fondant icing
icing sugar, for rolling and moulding
100 g /4 oz Glacé icing (see page 27)
red and blue food colouring

1 Heat the oven to 170C /325F /gas 3. Grease and flour 2 × 400 g /14 oz cans. Grease and line a 28 × 18 cm /11 × 7 in baking tin with greaseproof paper.
2 Make the sponge mixture. Half-fill the 2 cans and put the remaining mixture in the baking tin. Bake for 25–40 minutes. Let the cakes settle in the tins for 2 minutes then turn them out onto a wire rack. Peel off the paper and leave the cakes until cold, preferably 24 hours.
3 Cut off and discard the rounded tops of

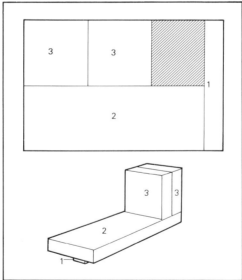

the 2 cylindrical cakes. Stick the 2 cylinders together end to end with butter cream.
4 Cut a strip 25 mm /1 in wide off the end of the rectangular cake, then cut the rest of the cake in half lengthways (see diagram above). Reserve one half and cut 2 × 7.5 cm / 3 in pieces from the other half. Discard the remaining piece. Sandwich the two equal pieces with butter cream to form the 'cab'.
5 Melt the apricot jam with 30 ml /2 tbls water. Cool it slightly, then brush it over the top and sides of the 'cab' and the 2 remaining rectangles.
6 Cover these sections with butter cream. Lay the 25 mm /1½ in strip in the centre of a foil-covered board with the flat piece on top (see diagram). Put the cab in position and smooth the icing.

Tanker lorry

7 Using a little of the butter cream, attach 3 liquorice wheels on each side.
8 Dissolve the sugar in 30 ml /2 tbls water and boil over a medium heat until it is golden. Turn the caramel onto an oiled baking sheet. When it begins to set, cut it into window shapes and position them on the cab with butter cream.
9 Put a little butter cream into a piping bag fitted with a small writing nozzle and pipe around the edges of the cake and windows. Pipe in a radiator grid.
10 Position yellow chocolate buttons on the cake as lights. Put a line of silver balls above the windscreen. Cut liquorice strips for the bumpers and attach.
11 Brush the 'can' cakes with apricot glaze. On a flat surface dusted with icing sugar, roll the fondant icing out thinly. Cut a rectangle 23 × 11 cm /9 × 4½ in and roll it round the cakes.
12 Cut 2 × 7.5 cm /3 in circles from the icing and position them at each end of the cylinder made with the 'can' cakes. Dip your fingers in icing sugar and mould the icing to the cake cylinder by rubbing it lightly with a circular movement. Mould the icing joins together in the same way.
13 Colour half the glacé icing red and the other half blue.
14 Using a piping bag fitted with a small writing nozzle, pipe a blue circle on each side. With another bag and red icing, pipe a trade name in the circle and 2 stripes along each side.
15 Lay the 'tank' in position on the chassis. Attach 4 coloured chocolate buttons to the top of the tank with a little icing.

CHILDREN'S DRINKS

Try some of my party drinks recipes — they're bright and inviting, perfect with your special party food. And when it comes to cooling down your young guests after party games, these drinks are ideal thirst-quenchers.

Crisps, cakes, biscuits and much of the popular party foods on offer are likely to be very thirsty work for children. It is therefore important to provide plenty of cooling liquid refreshment.

Your choice of drink will depend on the age group of the children as well as the size and location of the party. A sensible general rule is to avoid anything very cloying, or too many fizzy drinks. Stock up on unsweetened fruit juices, but don't be offended if some children also seem to want a drink of cool mineral water or a glass of tap water.

The drinks I suggest here span a wide range of attractive colours and flavours — milky, tangy, fruity and so on. They will suit children aged six to eleven, although most toddlers would enjoy Orange barley water (see recipe) and Banana malt shake (see recipe).

Most of the drinks can be prepared in advance or they can be made quickly, just before serving. Choose one or two drinks to make. Prepare one of them in advance, keep it chilled, if necessary, and add ice before serving. Make up the other drink as the children arrive. With gentle supervision, older children can make several of the drinks themselves, if the party is small.

Use plastic or paper cups and mugs for the younger children, sturdy glasses and tumblers for older children. There are plenty of attractive shapes and colours of both glasses and plastic or paper cups to choose from. A word of caution — don't be over-generous when you pour the drinks — it is better to top up rather than mop up!

Special effects

Jazz up disposable cups with stars or other gummed shapes stuck on the outsides. Novelty straws add extra sparkle to the look of the drinks, and the range available is vast. Or you could decorate the drinks with cocktail accessories, such as colourful little umbrellas. Fruit garnishes are attractive, too — a pair of fresh cherries still joined by their stalks, a slice of orange or lime or a glacé cherry on a cocktail stick make a simple fruit juice look like an adult cocktail.

For a sophisticated style, brush the rims of clear tumblers with lightly beaten egg white or lemon juice, then dip the rim into caster sugar. For a more colourful effect, add a few drops of food colouring to the sugar and stir well until all the sugar is tinted, then dip the glasses in it.

If the party has a special theme, you could carry this through in the drinks. Milk shakes or ice cream sodas are ideal to serve at a gangster or other American-style party. Or for a Hallowe'en party (see pages 70–73), dilute lime cordial with soda water, garnish it with slices of lime and white marshmallows and serve it as a garish brew for small visiting witches and ghosts.

Strawberry shake

If you do not possess an ice cream scoop, remember that 1 scoop equals 60 ml /4 tbls. You can decorate the drinks with a few whole tiny strawberries or fan wafers.

⏱ 10 minutes

Serves 2
lightly beaten egg white
caster sugar
4 scoops vanilla ice cream
150 ml /5 fl oz cold milk
100 g /4 oz strawberries, hulled and crushed
30 ml /2 tbls strawberry syrup

1   Brush the rims of 2 tall, 250 ml /10 fl oz glass tumblers with beaten egg white, then dip them in caster sugar to give a frosted effect. Chill the glasses in the refrigerator while you make the shakes.
2   Put the ice cream, the milk, the strawberries and the strawberry syrup in a blender and blend, covered, at maximum speed for 60–90 seconds until frothy. Pour into the prepared glasses.
3   Serve with 2 straws in each glass.

● For an extra thick shake, replace the milk with an equal quantity of ice cream.
● For strawberry and banana shake, omit the strawberry syrup and add a small peeled and sliced banana and 1–2 drops of red food colouring (to give a good colour).

Cherry cooler

⏱ 15–20 minutes, plus chilling

Makes 6–8 drinks
425 g /15 oz canned cherries
60 ml /4 tbls caster sugar
600 ml /1 pt yoghurt
fresh cherries, in pairs, to decorate

1   Drain and stone the cherries, reserving the syrup. Transfer them to a blender, then add a little syrup and purée until smooth.
2   Sieve the purée into a large jug or bowl, then stir in the caster sugar. Whisk in the yoghurt, adding a little at a time.
3   Make up the reserved cherry syrup to 425 ml /15 fl oz with cold water, then stir into the yoghurt mixture. Cover and chill for 30 minutes, or up to 12 hours.
4   When ready to serve, stir well and pour into small tumblers. Dangle a cherry 'ear-ring' on each tumbler and serve.

At the back, Tropical sunset; in the front, Cherry cooler and Blackcurrant frostie

Tropical sunset

⏱ making the garnishes, then 5–10 minutes

Makes 8 drinks
ice cubes
350 ml /12 fl oz apricot or peach nectar
1 L /1¾ pt unsweetened pineapple juice, chilled
1 L /1¾ pt unsweetened orange juice, chilled
grenadine syrup
To garnish
16 maraschino cherries
2 slices of fresh pineapple, quartered
4 slices of orange, halved

1   To make the garnish, spear a cherry, a piece of pineapple and orange and another cherry on 8 cocktail sticks.
2   Put the ice cubes in a jug and then add the nectar, the pineapple juice and the orange juice.
3   Half-fill 8 large glasses (about 450 ml /16 fl oz capacity) with ice cubes and add the blended juices. Pour a thin stream of grenadine into each glass. It will sink and form a rosy layer at the bottom.
4   Add the prepared garnish. If liked, add a paper parasol and two straws to each glass. Serve immediately.

Banana malt shake

| 15 minutes

Makes 8 drinks
4 bananas, chopped
90 ml /6 tbls malt extract, warmed in a
 bowl over a saucepan of hot water
90 ml /6 tbls cocoa powder
60 ml /4 tbls icing sugar
16 ice cubes, crushed
1.1 L /2 pt milk
16 chocolate finger biscuits

1 Make the malt shakes in batches, two at a
time, putting one-quarter of the banana, the
warmed malt, the cocoa, the icing sugar and
the ice into a blender. Add 275 ml /10 fl oz
milk and blend for 2 minutes, until the
mixture is frothy.
2 Pour into 2 tall glass tumblers. Pop 2
biscuits into each glass and decorate with 2
straws, then serve immediately.
3 Make the remaining malt shakes in the
same way.

● You can blend the shake several hours in
advance. If you do this, pour each batch into
screw-top jars and keep in the refrigerator.
When ready to serve, shake the jars vigorously to aerate the liquid.

Lemon 'n' limeade

| 10 minutes,
| plus cooling

Makes 8–10 drinks
finely grated zest and juice of 3 lemons
finely grated zest and juice of 2 limes
175 g /6 oz sugar
a block of ice
soda water or sparkling mineral water, chilled
To decorate
slices of lemon and lime
a sprig of mint

1 Put the lemon and lime zest into a heavy-
based saucepan. Add the sugar and 600 ml /
1 pt water. Stir over low heat until the sugar
has dissolved. Bring to the boil and boil,
without stirring, for 2 minutes.
2 Pour the syrup into a heatproof jug and
leave it to stand for 2 hours, or until it is
completely cold. Then stir in the juice of the
lemons and the limes.
3 Place a block of ice in a large jug, then
strain the lemon and lime syrup over it. Stir
well, then top up with soda or mineral water.
Garnish with slices of lemon and lime and a
sprig of mint. Serve immediately.

Raspberry ice cream soda

| 15 minutes

Makes 8 drinks
1 L /1¾ pt raspberry ripple ice cream
225 ml /8 fl oz raspberry milk shake syrup
soda water, from a syphon
fresh raspberries, washed and hulled, to
 decorate

1 Cut the ice cream into 16 equal cubes.
2 Pour the raspberry milk shake syrup into
8 tall goblets or tumblers of at least 175 ml /
6 fl oz capacity each.
3 Dilute the syrup with a dash of soda
water, then add 2 cubes of ice cream to each
goblet.
4 Fill the goblets to the brim with soda
water, decorate with the raspberries and serve
immediately.

St Clement's sparkle

| defrosting the orange juice,
| then 5 minutes

Makes 10–12 drinks
2 × 184 g /6½ oz cartons frozen
 concentrated orange juice, defrosted
2 × 1 L /1¾ pt bottles bitter lemon,
 chilled
slices of orange and lemon, to garnish

1 Pour the orange juice into a jug and add
the bitter lemon gradually, stirring it in well.
2 Pour the drink into tall tumblers, garnish
them with slices of orange and lemon and
serve immediately.

Orange barley water

| 5 minutes, then 1½ hours,
| plus cooling

Makes 8–10 drinks
75 g /3 oz pearl barley
thinly pared zest and strained juice of
 3 large oranges
40–50 g /1½–2 oz sugar
ice cubes

1 Put the pearl barley into a large, heavy-
based saucepan with cold water to cover.
Bring to the boil and simmer for 2 minutes,
then drain well.
2 Rinse the barley under cold running
water, drain again, then return to the pan
with 1.7 L /3 pt cold water. Add the orange
zest and bring to the boil. Cover and simmer
gently for 1½ hours until the pearl barley is
tender.
3 Strain the liquid into a large, heatproof
jug, discarding the barley and the orange
zest. Stir in the sugar to taste and leave the
barley water to cool completely.
4 Stir in the orange juice and serve in tall
tumblers with plenty of ice.

Blackcurrant frostie

|| 5 minutes, then 4 hours freezing,
|| plus 5 minutes finishing

Makes 8 drinks
350 ml /12 fl oz blackcurrant cordial
strained juice of ½ a large orange

1 Pour the cordial into a large jug and add
800 ml/1 pt 8 fl oz cold water. Next, pour
the liquid into a shallow freezerproof container, cover and freeze for about 2 hours,
until it is frozen around the edges.
2 Using a fork, thoroughly stir the half-
frozen mixture. Stir in the orange juice and
mix well. Cover and freeze for a further 2
hours, until icy but not solid.
3 Remove from the freezer and mash the
mixture well with a fork until it is evenly
slushy. Divide the mixture among 8 small
chilled glasses and serve immediately with
long-handled spoons.

Fruit cup

| preparing the grapes, then 5 minutes

Makes 8–10 drinks
700 ml /1 pt 5 fl oz white grape juice, chilled
575 ml /1 pt sparkling apple juice, chilled
ice cubes
2–3 bananas
225 g /8 oz white grapes, halved and seeded

1 Pour the grape and apple juice into a
large jug or a glass bowl.
2 Add the ice cubes. Peel and slice the
bananas thinly. Add the bananas and the
grapes to the jug or bowl and serve it
immediately, pouring it into tumblers or
ladling it out of the bowl with a spoon.

Cola cup

Add a surprise element to a favourite drink
with fresh fruit.

freezing the ice block,
then 10 minutes

Makes 1 L /1¾ pt
2 bananas
1 orange
1 lemon
1 L /1¾ pt cola, chilled

1   Pour water into a clean household glove,
seal it with a freezer tie and put it in the
freezer until solid.
2   Slice the bananas, the oranges, and the
lemons. Place them in the jug or bowl and
pour the cola over them.
3   Remove the glove from the freezer. Peel
off the glove. Add the shaped ice block to the
bowl and serve.

Strawberry froth

10 minutes,
plus chilling

Makes 500 ml /18 fl oz
225 g /8 oz strawberries, defrosted if frozen
275 ml /10 fl oz fresh orange juice
sugar, to taste
To garnish
*extra strawberries, or strawberry ice cubes
   (optional)*

1   Blend together the strawberries, the
orange juice and the sugar. Place in a jug or
bowl and chill in the refrigerator.
2   Make strawberry ice cubes by putting
whole strawberries in ice cube trays. Cover
them with water and freeze. Alternatively,
simply slice the strawberries for a garnish.
3   When ready to serve, add the strawberry
ice cubes or sliced strawberries. Each person
should get some slices of fruit.

Gingerbeer

5–10 minutes for 8 days,
then 1 week storage

Makes 5 L /8¾ pts
*25 g /1 oz fresh yeast or 15 g /½ oz
   dried yeast*
1 kg./2¼ lb sugar
40 ml /8 tsp ground ginger
juice of 2 lemons

1   Put the yeast into a large clean jar. Pour
in 275 ml /10 fl oz water and stir well. Stir in
10 ml /2 tsp sugar and 10 ml /2 tsp ground
ginger. Cover the jar and leave it to stand for
24 hours.
2   On each of the following 6 days, stir in 5
ml /1 tsp sugar and 5 ml /1 tsp ground ginger
and cover the jar each time. After the last
addition, leave the solution to stand, covered,
for another 24 hours.
3   Line a sieve with muslin or cheese-cloth.
Strain the solution, reserving both the liquid
and the sediment.
4   Put 900 g /2 lb sugar into a large saucepan and pour in 575 ml /1 pt water. Stir over
a low heat to dissolve the sugar, then bring
the syrup to the boil and boil for 3 minutes.
5   Pour the syrup into a large bowl and stir
in the lemon juice, ginger liquid and 3.5 L /
6 pt water. Stir well.
6   Pour the ginger beer into clean, rinsed-
out bottles. Secure the bottles with corks
(do not use screw tops because fermentation
could cause the bottles to explode).
7   Store for 1 week before serving. Serve
well chilled.

● Half of the reserved ginger sediment will
be enough to start your next batch of ginger
beer.
● For a real thirst-quencher, pour 45 ml /3
tbls lime cordial into a tumbler, then add lots
of crushed ice and top it up with the home-
made ginger beer.
● To make a drink called Evesham shandy,
mix half-and-half ginger beer and chilled
sweet cider.

Sparkling fruit cup

5 minutes

Makes approximately 2.3 L /4 pt
200 g /7 oz canned crushed pineapple
600 ml /1 pt pineapple juice, chilled
600 ml /1 pt orange juice, chilled
1 L /1¾ pt lemonade, chilled
To serve
a block of ice
2 small oranges, sliced

1   Put the crushed pineapple with its juice
into a large jug or bowl. Add the fruit juices
and the lemonade, giving the mixture a good
stir to blend it well.
2   Put in the block of ice, decorate with the
slices of fresh orange and serve.

*Cool and refreshing: Strawberry froth and
Cola cup*

Weddings

A FORMAL RECEPTION

Whatever the style of reception you choose, there will be a lot of preparation beforehand. To ensure that everything runs smoothly and according to plan on the day, simply follow these basic guidelines.

Before you begin planning, decide what kind of reception would suit you best if you are going to be doing all the cooking yourself. There are two main factors to bear in mind when deciding: the number of guests the bride and groom wish to invite and the time of the wedding ceremony. For instance, if you have a big family and many friends coming from far and wide, and are working to a limited budget, you may find that a noonday ceremony followed by lunch would be too costly. A less expensive alternative might be a tea-time reception — serving small sandwiches, cakes and desserts — or a canapé reception which you can prepare in advance at your leisure and then freeze until the day the food is needed.

Here I give you the frameworks for various menus, and for the more elaborate dishes (marked with asterisks) I have given you the full recipes.

If possible, relate the time of the reception to the couple's going-away plans. With the best will in the world, the bubbly atmosphere tends to fizzle out once the bride and groom leave on their honeymoon. So if they have a train or plane to catch, work backwards from their deadline and plan for the party to end soon after their departure. Consider your guests, too. If they will be travelling long distances, allow them enough time to arrive comfortably.

One last, but most important, point: do remember to book the wedding in good time, to ensure that the church or registry will be able to accommodate your wishes.

Quick party check list

- Book the church or registry office.
- Decide where and when the reception is going to be held. Decide exactly what kind of reception it's going to be. Do any necessary booking. Write your own personal check list.
- Draw up the guest list and send out the invitations.
- Select the menu and drinks and made a comprehensive list of the equipment you will need — tableware, cooking utensils, linen, etc. Place any necessary orders and arrange to borrow what you are going to need.
- Order flowers.
- Write a shopping list and draw up your own cooking schedule.
- Start shopping and prepare any food that can be frozen.
- Draw up a party timetable.
- Finish the shopping. Prepare and chill as much of the food as possible.
- Check and lay out the tableware. Have all the utensils ready.
- Decorate the rooms that are going to be used.
- Finish the cooking.

The location

Once you've drawn up the guest list, decide where the reception will be held. Can you cope with the numbers at home? Will you have to hire a hall? Would a marquee be the answer?

Unless you're planning a quick cocktail party, you should allow for all the guests at the reception to be able to sit or perch somewhere — even if only on floor cushions. You can shift your furniture temporarily to the garage and hire folding chairs and tables.

If you hire a local hall, space won't be a problem, but don't be tempted to invite more guests than you can comfortably cater for. And do check when the hall has to be cleared and whether hired help is available.

If you have a garden (and if expense isn't the main consideration) you could hire a marquee. Contractors are very clever at erecting elegant marquees on the smallest and unlikeliest of plots or gardens — and a yellow or pink-and-white striped awning with table settings to match certainly does look effective. You needn't think of a marquee only in terms of warm-weather weddings; with off-the-ground wooden platform flooring and portable gas heaters they adapt well to cooler, muddier days too. Hire firms invariably offer a complete package including chairs, folding tables and long trestle tables.

What style of party?

If the reception is to be at lunchtime, you should choose between a sit-down meal and a cold, help-yourself buffet.

If the guest list has crept up to near 100, then the most practical meal to consider is a fork-and-finger buffet. This can be given either early in the day, around noon after a morning wedding, or in the early evening. But another very easy way to entertain large numbers of guests is to serve afternoon tea and champagne.

In general very small, intimate weddings are suited to the morning with drinks and a sit-down lunch to follow. For a slightly larger wedding party, a cold buffet lunch is the ideal answer.

If you are going to have a wedding breakfast for family and close friends, you might even consider a hot menu. Only choose this, however, if you feel sufficiently calm and confident about going off to the ceremony and leaving the food. A reliable friend or hired help — to whom you can entrust such an important meal — is a great asset here. Bear in mind, too, that you won't want to miss the pre-lunch champagne toasts by being away in the kitchen for any great length of time, finishing a sauce or seeing to other last-minute preparations. If you do decide on a hot menu, hire or borrow enough heated trolleys to keep all the food at the right temperature until the moment that it is actually served.

Whether they are large or small, wedding receptions call for dishes with a touch of luxury — after all, a wedding is a very special occasion, and one to be remembered long afterwards. On the following pages I give you useful suggestions for elegant and delicious dishes that will grace your reception, and I also give the full recipes for those marked with asterisks.

A buffet reception

The main-course dishes I suggest for a cold buffet are Poached salmon in aspic, Mayonnaise chicken chaudfroid, Ballotine of veal and Cold loin of pork with courgette stuffing (see recipes). All these have an essential common factor — you can prepare them right up to the garnish stage ahead of the reception.

filled with a mixture of fresh or canned fruits, both served with rich whipped cream.

Finger food

For a fork-and-finger buffet, choose a main fork dish from amongst those already suggested. Prepare in addition, a wide variety of canapés. Make batches of the tiniest vol-au-vent cases, pastry boats and tartlet cases in advance and freeze them. Freeze with them, a selection of fillings which can be used such as mushroom, prawn, chicken, salmon and ham. Make bite-sized choux buns to fill just before the reception with cream cheese or a thick sauce flavoured with fish, herbs or spices. Have colourful sticks of fresh raw vegetables, all cut the day before and chilled in the refrigerator, to surround cheese or spicy dips, and have watercress, fresh herbs and lemon wedges at hand for garnishing.

On the morning of the buffet make up some mini kebabs on cocktail sticks, offering a selection of low-calorie and refreshing 'bites' such as pineapple cubes, melon balls or melon cubes, prawns, celery and carrot strips. Make sure you enlist enough help to put the finishing touches to the table and to see that everything is ready in plenty of time.

At a stand-up celebration, pamper sweet-toothed guests by serving tiny cakes flavoured with coffee, chocolate, lemon and orange, and iced in soft pastel colours. These can be made two or three days ahead as the icing will seal the freshness into the cakes. Avoid triple-layer gateaux or very gooey cakes because they are so very difficult and messy to eat with one hand. Offer a selection of desserts served in individual wine glasses or tumblers that can be hired along with the rest of the equipment. Fruit fools and mousses of all kinds, an old-fashioned trifle or fresh fruit set in a clear jelly flavoured with port or wine — these will all be popular and involve you in no last-minute work.

Drinks

● Turn your attention to the drinks once you have worked out the food and organized your crockery and other requirements.
● Select your drinks carefully, to keep within your budget and to satisfy your guests.
● For greeting people, serve trays of medium or dry sherry, glasses of sparkling white wine or a simple wine cocktail. Pour a small measure of brandy into each glass in advance and top up at the last minute with sparkling white wine — this will give a quick 'lift' at the beginning of the reception!
● Buy the best champagne or sparkling wine you can afford for the wedding toast. Keep it separate from the other drinks.
● Provide plenty of sparkling mineral water and a good selection of fruit juices for non-drinkers, children and drivers.
● Order the drinks and glasses in good time — remember that many suppliers offer a free loan service with a large order for wine, so it is worthwhile shopping around.
● Don't forget to order plenty of ice — white wines, sparkling wines, and most wine and fruit cups flavoured with fruit syrup juices and liqueurs taste much better chilled.

Mayonnaise chicken chaudfroid (page 89)

For an attractive and economical cold buffet, a selection of savoury flans, quiches and savoury mille feuilles tastefully decorated and filled with tempting prawn, chicken or turkey mixtures is an excellent choice. All the pastries can be cooked ahead and frozen ready for filling on the day. The day before the party you can hard-boil eggs, split them lengthways and pipe assorted creamed mixtures onto them.

With the main course you should serve a good variety of salads. A food processor is a tremendous asset here: it makes salads in a twinkling. Thinly sliced raw mushrooms, grated carrot, strips of red, green and yellow pepper, matchsticks of cucumber or celery can all be quickly prepared a day ahead, chilled, tossed in a home-made vinaigrette dressing and then blended in countless permutations on the morning of the day.

If the wedding is planned for a chilly time of year, you can welcome the guests with a hot soup — something light and seemingly exotic is just the thing. Mock turtle, lobster bisque or sherried consommé are all perfect before a cold main course. If you want something unusual for such a special occasion, try hiring (or borrowing) Chinese bowls complete with china spoons. If you want to serve a hot main dish, choose something that is neither too heavy nor too strongly spiced.

For a buffet dessert, a refreshing choice — in the summer — is a colourful selection of fresh berries or just strawberries tossed in a raspberry sauce, and light sponge flan cases

Tea-time celebration

The cakes and desserts I have mentioned previously are just as appropriate for a tea-time reception too, though you may feel the wedding cake itself is sufficent (see recipe, page 96). However, Sweet pastry bites (see recipe, page 106) will be spectacular attractions on your tea table.

If you want to include savoury food too, serve small sandwiches made from the thinnest possible slices (an electric carving knife does the job beautifully), cut into fancy shapes with a pastry or biscuit cutter. Make up a selection of moist and refreshing fillings ahead of time and freeze them, or prepare and refrigerate them the day before. Tasty combinations of cream cheese and watercress, orange butter and minced ham, cottage cheese and minced pineapple, liver sausage and herb butter are just a few ideas. Asparagus, enclosed in wafer-thin brown bread, and chequer-board sandwiches made with half white and half wholewheat bread are also most suitable. Prepare them in advance, cover them with cling film and chill until the last minute. Party sandwich loaf (see recipe,

Cold loin of pork with courgette stuffing (page 92), and a selection of salads

page 103) will also be an eye-catching and delicious addition to your menu.

Having decided on the numbers you are catering for, choose an appropriate menu. Below I give you four, with lots of different suggestions. Or choose one — or even more — main course dishes for a striking buffet or lunch centrepiece, remembering, however, to multiply up recipe quantities to feed the number of guests invited. If you follow my recipes carefully — the preparations require patience, but they aren't difficult — your centrepiece will be beautiful.

One word of advice: cleverly glazed dishes are best very simply presented. Do not crowd the serving plate with too many extra decorations — they will only detract from the impact of the food. Just make sure the dish has pride of place and plenty of space on your buffet table.

Wedding breakfast for 10–12

In bygone days a wedding breakfast meant a very grand banquet. Nowadays, it usually means a small and rather formal sit-down luncheon — either mid-morning or at noon but very rarely as early as breakfast time.

This is a delicate but very luxurious menu requiring little last-minute attention as most

An asparagus salad
or
An artichoke heart salad

Poached salmon in aspic
or
Mayonnaise chicken chaudfroid

A dessert-wine jelly, with thick cream
or
Summer fruit salad

of the food can be prepared the day before the wedding. If you choose asparagus, keep the cooked spears in a bowl covered with cling film and stored in a cool place (not the refrigerator). If asparagus is not in season, choose artichokes instead.

The Poached salmon in aspic (see recipe) can be prepared and garnished the day before. For an equally gracious main course, serve Mayonnaise chicken chaudfroid (see recipe). Accompany the main course with a selection of seasonal vegetables.

Make your dessert-wine jelly stunningly pretty by floating a flower — a violet, pansy or rose-bud — in it before it sets completely, then covering the flower with a little more

jelly to seal it. If you've chosen the chicken for a main course, the Summer fruit salad with cream would be a better dessert choice.

Buffet lunch for 15–20

For a slightly larger reception it is easier to serve a buffet lunch and let people help themselves. However, do make sure that you provide plenty of chairs and perhaps some small tables so that your guests can sit down and eat in comfort.

Gruyère and ham tartlets
or
Herring croustades (see page 94)

Loin of pork with courgette stuffing
or
Ballotine of veal

A green salad with Roquefort
or
A salad with celeraic and apple

Eight-fruit salad
or
A creamy moulded pudding

Everything on this menu can be prepared in advance and refrigerated until the moment you need them. The only last-minute thing to do will be to toss the salad.

Mille-feuilles are simple to make, a fish terrine will be more complicated.

The loin of pork is most attractive, and is just as delicious served cold or hot. In this case, remove the joints from the dish once cooked, skim the juices and reduce slightly to make a gravy. The ballotine of veal, with its attractive stuffing, is also ideal for a buffet.

The Eight-fruit salad is an eye-catching dessert to grace your table. For a more subtle effect, however, serve a creamy moulded pudding and flavour it with soft fresh fruit of the season.

Afternoon tea for 30–50

It's very pleasant to hold an afternoon reception out of doors, but if you can't depend on the weather, hire a marquee.

While the emphasis will naturally be on

A selection of open sandwiches together with asparagus rolls

A selection of stuffed eggs
Party sandwich loaf (see page 103)

A walnut roll
or
A chocolate cake
A pound cake
Spiced chocolate biscuits (see page 23)
and *Almond biscuits* (see page 52)

Allspice flowers with nectarine mousse
or
Seasonal fresh fruit tartlets

Whatever champagne you choose — from dry to sweet — it should be served chilled

sweet, tea-time foods, it is a good idea to offer a selection of sandwiches and a fairly substantial savoury dish, which can be easily eaten with a fork.

For a special touch, wrap asparagus in thin slices of smoked salmon. Stuffed eggs are pretty when made with different coloured fillings, while for your centrepiece, make two or three Party sandwich loaves.

Some people love creamy cakes while others prefer something plainer; a deliciously gooey chocolate cake makes a good contrast to a walnut roll, while a pound cake is less rich but very moist.

Spicy biscuits filled with nectarine mousse make delicious mouthfuls, but if nectarines are unavailable, tartlets with a fresh fruit and nut filling are a good alternative.

Evening reception for 50 plus

For this kind of party, the emphasis is on bite-sized savoury foods. Offer at least six sorts of canapé — up to ten if you feel really ambitious!

It's important to have a variety of tastes and textures, and it's a good idea to provide bowls of raw vegetable slices for a fresh contrast to the richer canapés or to eat with spicy and savoury dips.

Allow at least eight canapés per person and serve something hot halfway through. The decorative Sweet pastry bites — well worth the time they take to prepare — are just the thing to hand round with a cup of coffee towards the end of what is sure to be a very successful party.

A selection of appetizers (see page 94)
Garnished cucumbers and celery sticks
A selection of chopped meats in aspic
Fillet steak balls
Potted Stilton dates (see page 27)
Smoked salmon barquettes
Brie on French bread
Pastry boats with varied savoury fillings

Ginger prawns in soured cream
(see page 104)
or
Savoury crêpes

Sweet pastry bites (see page 106)
or
Orange-almond petits fours
(see page 108)

Canapés: if you are planning to do all the cooking for the reception yourself, your greatest ally is your freezer, providing you have enough space. If necessary, start eating up non-party items from your freezer as soon as you've sent out the wedding invitations. By the time you come to cooking for the reception, you should have plenty of space in the freezer.

Planning the food

As I have said, you will want several sorts of canapés to give variety, bearing in mind that as many as possible should be prepared and frozen ahead. Some canapés, such as Gruyère and ham tartlets (see recipe) will need to be filled on the day of the party. Balance your work load by choosing others, such as Herring croustades (see recipe), which can be frozen completely finished. (The garnish takes no more than a minute or two to complete, and can be done quite quickly on the morning of the reception.)

Bases for freezing

Little pastry cases, either shortcrust or puff, round or boat-shaped (called barquettes), can be made ahead and frozen or stored in an airtight container for up to a week.

Croustades (small round or fancy-shaped pieces of bread) can be fried, then frozen either with or without their topping.

Fillings

Some fillings, such as spinach and cream cheese or smoked salmon pâté (see recipes), can be frozen in the prepared base. Topped with an asparagus tip, smoked salmon paté makes a delicious, and less expensive, alternative to a slice of smoked salmon wrapped around an asparagus spear.

If you are planning a mayonnaise-based filling, then make it the day before the reception and assemble the canapés once the bases are defrosted. The mayonnaise itself can be made up to five days before the reception and kept in an airtight jar in the refrigerator. Spoon out the amount you need and flavour it according to the recipes selected.

Garnishes

Chopped parsley, olives and nuts can all be prepared a couple of days in advance and then stored, covered with cling film, in the refrigerator. A day in advance, cut out tiny fancy shapes, such as stars or moons, from ham, cheese or pimento, using aspic cutters. Add a little aspic to the mayonnaise piping if you wish.

Freezing the canapés

It is easiest to freeze canapés laid flat on trays — for this you may need to borrow baking sheets or domestic trays to hold them all. Arranged like this, you can put them all in the freezer and get them out again to defrost them without touching them. In an upright freezer store one tray on top of the frozen goods on each shelf; the trick is less easy to manage in a chest freezer.

As an alternative, freeze as many canapés as possible on a tray. When frozen solid, pack them in a rigid container, layering with greaseproof paper. Take particular care with unfilled pastry cases, which will break if knocked. When they are frozen, pack them in a rigid container, stacked in sets of 5–6. Unpack and defrost all canapés, unwrapped, in a single layer. They will defrost in about an hour, but it is better to allow longer if you can.

While you are having your big cook-and-freeze session, make a big, homely stew or a casserole and freeze that, too. After the last guests have gone, and after all the hard work, you, your family, and any helpers may well appreciate a ready-made meal.

Ballotine of veal

making the stock and aspic, then 3 hours, plus chilling

Serves 24
1.4 kg /3 lb chicken
3 kg /6¾ lb boneless breast of veal
salt and freshly ground black pepper
30 ml /2 tbls chopped fresh parsley
5 ml /1 tsp chopped fresh thyme
2.5 ml /½ tsp dried chervil
a pinch of celery salt
cayenne pepper

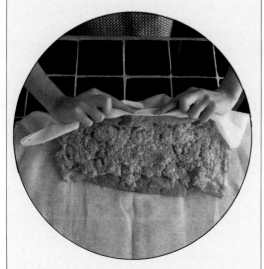

Preparing the ballotine

Roll the veal tightly to form a cylinder, neatly tucking in the ends.

For the stock
1 veal knuckle bone
2 medium-sized onions
2 medium-sized carrots
2 celery sticks
1 chicken stock cube, crumbled
For the stuffing
salt and freshly ground black pepper
225 g /8 oz finely chopped onion
1 garlic clove, finely chopped
2.5 ml /½ tsp dried rosemary
50 ml /2 fl oz port
50 ml /2 fl oz dry sherry
60 ml /4 tbls white breadcrumbs
1 egg
75 g /3 oz pâté de foie gras
75 g /3 oz salt pork fat
100 g /4 oz cooked tongue
25 g /1 oz pistachio nuts, shelled
50 g /2 oz cocktail gherkins, drained
For the chaudfroid sauce
15 g /½ oz butter
30 ml /2 tbls flour
5 ml /1 tsp tomato purée
60 ml /4 tbls port
30 ml /2 tbls red wine
5 ml /1 tsp powdered gelatine
For the garnish
1 envelope (45 ml /3 tbls) savoury aspic powder
1 small red pepper, cored, seeded and cut into small heart shapes
fresh chives
green parts of 2 spring onions, cut into leaf shapes
crisp lettuce leaves
watercress leaves
fresh dill

1 At least a day before serving, skin and bone the chicken, keeping the breasts whole. Reserve the meat for the stuffing and use the carcass for the stock.
2 Make the stock. In a large saucepan, combine the knuckle, chicken carcass, onions, carrots, celery and stock cube with 3.4 L /6 pt water. Bring them to the boil, skim off any scum and simmer for 1 hour. Remove and discard the bones. Reserve the stock.
3 Meanwhile, trim and discard all the excess fat and membrane from the veal. Slip the knife under the edge where the rib bones were and cut off the top layer of meat. Reserve.
4 Remove and discard the fine membrane covering the flattish surface of the remaining meat. Where the meat is thickest, trim off the surface and add it to the pieces reserved for the stuffing, leaving an even thickness of meat. Place the meat between sheets of cling film and bat it out to a thin rectangle, about 45 × 30 cm /18 × 12 in.
5 Prepare the stuffing. Remove all fat and membrane from the veal trimmings, leaving about 500 g /1 lb meat. Pass it twice through the finest blade of a mincer into a bowl.
6 Proceed as above with the chicken leg meat and combine it with the veal. Season and add the onion, garlic, rosemary, port, sherry, 50 ml /2 tbls reserved stock, breadcrumbs and the egg. Mix thoroughly and adjust the seasoning. Reserve.
7 Cut the reserved chicken breast meat, pâté de foie gras, salt pork fat and tongue

into 75 × 15 mm /3 × ½ in strips. Reserve.
8 Put the pistachio nuts into a saucepan. Cover them with water and bring them to the boil. Drain them well, then rub the nuts in a clean tea-towel to remove the skins. Reserve.
9 Heat the oven to 220C /425F /gas 7.
10 Lay a large rectangle of double thickness muslin, about 90 × 60 cm /3 × 2 ft, on a work surface. Spread the veal out over the centre of the muslin. Season with salt and pepper and sprinkle with the parsley, thyme, chervil, celery salt and cayenne pepper.
11 Spread ⅔ of the mixture over the veal, leaving 5 cm /2 in free around the edges. Using half the remaining stuffing ingredients, arrange lines of chicken, foie gras, pork fat, tongue, gherkins and pistachio nuts across the width, that is down the centre of the stuffing.
12 Spread the remaining meat mixture over the decorative layer, then arrange the remaining stuffing ingredients on top.
13 Lift one long edge of the muslin and use it to fold one long side of the veal over the stuffing. Pulling upwards with the muslin, roll the veal tightly like a Swiss roll to form a cylinder, tucking in the ends.
14 Roll the meat to the edge of the muslin, then roll the muslin tightly around the veal and tie the ends firmly with string. Make a series of ties around the parcel, then tie once from end to end to hold it in a neat shape.
15 Strain the remaining stock into a roasting tin. Add the ballotine. Baste with stock, then cover loosely with foil and transfer to the oven. Cook for 20 minutes.
16 Reduce the temperature to 190C /375F /gas 5 and cook for 40 minutes.
17 Remove the tin from the oven and turn

the ballotine over in the stock. Cover with foil and return it to the oven for a further hour, or until it is cooked.

18 Remove the tin from the oven and leave the ballotine to get cold in the stock.

19 Remove the ballotine from the stock. Remove the strings and muslin, then wrap the ballotine tightly in cling film and chill. Reserve 425 ml /15 fl oz of the stock.

20 Meanwhile, prepare the chaudfroid sauce. In a saucepan, heat the reserved stock. In a separate pan, melt the butter. Add the flour and stir over a low heat for 2–3 minutes to make a pale roux. Gradually pour in the stock, stirring constantly. Bring to the boil and simmer for 5 minutes, stirring occasionally, until thickened.

21 Stir in the tomato purée, port and red wine and season to taste with salt and freshly ground black pepper. Leave to get cold.

22 In a small bowl, sprinkle the gelatine over 30 ml /2 tbls water and leave it to soften. Place it over simmering water until the gelatine is dissolved. Leave it to cool slightly.

23 Stir the gelatine into the sauce and place this over a bowl or ice. Stir from time to time until the mixture gets syrupy and is on the point of setting.

24 Remove the ballotine from the refrigerator and discard the cling film. Place it on a wire rack over a tray and spoon over the setting chaudfroid sauce to coat it completely. Return it to the refrigerator with the rack.

25 Make the aspic: place 600 ml /1 pt water in a saucepan with the aspic powder and bring slowly to the boil.

Ballotine of veal

26 Prepare the pepper, chives and spring onion garnish. Put 150 1 /5 fl oz liquid aspic in a small bowl and stir it over ice until it is almost setting. Using a skewer, dip each piece of garnish in the aspic and position it as shown in the picture. Return the garnished ballotine to the refrigerator to set.

27 Spoon half the remaining aspic into a small bowl and stir it over ice until it is beginning to set. Spoon over the set ballotine to coat the garnishes. Chill until set.

28 In a bowl, stir the remaining aspic over ice until it is beginning to set and spoon it carefully over the ballotine to give it a glossy coating. Chill until firmly set.

29 About 1 hour before serving, place the ballotine on a long serving dish. Garnish with lettuce leaves, watercress and dill.

Mayonnaise chicken chaudfroid

The breasts of the poached chicken are replaced with a mousse of brandied chicken livers. The breast meat is shaped into medallions and heaped with the mousse.

⏲🍴 making stock and aspic, several hours preparation and chilling

Serves 12
2–2.3 kg /4½ lb chicken
about 1.1 L /2 pt chicken stock, home-made or
*   from a cube*
For the brandied chicken liver mousse
50 g /2 oz butter
175–225 g /6–8 oz chicken livers, trimmed
1 shallot, diced
salt and freshly ground black pepper
30 ml /2 tbls powdered aspic, dissolved in
*   50 ml /2 fl oz hot water*
15 ml /1 tbls brandy
15 ml /1 tbls Maderia
275 ml /10 fl oz thick cream, whipped to soft
*   peaks*
For the mayonnaise chaufroid sauce
600 ml /1 pt mayonnaise (see page 90)
150 ml /5 fl oz thick cream
15 ml /1 tbls powdered aspic, diluted in 15 ml /
*   1 tbls hot water*
salt and freshly ground white pepper
lemon juice
Choice of ingredients, for garnish
canned pimento, cut into flowers or strips
radishes, thinly sliced
fresh tarragon leaves
1 hard-boiled egg, shelled and thinly sliced
tomatoes, blanched, skinned, seeded and
*   cut into wedges*
cucumber, thinly sliced or cut into strips
1 carrot, thinly sliced
shredded lettuce
sprigs of fresh chervil
softened butter mixed with paprika
For the aspic finish
1 envelope (45 ml /3 tbls) savoury aspic
*   powder for:*
*   275 ml /10 fl oz cold aspic jelly*
*   150 ml /5 fl oz hot aspic jelly (optional)*

1 Two days before you are going to serve the chicken, truss it into a good even shape.

2 Place the trussed chicken in a saucepan just big enough to hold it, cover with chicken stock and bring gently to the boil, skimming off all impurities as they rise to the surface. Simmer for 35–40 minutes or until the chicken is tender.

3 Remove the saucepan from the heat and allow the chicken to cool completely in the stock. Remove the chicken from the stock and chill both separately overnight.

4 Cut away the chicken's trussing string. Take the chicken and ease the legs away from the body without quite separating them from the joint. Carefully cut around the legs next to the breast to loosen the skin but do not remove the legs from the carcass. Carefully cut down the breast bone and ribs to remove each breast in 1 piece. Leave the breast bone in place. Chill the carcass.

5 To make the chicken medallions, cut each breast diagonally into 4 or 5 slices and put them on a rack in the refrigerator.

6 To make the brandied chicken liver mousse, heat the butter in a frying-pan and sauté the chicken livers and shallots over a medium-low heat until cooked (about 5–7 minutes) and remove from the heat. Season with salt and freshly ground black pepper.

7 Put the chicken livers and 150 ml /5 fl oz of the reserved chicken stock in a saucepan, bring to the boil, remove it from the heat and allow it to cool. Finely mince the mixture then pass it through a fine sieve into a bowl.

8 Add the liquid aspic, brandy and Madeira to the puréed mixture. Fold in the whipped thick cream and chill until it is set.

9 To make the mayonnaise chaudfroid sauce, warm 75 ml /5 tbls of the reserved chicken stock, strain it, and fold it into the mayonnaise. Mix the mayonnaise well, then whisk in the thick cream. Add the liquid aspic, then season with salt, white pepper and lemon juice and reserve.

10 Remove the chicken from the refrigerator and put it on a wire rack with the breast slices. Place it over a clean tray.

11 Spoon the chaudfroid sauce over the chicken and medallions of breast until they are well coated. Refrigerate until the sauce is well set (about 5 minutes), then remove the rack and chicken from the refrigerator. Coat the chicken and medallions once again with the chaudfroid sauce. Chill for 5 minutes.

12 To finish, remove, the chicken from the refrigerator and pipe the brandied chicken liver mouse onto the breast bone, mounding the mousse up to resemble the complete bird, but replacing the breast with the mousse. Smooth the mousse with a palette knife.

13 Make the aspic finish: place 600 ml /1 pt water in a pan with the aspic powder and bring it slowly to the boil. Cool before using.

14 Prepare the garnishes of your choice and dip them carefully into the melted aspic.

15 Position the chicken on a dish, decorating it with the medallions and the garnishes. Return the dish to the refrigerator for about 10 minutes or until chilled.

16 Remove the dish from the refrigerator and spoon liquid aspic jelly over the chicken and garnishes. If the aspic is not liquid enough, add a little hot jelly to 'soften' it; be careful not to add too much. Chill until about 20 minutes before serving. Chill any remaining aspic and chop it up, to use as a garnish, if wished.

Poached salmon in aspic

🕐 🍴 3 hours, plus cooling, 1½ hours decorating, then chilling

Serves 12
1.8 kg /4 lb salmon with head and tail, cleaned
For the court bouillon
75 cl bottle dry white wine
1 large Spanish onion, sliced
4 medium-sized carrots, sliced
3 mushrooms
2 bay leaves
10 white peppercorns
bouquet garni
4 celery sticks, sliced
For the aspic
3 egg whites, whisked until frothy
100 g /4 oz raw white fish, minced
½ Spanish onion, finely chopped
1 carrot, finely chopped
1 leek, white part only, finely chopped
3 parsley stalks
3–4 mushroom stalks, finely chopped
10 white peppercorns
1 bay leaf
a pinch of dried thyme
1.5 ml /¼ tomato purée
juice of 1 lemon
1.5 ml /¼ tsp salt
40 g /1½ oz powdered gelatine

For the decoration
1 large cucumber
1 spring onion, green part only
2 slices stuffed olive
mustard and cress
For the Mayonnaise
Makes about 450 ml /15 fl oz
3 medium-sized egg yolks
22.5 ml /1½ tbls wine vinegar or lemon juice
4 ml /¾ tsp mustard powder
4 ml /¾ tsp salt
a pinch of freshly ground black pepper
450 ml /15 fl oz olive oil

1 Two days before serving, put the court bouillon ingredients and 2.3 L /4 pt cold water in the fish kettle. Bring it to the boil and skim off any scum that rises. Lower the heat and simmer the court bouillon gently for 20 minutes.
2 Remove the kettle from the heat and leave the contents to cool slightly. Lay the salmon carefully on the removable rack and lower it gently into the court bouillon to cover.
3 Cover the kettle tightly. Return it to the boil (about 3 minutes), then leave the fish in the court bouillon until cold or overnight. Check that the fish is cooked by looking into the stomach cavity: there should be no traces of blood along the backbone.
4 When the salmon is cold, lift it out, on the rack, then drain it thoroughly. Transfer it to a board and, using a sharp knife, slit the

skin across the head and tail, along the backbone and belly. Pull out the fins and bones attached to them. Remove the skin and the brown flesh along the central line of the fish, leaving the head and tail intact.
5 Using 2 fish slices, carefully transfer the salmon to the serving dish, best side up. Chill.
6 Strain off 1.1 L /2 pt of the court bouillon and use it, together with the listed ingredients, to make the aspic: mix the frothy egg whites in a large heavy-based saucepan with the fish, onion, carrot, leek, parsley stalks, mushroom stalks, peppercorns, bay leaf, thyme, tomato purée, lemon juice and the salt.
7 Bring the fish stock slowly to the boil in a separate pan. Pour the fish stock, a little at a time, onto the egg white mixture in the other pan, stirring constantly with a whisk or a wooden spoon.
8 Bring slowly to the boil, stirring. When the mixture boils, stop stirring and reduce the heat. Allow the foam to rise, then simmer the mixture for 5 minutes, uncovered, without stirring. Remove the pan from the heat, cover and infuse for 10 minutes.
9 Line a large sieve or colander with muslin and stand it over a bowl. Gently draw the scum away from one-quarter of the clarified stock. Lower a ladle into the gap and, disturbing the scum as little as possible, ladle the clarified stock into the muslin-lined sieve. (If, when you have finished, you find

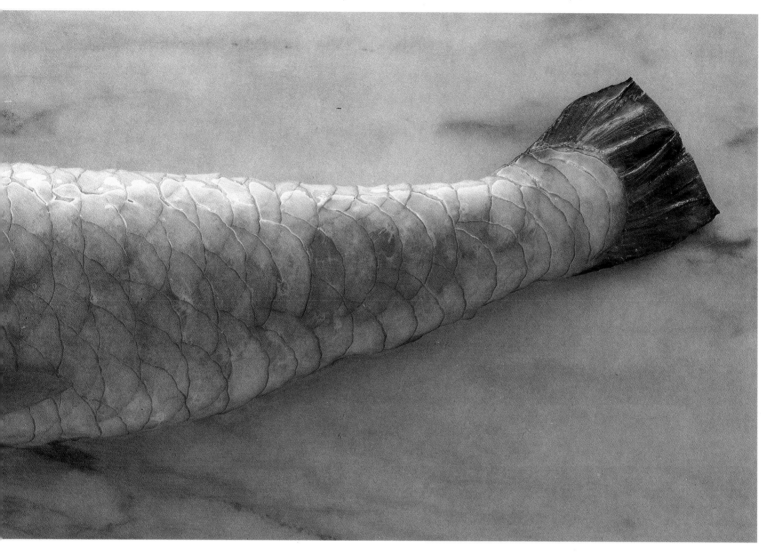

that the resulting consommé is not absolutely clear, strain it and then start again.) Measure 60 ml /4 tbls of the consommé into a small bowl and leave it to get cold.

10 Sprinkle the 40 g /1½ oz powdered gelatine over the consommé in a small bowl. Leave it to soften, then stand the bowl in a pan of simmering water until the gelatine has dissolved.

11 Strain the dissolved gelatine mixture into the remaining warm consommé and stir thoroughly. Allow the mixture to cool until it is very syrupy (the consistency of unbeaten egg white) and on the point of setting.

12 Meanwhile, prepare the decorations. Peel the cucumber and cut it into paper-thin slices, preferably using a mandolin cutter or food processor. Halve the slices. Cut the green part of the spring onion into strips. Chill all the decorations until they are needed.

13 Put 150 ml /5 fl oz liquid aspic in a bowl and chill it until it has started to set and has the consistency of unbeaten egg white. Keep the remaining aspic at room temperature to stop it setting.

14 Brush the fish with the syrupy aspic until it is evenly coated. Chill more aspic as you need it — and return the fish to the refrigerator as well if it starts to warm up. Don't worry about trying to keep the serving dish clean as you can very easily clear it afterwards.

15 When the fish is well coated, chill it for 20–30 minutes, to set the coating. Chill another 150 ml /5 fl oz aspic.

16 Remove the coated fish and chilled decorations from the refrigerator. Using the tip of a pointed knife or a skewer, and your fingers, carefully dip each halved cucumber slice in the syrupy aspic, one after another, and arrange them carefully on the glazed fish as overlapping 'scales'. Use some small wooden toothpicks to hold the cucumber slices in place. If necessary, while decorating, return the salmon to the refrigerator to chill it again.

17 Use the strips of spring onion to make 'fins', arranging them carefully on the salmon. Use the slices of stuffed olive to make eyes. Refrigerate the fish for 20–30 minutes, or until the aspic is set.

18 Chill the remaining aspic. When syrupy, carefully brush or spoon a layer of aspic over the fish, to finish the glazing. Chill the salmon again until set.

19 When the aspic is firm, remove the toothpicks. Clean up the serving dish, scraping off any split aspic with a knife, then wiping the dish with a cloth wrung out in very hot water.

20 Keep the salmon chilled until 20–30 minutes before serving. Arrange the mustard and cress under the head, to make 'gills'.

21 To cut a portion, use a spoon or fish server to remove a short length across the fish from the upper side of the bone. Remove the entire upper fillet of the salmon, a

Poached salmon in aspic

portion at a time. Next, snip through the bone at each end with a pair of scissors and pull it out and discard it. Repeat with the lower fillet.

22 Make the mayonnaise: place the egg yolks in an electric blender with the wine vinegar or lemon juice, mustard, salt, freshly ground black pepper and 30 ml /2 tbls cold water. Cover and blend at maximum speed for 5 seconds, or until well mixed. Remove the centre of the lid of the blender and, with the motor turned to maximum, add the oil in a thin, steady trickle. Taste and adjust the seasoning, if necessary, and use as required.

23 Serve the salmon with the mayonnaise.

● You may wish to offer your guests an additional mayonnaise for choice. I suggest Herb mayonnaise, a fresh tasting sauce which complements the delicate flavour of salmon beautifully. To make this, pound 45 ml / 3 tbls finely chopped mixed herbs (tarragon, dill, chervil, chives, parsley) and press them through a sieve, along with 4 large, blanched spinach leaves. Beat the purée into 450 ml / 15 fl oz Mayonnaise (see above) and add salt and freshly ground black pepper if wished.

● You will need a proper fish kettle for this recipe. I use a kettle of 13.5 L /3 gal capacity. Measure the kettle before buying your salmon to make sure that your fish actually fits into it comfortably.

Cold loin of pork with courgette stuffing

🕐 ∥∥ 4–4¾ hours, plus overnight setting

Serves 20

4.3–4.5 kg /9½–10 lb loin of pork, boned
  weight (bones and rind reserved)
125 g /4 oz smoked back bacon, finely chopped
450 g /1 lb small courgettes, coarsely grated
225 g /8 oz ricotta cheese
30 ml /2 tbls finely chopped fresh basil
15 ml /1 tbls crushed fresh thyme
15 ml /1 tbls coriander seeds, crushed
1 garlic clove, finely chopped
salt and freshly ground black pepper
2 medium-sized eggs, beaten
50 g /2 oz salted almonds
275 ml /10 fl oz dry white wine
slices of lime, to garnish
sprigs of fresh thyme, to garnish

1 Ask your butcher to bone the loin and remove the rind, then cut it into 2 joints, leaving it unrolled and untied.
2 Put the chopped bacon into a large, heavy-based saucepan over a moderate heat and cook for 3–4 minutes, stirring, until the fat begins to run. Add the grated courgettes and cook for 4 minutes, stirring.
3 Transfer the courgettes and bacon to a large bowl. Add the ricotta cheese, basil, thyme, coriander and garlic. Mash well, season with salt and freshly ground pepper and bind with the beaten eggs.
4 Lay the pork joints out flat, fat sides down, and divide the stuffing between them,

spreading it evenly. Roll up the joints very carefully, enclosing the stuffing as much as possible, then tie them in several places with fine string. Heat the oven to 180C /350F / gas 4.
5 With the tip of a sharp knife, make little incisions in the fat side of the pork. Insert a salted almond into each, pushing them in well. Sprinkle the joints with pepper.
6 Put the joints into a large ovenproof dish, side by side. Surround them with the bones and rind so that the joints fit snugly. Cover them with the wine and 1.7 L /3 pt water and cook uncovered on the top shelf of the oven for 30 minutes or until the fat has taken on colour.
7 Lower the heat of the oven to 150C / 300F /gas 2. Cover the meat with a double thickness of foil and cook it for a further 2½ hours.
8 Remove the meat from the oven and discard the bones and rind. Leave the joints, covered, in a cool place overnight.
9 Remove the jellied juices from the dish and chop finely. Reserve.
10 Carve the pork into 5 mm /¼ in slices and arrange them attractively on 1 or 2 serving platters. Garnish the pork with the finely chopped jelly, slices of lime and sprigs of thyme and serve.

Eight-fruit salad

With many more exotic fruits becoming increasingly available, this special fruit dish is an attractive choice for a buffet.

∥∥ 45 minutes preparation, chilling, then bringing to room temperature

Serves 12

2 small pineapples
2 ripe papayas
2 ripe mangoes
4 kiwi fruit
16 strawberries, hulled and sliced
4 passion fruit, halved and seeded, seeds
  reserved
20 mint leaves
juice of 6 oranges
juice of 2 lemons
icing sugar (optional)

1 Cut off both ends of the pineapples and remove the skins with a sharp knife. Cut the pineapples into neat quarters and carefully remove the cores. Cut approximately 20 chunks from each pineapple and reserve the remainder for the dressing.
2 Peel the papayas, cut them in half and remove the pips. Reserve 30 ml /2 tbls of the pips. Cut half the papaya flesh into 8 mm / ⅓ in dice. Reserve the remainder for the dressing.
3 Peel the mangoes and cut each one lengthways into 3 slices. Cut half the mango slices into 8 mm /⅓ in dice and reserve the remainder for the dressing.
4 Peel the kiwi fruit and slice them thinly.
5 Put the prepared fruit in a large bowl. Arrange the sliced pineapple and kiwi at the bottom, then cover with the diced papaya and mango and top the fruit with half of the sliced strawberries; set this aside. Reserve the remaining sliced strawberries for the final decoration.
6 Make the dressing. Put the reserved pineapple, papaya and mango, the passion fruit,

Eight-fruit salad

reserved seeds and 10 mint leaves in an electric blender and blend to a pulp. Add orange juice and lemon juice to taste. Press through a fine sieve into a bowl. If the dressing is too thick, thin it with a little more orange juice. Add a little icing sugar to taste, if wished.

7 Pour the dressing over the prepared fruit, cover the bowl and chill.

8 At least 45 minutes before serving, remove the fruit salad from the refrigerator. Toss it lightly with a large metal spoon and divide it among 12 individual glass serving dishes or coupes. Sprinkle with the reserved papaya pips. Top with the reserved sliced strawberries.

9 Cut the remaining 10 mint leaves into a fine julienne and decorate each serving with a few strips of it. Leave to come to room temperature before serving.

Allspice flowers with nectarine mousse

frosting the mint leaves, then 3 hours

Makes 48
75 g /3 oz butter, softened
100 g /3½ oz sugar
1 medium-sized egg
2 medium-sized egg whites
125 g /4 oz flour
2.5 ml /½ tsp vanilla essence
5 ml /1 tsp ground allspice
oil, for greasing
For frosted mint sprigs
48 mint sprigs
2 egg whites, lightly beaten
caster sugar, for dipping
For the nectarine mousse
450 g /1 lb nectarines, blanched, skinned,
  stoned and chopped
50 g /2 oz butter
7.5 cm /3 in cinnamon stick
15 ml /1 tbls clear honey
15 ml /1 tbls orange juice
15 ml /1 tbls gelatine
150 ml /5 fl oz thin cream
150 ml /5 fl oz thick cream
15 ml /1 tbls peach brandy

1 The day before you need them, prepare the frosted mint sprigs: holding each sprig by its stalk, dip them into the lightly beaten egg white, making sure they are covered. Dip them in caster sugar, place them on a baking sheet lined with greaseproof paper and refrigerate them overnight to set.

2 Heat the oven to 150C /300F /gas 2 and brush a baking sheet with oil.

3 In a large bowl, beat together the butter and sugar until they are light and fluffy. Add the egg and egg whites and beat lightly. Sift in the flour and beat thoroughly until smooth. Stir in the vanilla essence and allspice.

4 Drop the batter, 4 ml /¾ tsp at a time, onto the sheet at 10 cm /4 in intervals and spread each into a 5 cm /2 in circle. Bake for 10–20 minutes, until the edges of the biscuits have turned golden brown, checking frequently after the first 10 minutes.

5 Meanwhile, prepare the moulds: use 12

egg cups, milk or other bottle tops. Lightly oil the outside of 6 of them and have the other 6 standing near by.

6 When the biscuits are cooked, lift them off one at a time and place in an oiled mould, pressing down around the mould to obtain a flower shape. Working quickly, repeat with the next 5 biscuits, then transfer the 'flowers' to the unoiled moulds to hold them in shape.

7 Repeat with the remaining biscuits (keep them in the oven with the door ajar so that they don't harden too soon).

8 When the flowers have set on the unoiled moulds, transfer them to a platter to finish cooling, right way up. Continue until all the batter is used up.

9 Make the nectarine mousse: put the chopped nectarines into a heavy-based saucepan with the butter, cinnamon, honey and 30 ml /2 tbls water. Cover and cook gently for 30 minutes, or until the fruit is very soft.

Allspice flowers with nectarine mousse

10 Purée the fruit mixture and the orange juice in a blender or food processor. Transfer the purée to a large bowl and reserve.

11 Sprinkle the gelatine over 45 ml /3 tbls water in a cup, then stand the cup in a pan of gently simmering water to dissolve. Stir it into the purée; leave to cool slightly.

12 Whip together the thin and thick creams until soft peaks form, then stir in the peach brandy. Fold the cream into the fruit purée gently but thoroughly.

13 When the allspice flowers have cooled and set, but no more than 2 hours before serving, put a scant 15 ml /1 tbls of the mousse into each of them, smoothing over the top. Put the mousse-filled flowers into the refrigerator to set.

14 Just before serving, garnish each flower with a frosted mint sprig.

Smoked salmon barquettes

For speed, lay out the tiny greased barquette moulds a little apart and unroll the pastry from the pin over them. Working from one side across the batch, carefully press the pastry into each indentation. Cut away any spare pastry.

🕐 🍴 making the shortcrust pastry, plus 1 hour

Makes 50
flour, for dusting
225 g /8 oz made-weight shortcrust pastry, defrosted if frozen
butter, for greasing
200 g /7 oz smoked salmon trimmings, finely chopped
25 g /1 oz butter
15–30 ml /1–2 tsp lemon juice
freshly ground black pepper
450 g /1 lb canned green asparagus tips, drained
60 ml /4 tbls Mayonnaise (see page 90)
5 ml /1 tsp tomato ketchup
5 ml /1 tsp aspic jelly, made from aspic powder, slightly warmed
watercress sprigs, to garnish

Smoked salmon barquettes

1 Heat the oven to 190C /375F /gas 5.
2 Flour the work surface and rolling pin and roll out the pastry to 3 mm /⅛ in thick. Using a 7 cm /2½ in long barquette cutter, if you have one, cut out 50 shapes, or use the suggestion in the introduction to this recipe to fit the pastry to the barquette moulds. Re-roll the pastry as often as is necessary.
3 Grease 50 × 50 cm /2 in long barquette moulds with the butter and line them with the pastry shapes. Line the pastry with foil and beans and bake blind for 10 minutes.
4 Remove the foil and beans and bake for a further 10 minutes. Let the pastry cases cool in the moulds, then take them out.
5 Mash together the smoked salmon, the butter, lemon juice and freshly ground black pepper to taste in a bowl. Divide the mixture among the barquettes, then top each with 1 asparagus tip.
6 Put the canapés on a flat freezer-proof tray, cover with cling film and chill. Cover with foil and freeze them.
7 Defrost the barquettes 24 hours before the reception.
8 On the day of the reception, mix together the mayonnaise, tomato ketchup and apsic jelly. Fit a small piping bag with a 3 mm / ⅛ in nozzle and spoon in the mayonnaise mixture. Pipe a thin line of pale pink mayonnaise around the asparagus tip on each salmon barquette.
9 Arrange the barquettes on a platter and garnish with watercress.

Spinach and cream cheese puffs

🕐 🍴 45 minutes, plus cooling and chilling

Makes 52
flour, for dusting
225 g /8 oz made-weight puff pastry, defrosted if frozen
2 medium-sized egg yolks, beaten
225 g /8 oz frozen spinach purée, defrosted and drained
25 g /1 oz butter
125 g /4½ oz cream cheese
freshly grated nutmeg
1.5 ml /¼ tsp ground allspice
a large pinch of cayenne pepper
salt and freshly ground black pepper
30 ml /2 tbls salted almonds, coarsely chopped
parsley sprigs, to garnish

1 Heat the oven to 220C /425F /gas 7. Flour a board and the rolling pin and roll the pastry out to a rectangle 3 mm /⅛ in thick.
2 Cut the pastry into 13 long slices, 25 mm /1 in wide. Brush a baking sheet with cold water, place the pastry strips on it, then brush the tops with the beaten egg yolks.
3 Bake the strips for 14 minutes, then remove them from the oven and let them cool slightly. Split them in half horizontally.
4 Put the drained spinach, the butter and cream cheese into a small saucepan and stir over a medium heat until well mixed.
5 Season with freshly grated nutmeg, then add the allspice, cayenne, salt and pepper. Stir in the almonds and leave to cool.
6 Spread some of the spinach mixture down the middle of the pastry bases on the cut surfaces. Cover each strip with its top half, then cut each across into 4. Place on a large freezerproof tray, cover with cling film and chill, then wrap in foil and freeze.
7 Defrost the puffs 24 hours before they are needed.
8 Thirty minutes before serving, heat the oven to 190C /375F /gas 5. Transfer the puffs to an ovenproof serving platter and cover completely with foil.
9 Five minutes before serving, put the puffs into the oven to warm. Remove them from the oven, take off the foil, garnish with parsley and serve the puffs immediately.

Herring croustades

🕐 🍴 40 minutes

Makes 50
12½ slices of medium-cut white sandwich bread
vegetable oil, for deep frying
225 g /8 oz soft herring roes, cooked
50 g /2 oz butter
¼ medium-sized Spanish onion, grated
½ large dessert apple
15 ml /1 tbls finely chopped fresh parsley
15 ml /1 tbls lemon juice
freshly ground black pepper
50 g /2 oz salted herring fillet, finely chopped

Canapés (left to right): Gruyère and ham tartlets, Herring croustades and Fillet steak balls

1 Using a 3 cm /1⅛ in round cutter, stamp out 50 rounds from the bread slices.
2 Pour oil to a depth of 5 cm /2 in into a large saucepan and heat it gently until the oil just begins to smoke.
3 Add the croustades to the pan and deep fry them over a medium heat for 3–4 minutes, until they are all golden brown. Remove them with a slotted spoon and drain them thoroughly on absorbent paper.
4 Put the herring roes into a large bowl and add the butter and grated onion. Peel and core the apple and grate it into the bowl. Sprinkle with the parsley and lemon juice and season generously with freshly ground black pepper.
5 Stir everything well. Fit a piping bag with a 15 mm /½ in star nozzle and spoon in the mixture.
6 Pipe a swirl of the herring mixture onto each croustade, then put the croustades on a large freezerproof tray. Cover with cling film and chill. When thoroughly chilled, cover with heavy duty foil and freeze.
7 Defrost the croustades in the refrigerator 24 hours before the buffet reception.
8 On the morning of the reception, put a piece of finely chopped herring fillet on top of each croustade. Transfer the croustades to a serving platter, cover with cling film and refrigerate until ready to serve.

Gruyère and ham tartlets

 making the mayonnaise,
 plus 45 minutes

Makes 50
flour, for dusting
225 g /8 oz made-weight shortcrust pastry, defrosted if frozen
butter, for greasing
125 g /4½ oz Gruyère cheese, cut into tiny dice
100 g /4 oz ham, cut into tiny dice
45–60 ml /3–4 tbls thick Mayonnaise (page 90)
10 ml /2 tsp Dijon mustard
freshly ground black pepper
5 ml /1 tsp aspic jelly made from aspic powder
1 large red pepper, cut into tiny strips

1 Flour a board and a rolling pin and roll out the pastry to 3 mm /⅛ in thick. Using a 5 cm /2 in round pastry cutter, stamp and cut out 50 rounds, re-rolling and cutting the pastry as necessary.
2 Heat the oven to 190C /375F /gas 5. Butter 50 × 4 cm /1½ in round tartlet moulds and line them with the pastry. Line the pastry with foil and beans and cook for 10 minutes.
3 Remove the foil and beans from the pastry and cook for a further 10 minutes to brown the pastry. Cool the tartlets in their tins, then open freeze them, transferring them to a rigid container once they are frozen.
4 Defrost them the day before they are needed.
5 On the day of the reception, combine the Gruyère and ham with the mayonnaise and mustard. Season the mixture to taste with freshly ground black pepper and then stir in the aspic jelly.
6 Put 5 ml /1 tsp of the mixture into each pastry case.
7 Decorate the tartlets with a cross of fresh red pepper, arrange them on a platter and cover with cling film. Refrigerate the Gruyère and ham tartlets until just before they are to be served.

Fillet steak balls

 1 hour freezing, making the
 mayonnaise, plus 30 minutes

Makes 50
225 g /8 oz fillet steak, raw, in 1 small round piece
60 ml /4 tbls thick Mayonnaise (page 90)
10 ml /2 tsp capers, v finely chopped
5 ml /1 tsp fresh marjoram, finely chopped
2.5 ml /½ tsp Dijon mustard
2.5 ml /½ tsp horseradish sauce
1.5 ml /¼ tsp cayenne pepper
20 ml /4 tsp grated onion
freshly ground black pepper

1 If you have an electric slicing machine, put the steak in the freezer for about 1 hour to firm it up slightly, then slice it very thinly on the machine into about 25 slices. Otherwise, get your butcher to do this for you.
2 Arrange the slices, side by side, on sheets of cling film. Cover each layer carefully with cling film, roll them up, then wrap them in foil before freezing.
3 Defrost them in the refrigerator 24 hours before the reception.
4 The evening before the reception make the sauce by mixing together the mayonnaise with the capers, marjoram, mustard, horseradish sauce, cayenne and onion. Put the mixture into an airtight jar and refrigerate.
5 On the morning of the party, unwrap the beef slices and sprinkle them generously with pepper. Cut each slice in half.
6 Spread 1.5 ml /¼ tsp of the spicy mayonnaise on each slice and then roll it up into a little ball. Spear each with a cocktail stick.
7 Arrange the balls on a platter, cover them with cling film or foil and refrigerate them until ready to serve. Serve chilled.

THE WEDDING CAKE

The cake is a very important part of the wedding reception, so it is well worth creating something suitably special for the occasion. My cake looks stunning, and it is fairly simple to make.

My beautiful three-tier cake is designed to be within easy reach of the amateur cake-maker. The cake itself — a delicious rich fruit cake — requires the minimum of fuss and very little specialized icing and piping (the latter calls for considerable practice and application and is best left to the professionals).

The wedding cake is fresh and elegant and relies for its effect on the overall subtle colour and design. It is planned to make the maximum use of seasonal flowers and pretty ribbons. The sides of a cake are always most exposed to view and are difficult to pipe neatly so this cake cleverly uses heavy lace and ribbons to cover them.

Planning the cake

Rich fruit cakes are traditional in Europe for weddings, standing in two or three impressive tiers, with little plaster or plastic columns to raise each one. This type of cake requires a minimum of three months' preparation to allow it to be properly matured and decorated, so follow my wedding cake countdown (see page 98) carefully.

What size cakes? Use the master recipe for Rich fruit cake (see page 98) to bake the basic cakes. The number of tiers you choose will largely depend upon how many people will be attending the wedding and whether you want to follow the custom of sending a piece of cake to guests who couldn't attend. Traditionally the slices from a wedding cake are small. An 18 cm /7 in round cake will give 30 portions, a 23 cm /9 in cake 50 portions and a 28 cm /11 in cake 70 portions. You can, of course, increase the size of the slices if you wish. As a guide, you can expect 10 portions from 500 g /1 lb of uncooked cake mixture.

Planning the tiers: for the best effect, allow 5–7 cm /2–3 in difference in size between each cake. For example, a top tier of 18 cm / 7 in, a middle tier of 23 cm /9 in and a bottom tier of 28 cm /11 in. It is important that a pyramid is formed and that it does not look clumsy. Do not make the top cake too large. On a three-tier cake a maximum size of 18 cm /7 in, and on a two-tier cake a maximum size of 23 cm /9 in is best.

If you choose to make a single tier cake, remember that the top of the cake will need considerably more piping and decoration, demanding more skill. If you are not completely sure of your talents, a two-tier cake looks extremely impressive, while actually demanding less expertise on the part of the cook.

Round or square? Although a square cake may be marginally easier to cut, a round cake is easier to ice. A square cake can prove difficult to coat because it takes proficiency to make perfect right-angled corners.

Cake boards and bases: buy your cake boards well in advance because it may be difficult to obtain the large board needed for the bottom tier. To be on the safe side, buy the boards before baking, or buy cake boards and cake tins together.

To calculate board sizes, add 25 mm /1 in to the diameter of each of the top two cakes in a tier, and 5 cm /2 in to the bottom one.

Cake-stands: most outside caterers and hire companies hire out silver cake-stands and knives, as do some bakers. If you are making the cake yourself, you may not mind the extra expense of the stand. It has the advantage of lifting up the cake where it can be seen, and adding extra glamour.

Pillars: between the tiers give a cake height. Buy these well in advance; plaster looks more attractive than plastic. If you want good luck charms — such as silver horseshoes — buy these early, too, and incorporate them into your overall plan.

Colour scheme: an all-white cake is traditional, so a little variation on the theme will be very effective. As a general rule pastel shades look most inviting.

Use a coloured icing for flat coating the cake and then pipe on it in white; this is generally more effective than piping with a colour on a white background. Any really vivid colours should be used sparingly. The main thing to remember is that the colours must be in complementary tones — and to make one big batch of icing so that all the tiers are identical in colour.

Match any ribbons — and lace — with the chosen colour scheme. Remember that wide trimmings look best in plain white. Keep bright colours for narrow trimmings. If you are using curled paper ribbons, for instance among the flowers, buy these at the same time for a perfect match.

Ribbons and flowers: order a posy for the top of the cake at the same time as the other wedding flowers. Choose flowers that are light and do not wilt too quickly: freesias, Michaelmas daisies, rosebuds and chrysanthemums are all suitable. Explain your colour scheme to the florist and ask for advice. Smaller flowers are more effective on the side of the cake.

The posy bowl on the top of the cake should be planned to form the top of the pyramid, which means the flowers should be arranged upwards and sidewards and with some arching downwards. Work to a maximum height of 15 cm /6 in from the top of the cake to the top of the flowers for any two- or three-tier cake. You can order the posy from a florist ready-made or arrange the flowers yourself. It is easiest to arrange them in a small block of florist's green foam standing in a small bowl. If the flowers are ready-made, collect them on the morning of the wedding or arrange them on the previous night and keep the posy in the refrigerator. Place the flowers on the cake at the last minute.

You can use curled paper ribbons with the flowers. To curl them, draw scissors rapidly down the length of the ribbon (but, like the flowers, they will droop if left for a long period in a very hot room).

Making the cake

Baking: make the cakes, following the recipe in this chapter. Bake the two smaller cakes on the first day, making a note of whether they cooked within the given time. Bake the largest cake the next day, allowing extra time to complete the cooking, because the performance of different ovens at very low temperatures varies considerably. Mature the cakes for up to three months, well wrapped. If you wish, prick them every 14 days and 'feed' them with brandy.

Marzipan coating: home-made almond paste (see recipe) is undoubtedly the most delicious. However, ready-made marzipan is cheaper and less sticky to work with. You may be able to buy it in bulk from your local baker. It is worth taking a lot of care with the marzipan covering as it provides the smooth base for the icing; uneven marzipan means a poor finish to the cake. Roll over the marzipan-covered cake with the rolling pin when you have finished to get a perfectly flat, even surface — and round the sides with a jar. Do not worry if the marzipan is thicker in some places than others; use it to fill out any uneven patches on the surface of the cake to get a smooth finish.

Icing: a wedding cake requires at least two coats of icing. It is sensible to make one big batch of icing (big enough for three coats, even if the latter is not needed). Like this there will be no variation between the colour of the layers. Keep the icing covered in the refrigerator until the whole job is complete.

A cake is far easier to coat if the icing is just the right texture. It should be light and form peaks like meringue. This is achieved not by adding extra egg white or sugar but by beating the mixture to aerate it. Store the icing for 24 hours before use. Keep it covered when not working with it. When it gets harder, after a couple of weeks, thin it with a little egg white.

Colour the icing the day you ice the cakes. Add the colour a few drops at a time — especially towards the end — and match it carefully to any fabric; icing always dries a shade darker than when first mixed.

The icing on wedding cakes is traditionally very hard. This is so that the pillars, which bear the weight of the cake(s) above, do not sink into it.

Organizing the pillars: to spread the weight of the pillars I put another thin cake board on the surface of the bottom cake(s). This scheme has other advantages, too. When these boards are iced and in place they give a pretty decoration to the surface of the lower cake(s). Having the pillars ready on separate platforms makes the task of assembling the cake much easier. Flat ice the thin cake boards at the same time as the cakes, then stick four pillars in place in the wet icing. When it comes to assembling, all you need do is put the flowers in place between the pillars and then position the little board on the cake.

The wedding cake

Wedding cake countdown

Three months before the wedding
(Takes 2 days.) Make the two smaller cakes on the first day, checking the cooking time carefully. The next day make the largest cake. Do not remove the greaseproof paper from the base of the cakes — this helps keep them moist. When cold, wrap them in foil and store them in airtight containers.
(Takes 15 minutes per fortnight.) Once every 14 days prick the cakes with a skewer and feed them with a few spoonfuls of brandy.

Two months before the wedding
Buy cake boards, pillars, ribbons and order fresh flowers for the actual day, if needed. Buy or make the almond paste and store it in a cool place. Order the cake-stand and knife.

Five weeks before the wedding
(Takes 1½ hours.) Cover the cakes with apricot glaze and almond paste. Place on cake boards. Cover loosely with foil and leave in a cool, airy place for 1 week.

Four weeks before the wedding
(Takes 1½ hours on each of 2 days.) Make up the Royal icing and allow it to stand for 24 hours. The next day coat the cakes. Allow the icing to become dry before you cover it with greaseproof paper. Coat the two thin cake boards with icing and stick on the pillars. Leave the iced cakes and boards separately in a cool airy place. Cover the remaining icing with a damp cloth and cling film and then refrigerate.

Three weeks before the wedding
(Takes 1 hour.) Using a sharp knife, remove any uneven edges from the icing. Use the Royal icing thinned with egg white to coat the cake a second time. Cover with grease-proof paper and allow to dry for 1 week.

Two weeks before the wedding
If need be, trim again and apply a third coat of icing. Cover and allow to dry for 1 week.

One week before the wedding
(Takes 1½ hours.) Make fresh Royal icing. Pipe shells of icing around the top and base of each cake and around the edge of the cake boards on which the pillars are standing. Attach lace and ribbons to the cakes.

On the day of the wedding
Assemble the cake on the cake stand with the flowers and ribbons between each layer. Place the posy bowl on top.

Piping: home-made greaseproof paper bags are best for delicate piping because they are small and give you much more control. To make these, cut out a 25 cm /10 in square of greaseproof or silicone paper (available from department stores and supermarkets). Lay the sheet on a work surface and cut it in half from corner to corner. Curving one corner sharply in on itself, continue to fold the paper over until you have a firm cone. Secure with sticky tape. This makes a small, neat bag which is easier to use when full of icing than a larger one.

Snip off the tip of the bag and drop in a decorating nozzle. Aim to have 10 mm /½ in protruding. Like this the nozzle will fit tightly and icing cannot leak. Put in the icing to fill the bag three-quarters full. Fold the top flap down, enclosing the front edge and sealing the bag. Hold the bag with your thumb on top to keep it closed, and your forefinger down the side. Your second finger is curved underneath to squeeze the bag. Try to pipe steadily and evenly, and practise on the cake board before piping on the cake. Use a medium-sized writing nozzle to make a simple row of bold pearls or a medium-sized star nozzle for shell shapes.

Pipe around the rims of the cakes and again around the base of the cakes where they meet the boards, then around outside of the thin boards, on which the pillars are standing.

Quantities and timings for different size rich fruit cakes

TIN SIZES	18 cm /7 in round 15 cm /6 in square	20 cm /8 in round 18 cm /7 in square	23 cm /9 in round 20 cm /8 in square	28 cm /11 in round 25 cm /10 in square	30 cm /12 in round 28 cm /11 in square
INGREDIENTS					
flour	225 g /8 oz	350 g /12 oz	400 g /14 oz	700 g /1 lb 8 oz	1 kg /2 lb 3 oz
salt	a pinch	a pinch	a pinch	a pinch	a large pinch
mixed spice	2.5 ml /½ tsp	5 ml /1 tsp	7.5 ml /1½ tsp	10 ml /2 tsp	12.5 ml /2½ tsp
cinnamon	2.5 ml /½ tsp	2.5 ml /½ tsp	5 ml /1 tsp	10 ml /2 tsp	12.5 ml /2½ tsp
glacé cherries	75 g /3 oz	150 g /5 oz	175 g /6 oz	225 g /8 oz	400 g /14 oz
chopped mixed peel	75 g /3 oz	150 g /5 oz	125 g /4 oz	225 g /8 oz	350 g /12 oz
butter	225 g /8 oz	350 g /12 oz	400 g /14 oz	800 g /1 lb 12 oz	1 kg /2 lb 3 oz
soft brown sugar	225 g /8 oz	350 g /12 oz	400 g /14 oz	800 g /1 lb 12 oz	1 kg /2 lb 3 oz
eggs	3	5	6	11	17
black treacle	15 ml /1 tbls	25 ml /1½ tbls	30 ml /2 tbls	45 ml /3 tbls	60 ml /4 tbls
lemons (juice, zest)	½	1 small	1	2	3
oranges (juice, zest)	½	1 small	1	2	3
currants	350 g /12 oz	450 g /1 lb	625 g /1 lb 6 oz	1.1 kg /2½ lb	1.7 kg /3¾ lb
sultanas	200 g /7 oz	275 g /10 oz	350 g /12 oz	450 g /1 lb	725 g /1 lb 10 oz
raisins	200 g /7 oz	275 g /10 oz	350 g /12 oz	450 g /1 lb	725 g /1 lb 10 oz
almonds	75 g /3 oz	100 g /4 oz	150 g /5 oz	225 g /8 oz	350 g /12 oz
brandy or rum	15 ml /1 tbls	25 ml /1½ tbls	30 ml /2 tbls	45 ml /3 tbls	90 ml /6 tbls
TEMPERATURE	150C /300F /gas 2	150C /300F /gas 2	150C /300F /gas 2	150C /300F /gas 2	150C /300F /gas 2
COOKING TIME	3 hours	3½ hours	4 hours	5 hours, then reduce the temperature to 130C /250F /gas ½ for 2 hours	5½ hours, then reduce the temperature to 130C /250F /gas ½ for 2½ hours

Method

1   Line a 25 cm /10 in square or a 28 cm / 11 in round cake tin with a double thickness of greased greaseproof paper. Heat the oven to 150C /300F /gas 2.
2   In a bowl sieve together the flour, salt and spices. Wash and dry the cherries. Cut them into quarters. Wash and dry the peel.
3   Cream the butter and sugar together until the mixture is light and fluffy. In a bowl beat together the eggs, black treacle and the juice from the orange(s) and lemon(s). Gradually beat the egg mixture into the creamed mixture. Add a little flour with the last additions of egg.
4   With a metal spoon, fold in the remaining flour, finely grated fruit zests, dried fruits and blanched, chopped almonds. Next, add the brandy or rum. Fold in until the mixture has a dropping consistency.
5   Spoon the mixture into the prepared tin, spreading it out evenly and into the corners, and then make a small hollow in the centre.
6   Tie a double thickness of thick brown paper around the outside of the tin. Place the tin on a pad of brown paper on the lowest shelf in the oven. Bake the mixture (see chart above). Cover the tin if the cake browns too quickly.
7   When a skewer inserted in the centre comes out clean, the cake is cooked. Cool and remove the paper.
8   Wrap and store for at least 2–3 months.

Quantities of almond paste and Royal icing

Tin size:							
round	18 cm (7")	20 cm (8")	23 cm (9")	25 cm (10")	28 cm (11")	30 cm (12")	—
square	15 cm (6")	18 cm (7")	20 cm (8")	23 cm (9")	25 cm (10")	28 cm (11")	30 cm (12")
Almond paste	450 g (1 lb)	550 g (1¼ lb)	800 g (1¾ lb)	900 g (2 lb)	1 kg (2¼ lb)	1.1 kg (2½ lb)	1.4 kg (3 lb)
Royal icing	550 g (1¼ lb)	700 g (1½ lb)	900 g (2 lb)	1 kg (2¼ lb)	1.1 kg (2½ lb)	1.4 kg (3 lb)	1.6 kg (3½ lb)

How to make almond paste

Sift the caster sugar, icing sugar and the ground almonds into a bowl. Make a well in the centre.

Add the lemon juice, essences and some of the egg. Mix together well. Add more egg if it is necessary.

Mix to a smooth paste. Turn the paste onto a board sprinkled with icing sugar. Knead it for 3 minutes.

Cutting the cake

Apart from the ceremonial photograph, the wedding cake is taken to pieces before it is cut and the boards with the pillars are removed. Cut each cake across the full width in a 25 mm /1 in thick slice. Next cut each slice into slivers — only a small amount of rich cake is needed per guest.

Almond paste

Use almond paste to make an absolutely smooth base for Royal icing. If you have any surplus left over after covering your wedding cake, you can reserve it for another recipe.

 10 minutes

Makes 450 g /1 lb of paste

225 g /8 oz ground almonds
100 g /4 oz caster sugar
100 g /4 oz icing sugar, sifted, plus extra for
  rolling
2.5 ml /½ tsp vanilla essence
few drops almond essence
5 ml /1 tsp lemon juice
1 egg, lightly beaten

1 Combine the ground almonds with the sugars in a large bowl. Mix them well.
2 Add the vanilla and almond essences, lemon juice and egg. Knead the mixture thoroughly with your hands until the paste is smooth and pliable. If there is not enough liquid, add more egg.

● If you are not using the almond paste immediately, keep it wrapped in cling film in the refrigerator.

Royal icing

This icing is the grandest of the plain white icings and is the one traditionally used for wedding cakes. It sets very hard and is therefore ideal for a perfect, smooth surface and also for piping.

30 minutes, plus 24 hours standing for flat icing or piping

Makes 1 kg /2 lb of icing

4 egg whites
900 g /2 lb icing sugar
lemon juice
colouring (optional)

1 In a large bowl whisk the egg whites until just frothy. Sift the icing sugar into the bowl a little at a time, whisking well between each addition. Add colouring if you wish.
2 Add 10 ml /2 tsp of lemon juice. Continue to whisk the mixture until peaks form.
3 If you are flat icing or piping, it is best to let the icing stand for 24 hours so that the bubbles made by the mixer can subside. Cover the icing with a damp tea-towel when it is not being used to prevent it drying out and a crust forming.
4 If you find when you start to use the icing that it is too stiff to work, particularly for piping, soften it with a few extra drops of lemon juice. Remember to keep the surface of the bowl covered while you are working.

● If you are icing a cake other than a wedding cake, add a few drops of glycerine along with the lemon juice. This makes the icing softer. However, glycerine should not be added when you are icing a three-tier wedding cake as the surface needs to be very hard to support the pillars.

● If you are making rough icing, you can use the icing straight away after making it, without having to let it stand for 24 hours.

The wedding cake

This three-tier cake will serve 100–150 people. Start by making the three cakes (see page 98) at least 3 months before the wedding and use the countdown (see page 98) to guide you through.

Putting on almond paste

Cover the cake with almond paste at least 5 weeks before the wedding.

🕐 🔪🔪🔪 1½ hours,
then 1 week drying

18 cm /7 in round fruit cake, matured 8–12 weeks
23 cm /9 in round fruit cake, matured 8–12 weeks
28 cm /11 in round fruit cake, matured 8–12 weeks
5 × Almond paste (see previous page)
icing sugar, for dusting
180 ml /12 tbls apricot jam

1 Start with the large cake. Remove the greaseproof paper or foil from the cake. With a long, sharp knife trim the top of the cake level if it is uneven. Carefully brush away any loose crumbs; it is essential that no cake crumbs should become mixed with the almond paste.
2 Divide the almond paste into three pieces weighing 450 g /1 lb, 800 g /1¾ lb and 1 kg / 2¼ lb. Reserve the smaller pieces and divide the large piece again, into two: approximately one-third for the top and two-thirds for the side of the cake.
3 Dust the work surface with plenty of icing sugar to prevent the almond paste sticking. Roll the small portion into a circle 15 mm /½ in wider than the diameter of the cake.
4 Measure the circumference of the cake with a piece of string. Roll the remaining portion of paste into a strip as long as the string and as wide as the cake is deep.
5 For the apricot glaze, sieve the jam into a saucepan, add 60 ml /4 tbls water and heat it gently. When the jam has melted, brush some over the sides of the cake.
6 Holding the cake on its side, roll it onto the strip of almond paste. Pat the almond paste into place, making a neat join.
7 Warm the apricot glaze again and brush it over the top of the cake. Turn the cake upside down onto the almond paste circle. Using a palette knife, smooth the edges together, making a sharp right-angled edge.
8 Use an empty jar to roll round the sides of the cake (steadying it with your other hand) to make the sides absolutely straight.
9 Turn the cake the right way up and place it in the centre of the appropriate cake board. Remove any excess icing sugar with a clean pastry brush, then cover the cake with grease-proof paper or foil.
10 Cover the other two cakes with almond paste using 800 g /1¾ lb almond paste for the middle cake and 450 g /1 lb almond paste for the smaller one.
11 Leave all the fruit cakes to dry, lightly covered, for 1 week.

Assembling the cake

Coating with Royal icing

Put on the coats of basic icing 4 weeks before the wedding.

🕐 🔪🔪🔪 making the icing, 24 hours
setting, 1 hour, then 1 week

2.3 kg /5 lb Royal icing (see previous page)
few drops yellow food colouring

1 Mix the Royal icing and let it stand for 24 hours, covered.
2 Add a little yellow food colouring, a few drops at a time. Place the first cake on an icing turntable or an upturned plate.
3 Spoon a generous quantity of icing (enough for the top and sides) on top of the cake. Spread it evenly over the top of the cake, using an icing ruler to scrape it to a 5 mm /¼ in layer.
4 Work the icing around the sides of the cake. To make a right-angled edge, make a lip 15 mm /½ in above the top edge. Next, smooth the sides holding a cake scraper against them and gently revolving the cake.
5 Hold a palette knife at a 45° angle and draw it from the side of the cake to the centre, cleaning the knife after each pass. This will give a sharp right-angled edge.
6 Draw the icing ruler across the top of the cake to make it completely smooth. Ice the

other cakes in the same way. Allow the icing to set, then cover the cakes and dry them for 1 week.

Making the supports

Do this immediately after coating the cakes with Royal icing.

🕐 🔪🔪🔪 30 minutes,
then 3 weeks drying

2 × 15 cm /6 in diameter thin cake boards
8 × 8 cm /3 in high round plaster pillars

1 Use some of the remaining icing to coat 2 thin 15 cm /6 in cake boards.
2 Spread the icing thinly and evenly over the cake boards and smooth it with an icing ruler.
3 While the icing is still soft, mentally quarter each board, then make 4 symmetrical marks about 4 cm /1½ in in from the edge.
4 Press a pillar into the soft icing, placed centrally over each mark.
5 Leave it to dry, then cover and store.

Completing the flat icing

Complete the flat icing three weeks before the wedding.

🔪🔪🔪 1 hour,
then 1 week drying

Place one cake on an icing turntable or an
[up]turned plate. With a sharp knife remove
[a]ny rough or uneven edges. Brush off any
[fl]akes of icing.

[2] Remove the Royal icing from the refri-
[g]erator and thin it with extra lightly beaten
[e]gg white; it should be a thick pouring
[c]onsistency which will leave a trail.

[3] Place a little icing on top of the cake.
[S]mooth over the top with a palette knife,
[b]reaking up all the air bubbles. Draw an
[i]cing ruler across the top of the cake to
[s]mooth it completely.

[4] Spread the icing around the sides of the
[c]ake. Smooth with a cake scraper. Repeat
[w]ith the other cakes.

[5] Remove any excess icing from the top
[a]nd bottom edges of the cake. Clean the cake
[b]oard with a cloth wrung out in hot water.

[6] Allow it to dry, cover it when set and
[l]eave for 1 week. If necessary apply a third
[c]oat in the same way. Allow each cake 1 week
[t]o dry before piping.

Decorating the cake

**For decoration I have chosen white daisy
[l]ace with white and yellow ribbon to give a
[f]resh, delicate effect. You should pipe the
[c]ake and put on the ribbons one week before
[t]he wedding.**

1½ hours,
then 1 week drying

---

450 g /1 lb Royal icing (see previous page)
1½ m /1¾ yd of 5 mm /¼ in wide daisy lace
1½ m /1¾ yd of 25 mm /1 in wide white
ribbon
1½ m /1¾ yd of 5 mm /¼ in wide yellow
ribbon

1 Make a greaseproof paper piping bag (see
page 98). Fit it with a small shell- or star-
shaped nozzle. Fill the bag with a small
amount of icing.
2 Working on each cake in turn, hold the
nozzle close to the edge of the cake and pipe
shells of icing around the top and bottom
edge of each cake. As you use up each bag of
icing, make a new bag and fill it.
3 Pipe small shells around the edge of each
cake board, holding the pillars.
4 Attach the lace and ribbons as shown in
the picture on page 97.

● Piping may appear to be an extremely
complicated skill, and indeed the more
elaborate designs are difficult to get right.
However, if you start with a simple design
using a small star- or shell-shaped nozzle, you
can still produce professional-looking results.
Of course, the more you practise, the better
the results will be!

Piping requires a light yet firm hold and a
very steady touch. Hold the bag so that one
hand secures the twist at the top of the bag
ready for squeezing. Leave the other free for
guiding the bag as you work — start by
practising the simple designs, then gradually
progress to more complicated patterns. The
same technique applies to all forms of piping,
whether you are using icing or cream. When
piping with a shell nozzle, hold the nozzle
just above the surface of the cake at a 45°
angle. Squeeze out the icing to form a head,
then pull the nozzle away, gently releasing
the pressure, until the head tapers to a neat
point. Pipe the next shell onto the pointed
end of the previous shell and continue piping
to form a border.

The shell border can be piped either with a
star or a shell nozzle. The difference is that
the shell nozzle has more ridges than the star
nozzles, producing a fatter shell.

Assembling the cake

**The final stage of your preparation should
be carried out on the wedding day itself.
Assemble the cake on the table where it will
be displayed.**

1 hour

1 posy of flowers, up to 15 cm /6 in high
extra flowers

1 Place the biggest cake on the cake-stand
(if using). Place one of the thin cake boards
in the centre of the cake. Arrange a few
flowers between the pillars.
2 Position the middle cake. Decorate the
second thin cake board in the same way and
put it in place. Top with the third cake.
3 Arrange the posy of flowers in place on
top of the third cake.
4 Attach extra flowers to the sides of the
cake and base boards with icing, if wished.

Flat icing a rich fruit cake

Stick the cake to a cakeboard with a dab of
icing. Spread icing over the top. Draw an
icing ruler towards you to smooth it. Neaten
the edges with a knife. Stand for 24 hours.

Spread icing around the sides of the cake.
Hold a flat scraper or palette knife against the
side of the cake and revolve the turntable
away from you. Leave it for 24 hours.

Smooth over the rough edges with an emery
board or fine sandpaper. Re-ice the cake,
using icing thinned with egg white if wished.
Leave it for 24 hours before piping.

AN INFORMAL RECEPTION

If your personal preference is for a less formal reception, here are some very attractive alternatives — simply choose what is right for you, follow my planning suggestions, and look forward to a relaxed, enjoyable day.

A wedding is always a time for celebration, but there is no reason why it has to be a complicated formal affair. If you are planning an informal party — because it's a second marriage, or because you are away from home and you haven't a willing mother who will shoulder all the responsibility and the organization for you, or simply because you think that orange blossom and lace are not really your style — then make life as easy as possible for yourself on the big day.

The most important thing is to have a jolly good party and enjoy it. One solution may be to plan a buffet party. It may be a very informal occasion, but even then you will still have to prepare the setting and provide cake if you want one.

Try my Rose wedding cake (see recipe) — this is an unconventional wedding cake in that it is a sponge rather than a rich fruit cake, but its main advantage, apart from being cheaper to produce, is that it can be made just a few days before it is needed. It does not call for marzipan, which is time-consuming to make and use, just a pretty butter cream icing. After it is iced the cake will keep well for two or three days.

Remember that you will need to provide glasses, soft drinks, tea or coffee — with milk and sugar, too. In such a cheerful setting, a harlequin selection of crockery and cutlery, borrowed from family and friends, is not inappropriate.

Planning the menu

Plan your menu carefully so that you have a minimum of last-minute preparation and cooking. Most of the recipes included in this section are for at least 12 people and can be made in advance. Chicken legs are easy to eat and spread with curried butter (see recipe), they are an unusual and spicy way to start a meal.

The spectacular Party sandwich loaf (see recipe), with its mixture of flavours, colours and textures, is not only easier to make than conventional sandwiches but the creamy, cheesy coating keeps the loaf moist and inviting down to the very last slice.

Follow these starters with one main dish. Pies are a good idea: they can be made a couple of days ahead and are easy to cut up and serve. Layered pies (see recipe) are made using a delicious combination of minced lean pork (you could use less expensive sausage-meat, but the result would not be as good), grated onion, apple and potatoes, spiced with herbs and set in a light chicken jelly. On the other hand, a rabbit pie would make an unusual and tasty alternative.

Or try a sauce-based main course served with rice. Rice reheats more satisfactorily than potatoes and can also be made to look more exotic and festive. Three-coloured rice (see recipe) is decorative and provides a good base for the subtle Ginger prawns in soured cream (see recipe). Even if there are no vegetarians in the party, Chick-pea and aubergine casserole (see recipe) makes a substantial and interesting dish.

All sorts of seasonal salads can be mixed and offered to your guests — with a variety of dressings to excite the taste buds or contras with the piquant flavourings of the mai courses.

Serve a simple but delicious cheese boar with the salads if you wish: a half, ripe Bri and some mature farmhouse Cheddar or half Stilton would probably fill the bill.

You might like to offer a selection o puddings to round off the meal, say one ric and creamy and one cool and refreshing Fruit salads — particularly in the summer – are always very popular. Try the Summe fruit salad (see recipe). The dish has spectacularly colourful presentation whic makes it hard to resist. Ice creams an

sorbets are also a good choice — if, that is, you have enough fridge or freezer space to keep them until they are needed. The delightful little Sweet pastry bites are so rich, tangy, creamy and delicious that most of your guests will want to try one in each of the different flavours you have to offer.

With everything firmly under control, and good friends perhaps sharing the cooking and organization, you can enjoy your own reception and make it a memorable day for everyone else involved. There's a lot to be said for unconventional informality!

Party sandwich loaf

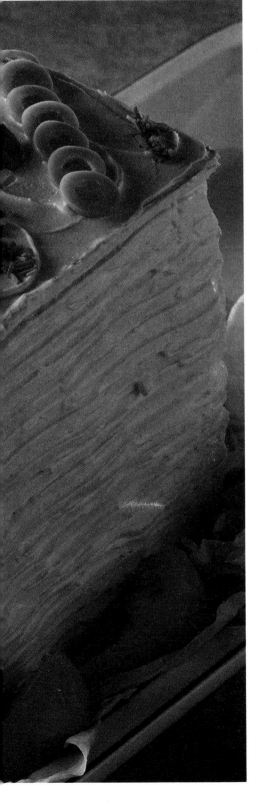

Party sandwich loaf

🍴🍴🍴 45 minutes, chilling, then 15 minutes

Serves 10–12
1 large white loaf, 1 day old
90 ml /6 tbls thick mayonnaise
15 ml /1 tbls tomato ketchup
a pinch of cayenne pepper
a dash of Worcestershire sauce
100 g /4 oz cream cheese
15 ml /1 tbls finely snipped fresh chives
salt
15 ml /1 tbls lemon juice
2.5 ml /½ tsp paprika
3 tomatoes, blanched, skinned and thinly sliced
2 eggs, hard-boiled and sliced
8 lettuce leaves, shredded
150 g /5 oz canned white crabmeat (drained weight), finely shredded
For the watercress mayonnaise
1 bunch watercress, finely chopped
150 ml /5 fl oz thick mayonnaise
green food colouring (optional)
For the cheese coating
250 g /9 oz cream cheese
salt
juice of ½ lemon
paprika
about 90 ml /6 tbls thick cream
For the garnish
stuffed olives, sliced
sprigs of watercress
freshly snipped chives
lettuce leaves
tomato wedges

1 First make the watercress mayonnaise: blend the watercress with the mayonnaise. Tint it green, if wished, and reserve.
2 Trim the crusts from the loaf, cutting it into a neat rectangle. Cut it lengthways into 6 even horizontal slices.
3 In a small bowl, blend the mayonnaise and tomato ketchup. Season to taste with the cayenne pepper and Worcestershire sauce.
4 In another bowl, combine the cream cheese with the chives and season to taste with salt, lemon juice and paprika; stir. Spread 1 slice of bread with this mixture.
5 Spread a second slice of bread with half the watercress mayonnaise. Using half the sliced tomatoes and 1 egg, cover the mayonnaise with slices of tomato and egg.
6 Spread a third slice with half of the ketchup-flavoured mayonnaise. Cover this with half the shredded lettuce, followed by half the crabmeat. Repeat with a fourth slice.
7 Spread a fifth slice with the remaining watercress mayonnaise, tomatoes and egg.
8 Neatly layer the slices in the order described, then top it with the remaining plain slice. Wrap the loaf in foil and chill for at least 2 hours or until firm.
9 Prepare the cheese coating. In a bowl, combine the cream cheese, salt, lemon juice and paprika. Beat until smooth, adding enough cream for a spreading consistency.
10 Spread the top and sides of the loaf with the coating, smoothing it with a palette knife. Garnish it with sliced olives, sprigs of watercress and chives, and serve it on a bed of lettuce leaves, surrounded by tomato wedges.

Chicken legs in curried butter

These interestingly spiced chicken legs in curried butter are simple to prepare and are delicious additions to any buffet meal.

🕐 🍴🍴 1 hour, plus cooling and chilling

Serves 24
24 chicken legs
1 large onion, halved but unpeeled
5 ml /1 tsp marjoram
5 ml /1 tsp dried savory
4 sprigs of parsley
2 sprigs of thyme
1 large lemon, halved
12 black peppercorns
225 g /8 oz butter, softened
5 ml /1 tsp ground cardamom
5 ml /1 tsp cumin seeds, crushed
5 ml /1 tsp ground ginger
2.5 ml /½ tsp ground turmeric
2.5 ml /½ tsp chilli powder
5 ml /1 tsp ground coriander
5 ml /1 tbls mustard powder
15 ml /1 tbls Worcestershire sauce
5 ml /1 tsp garam masala
a large pinch of ground fenugreek seeds
5 ml /1 tsp lime juice
salt
freshly ground black pepper
sprigs of watercress, to garnish

1 In each of two large saucepans put 12 chicken legs with half the onion, marjoram, savory, parsley and thyme sprigs, lemon and peppercorns. Pour 1.4 L /2½ pt cold water into each pan and bring them gently to the boil, then lower the heat and simmer for 25–30 minutes. Remove the chicken legs carefully from the pan with a slotted spoon, transfer them to a plate and leave them to cool. Reserve the liquid for another recipe. (If you have a very large casserole, the 24 legs can be cooked together, but you will need more than 2 L /3½ pt water to cover the joints.)
2 While the chicken legs are cooling make the curried butter: mash the softened butter in a large bowl with a fork until it is creamy.
3 Add the remaining ingredients (except the salt and black pepper) and thoroughly beat them into the butter, then season lightly with salt and freshly ground black pepper.
4 When the legs are cold, skin them and break off the bottom joint if it is still attached.
5 Using a palette knife, spread each leg with some of the butter mixture — spreading it evenly all around the leg and completely covering the flesh.
6 Transfer the legs to a large rigid container, or 2 smaller ones. Refrigerate them — preferably overnight but for at least 6 hours.
7 Remove the legs from the refrigerator one hour before serving; keep them in a cool place where the butter can soften slightly but not become mushy. Before serving the chicken legs, fit each one with a cutlet frill, garnish them with watercress and provide plenty of napkins for your guests.

Layered pies

 3¾ hours,
plus overnight chilling

Serves 16–20
700 g /1½ lb made-weight shortcrust pastry
flour, for dusting
butter, for greasing
900 g /2 lb lean pork, minced
10 ml /2 tsp freshly grated nutmeg
10 ml /2 tsp marjoram
10 ml /2 tsp ground allspice
2.5 ml /½ tsp ground sage
2.5 ml /½ tsp powdered bay leaves
salt
freshly ground black pepper
45 ml /3 tbls olive oil
900 g /2 lb onions, grated
900 g /2 lb potatoes, grated and squeezed of all
  excess moisture in a clean cloth
5 ml /1 tsp ground caraway seeds
900 g /2 lb cooking apples, peeled, cored and
  grated
4 sprigs of thyme
milk, for brushing
1 medium-sized egg yolk, beaten
275 ml /10 fl oz chicken stock, home-made, or
  275 ml /10 fl oz chicken stock made with a
  cube, mixed with 7.5 ml /½ tbls gelatine
  dissolved in 15 ml /1 tbls water
30 ml /2 tbls cider or medium-sweet white wine

1 Divide the pastry into 2, cut off one-third from each piece and keep for the lids. Roll out the larger pieces of pastry on a lightly floured board to fit two 1.7 L /3 pt loaf tins.
2 Grease the tins with butter and line each one with pastry, pressing it well into the corners; the pastry should project above the sides. Roll out the remaining pastry for lids.
3 Put the minced pork into a large bowl and mix with the nutmeg, marjoram, allspice, sage, and powdered bay leaves. Season with salt and the black pepper and reserve. Heat the oven to 200C / 400F /gas 6.
4 Heat the oil in a heavy-based frying pan, add the grated onion and sauté gently for 20 minutes until it is soft and golden. Remove it from the heat and allow it to cool.
5 Put one quarter of the grated onion into the bottom of each pie, spreading it in an even layer. Cover with one quarter of the grated potatoes, then season lightly with salt and pepper and sprinkle 1.5 ml /¼ tsp ground caraway seeds over each pie.
6 Next, put a layer of minced pork in each pie, again using one-quarter of the mixture, and cover with a layer of apple. Put 1 sprig of thyme on each layer of apple, then repeat the layers until all the ingredients have been used.
7 Brush the top edges of each pie with milk and then cover with the lids, pressing firmly to seal. Crimp the edges. Brush the tops of the pies with the beaten egg yolk and make 3 slits in each pastry lid.
8 Mix together the chicken stock and cider or white wine and then pour a little into each pie through a funnel in the centre slit. Reserve the remaining stock; you will probably have used about half.
9 Put the pies side by side in the oven and cook for 25 minutes.

10 Turn the heat down to 150C /300F /gas 2. Turn the pies round and cook for a further 1 hour 45 minutes, covering the tops with foil after the first hour.
11 Remove the pies from the oven and let them cool. When they are cold, pour in the remaining stock — reheat it gently if it has started to set. Put the pies in the refrigerator to chill overnight.
12 Take the pies out of the refrigerator 30 minutes before serving — they should be only slightly chilled.

Ginger prawns in soured cream

Serve these tasty prawns with a bowl of Three-coloured rice (see recipe below) for an unusual combination of flavours.

50 minutes

Serves 16–20
125 g /4 oz butter
4 large onions, finely chopped
3 garlic cloves, finely chopped
7.5 cm /3 in piece of fresh root ginger, finely
  chopped
1.8 kg /4 lb prawns, shelled
2 large cucumbers, peeled, seeded and chopped
  into thin 25 mm /1 in strips
24 sorrel leaves or 24 young spinach leaves
15 ml /1 tbls ground fennel
15 ml /1 tbls finely chopped dill
575 ml /1 pt soured cream
salt and freshly ground black pepper
60 ml /4 tbls chicken stock, home-made or from
  a cube

1 Melt the butter in a large heavy-based saucepan over a moderate heat, add the onions, garlic and root ginger. Sauté for 7–10 minutes, stirring, until they are soft and golden.
2 Add the prawns and stir-fry for 3–4 minutes, then add the cucumber strips and cook for a further 4–5 minutes.
3 Add the sorrel leaves or spinach, the ground fennel and the finely chopped dill. Stir-fry for 2 minutes, then pour in the soured cream. Bring it all gently to the boil, then simmer it over a very low heat for 25–30 minutes, stirring frequently.
4 Season with salt and freshly ground black pepper. Transfer the mixture to a large bowl or a rigid plastic container, allow to cool, then cover and refrigerate until needed. Reserve the stock in another container.
5 To reheat, put the prawns and sauce in a large shallow saucepan with the chicken stock and heat gently until the sauce has thickened again and the prawns are piping hot.

Three-coloured rice

This yellow rice, with green and red peppers mixed into it, makes a splendidly colourful dish for a buffet.

 1 hour

Serves 20–24
1.4 kg /3 lb long-grain rice
15 ml /1 tbls crushed saffron threads
225 g /8 oz butter
20 ml /4 tsp cardamom pods
10 cloves
6 cinnamon sticks
3 large onions, finely chopped
2 large green peppers, cored, seeded and finely
  chopped
2 large red peppers, cored, seeded and finely
  chopped
150 g /5 oz pine nuts
2.8 L /5 pt chicken stock, home-made or
  from cubes
15 ml /1 tbls salt
freshly ground black pepper
75 g /3 oz butter, for reheating

Chick-pea and aubergine casserole

overnight soaking,
then 4½ hours

Serves 20–24
450 g /1 lb chick-peas, soaked overnight
4 large aubergines
4 large onions, coarsely chopped
1 head of celery, trimmed, washed and cut into
  25 mm /1 in slices
450 g /1 lb courgettes, topped, tailed, washed
  and cut into 25 mm /1 in slices
450 g /1 lb mushrooms, wiped and quartered
450 g /1 lb mange tout, washed
4 garlic cloves, finely chopped
50 ml /2 fl oz olive oil
1.2 kg /2¾ lb canned tomatoes
7.5 ml /1½ tsp dried thyme
7.5 ml /1½ tsp dried basil
15 ml /1 tbls ground coriander
150 ml /5 fl oz thick coconut milk (see note)
salt and freshly ground black pepper
45 ml /3 tbls freshly chopped parsley, to
  garnish
60 ml /4 tbls grated Parmesan, to garnish

1 Drain the chick-peas, cover with fresh cold water and bring to the boil over a moderate heat. Lower the heat and simmer for 2½ hours or until the chick-peas are soft.
2 Cut the aubergines in half, sprinkle with salt and leave them to drain for 30 minutes. Prepare the rest of the vegetables and garlic.
3 When the chick-peas are cooked, drain them, discarding the cooking water.
4 Heat the olive oil in a large flameproof casserole (or divide the oil between 2 if necessary). When the oil is hot, add the onions and the chopped garlic cloves and sauté for 10 minutes until soft and golden.
5 Wash the aubergines thoroughly under cold water to rid them of the salt and bitter juices. Cut them into 25 mm /1 in cubes and add them to the pan. Sauté for 5 minutes.
6 Add the celery and sauté for another 5 minutes, then add the courgettes and cook for a further 5 minutes.
7 Put the tomatoes in a large bowl and break them up with a wooden spoon, then add them to the casserole with the chick-peas, thyme, basil and coriander. Bring to boiling point, then turn the heat down and simmer gently for 30 minutes, stirring occasionally.
8 Add the mushrooms, mange tout and coconut milk and simmer for a further 15 minutes until the sauce is rich and thick. Season fairly generously with salt and freshly ground black pepper.
9 Remove the casserole from the heat and let it cool, before covering it with cling film and refrigerating it overnight.
10 To reheat, bring the casserole to room temperature and heat the oven to 150C /300F /gas 2. Heat the casserole for 30–40 minutes, covered, and stirring from time to time. Garnish with the parsley and cheese.

● For thick coconut milk, blend 90 g /3½ oz desiccated coconut with 450 ml /16 fl oz hot water for 1 minute. Strain through a sieve. Discard the coconut.

1 Put the saffron threads in a bowl with 60 ml /4 tbls boiling water and leave to soak.
2 Melt half the butter in each of 2 large heavy-based saucepans, add half the cardamom pods, cloves and cinnamon sticks to each pan and fry for 3 minutes, stirring.
3 Add half the finely chopped onion to each pan and cook for 10 minutes until it is golden.
4 Add 1 red and 1 green chopped pepper to each pan and cook for a further 5 minutes.
5 Add half the rice and half the pine nuts to each pan, stir thoroughly and fry for 5 minutes, stirring.
6 Divide the chicken stock in half and pour a half into each pan, together with 30 ml / 2 tbls of the saffron mixture. Add 7.5 ml / ½ tbls salt to each pan (unless the chicken

Three-coloured rice and Ginger prawns in soured cream

stock was made with a cube in which case omit the salt at this stage and season to taste at the end of the cooking). Bring the rice to the boil, then turn the heat down very low and simmer for 30–35 minutes or until the rice is cooked and the stock absorbed, stirring occasionally.
7 Season with freshly ground black pepper, stirring it in well, then allow the rice to cool. When cold, cover it and refrigerate it.
8 To reheat the rice, melt the butter in a large casserole dish, add the rice mixture, stirring very thoroughly so that all the rice is coated with butter, then heat for 8–10 minutes, stirring. Serve immediately.

Sweet pastry bites

The tart shells, praline and pastry cream may all be made in advance.

 4½ hours

Makes 72
225 g /8 oz flour, plus extra for dusting
30 ml /2 tbls icing sugar
2.5 ml /½ tsp salt
150 g /5 oz cold butter, in 5 mm /¼ in dice
50 g /2 oz ground almonds
2 egg yolks
5 ml /1 tsp lemon juice
1.5 ml /¼ tsp almond essence
For the pastry cream
450 ml /16 fl oz milk
5 cm /2 in piece vanilla pod, split
4 egg yolks
60 ml /4 tbls caster sugar
30 ml /2 tbls flour
20 ml /4 tsp cornflour
30 ml /2 tbls butter, plus extra for greasing
30 ml /2 tbls maraschino
1.5 ml /¼ tsp vanilla essence
2.5 ml /½ tsp almond essence
For the chocolate praline
butter, for greasing
120 ml /8 tbls sugar
100 g /4 oz hazelnuts, chopped
100 g /4 oz semi-sweet chocolate
For the glazed fruit tartlets (use a selection)
seedless white grapes, halved
black grapes, halved and seeded
small canned apricot halves, drained
cherries, stoned
raspberries
canned lichees, halved
wild strawberries
large strawberries,halved
banana slices, dipped in lemon juice
redcurrants
For the apricot glaze
125 ml /4 fl oz apricot jam
15 ml /1 tbls Amaretto
For the chocolate icing
30 ml /2 tbls butter
90 ml /6 tbls sugar
50 g /2 oz unsweetened chocolate
1.5 ml /¼ tsp vanilla essence
For the vanilla icing
225 g /8 oz icing sugar, sifted
5 ml /1 tsp vanilla essence
15 ml /1 tbls cognac
orange or yellow food colouring (optional)

1 First make the pastry. Sift the flour, icing sugar and salt together into a large bowl. Add the diced butter. Using a pastry blender or 2 knives, cut the butter into the flour until the mixture resembles coarse breadcrumbs.
2 Rub in the butter using cool fingertips until the mixture resembles very fine breadcrumbs. Stir in the ground almonds until they are evenly blended.
3 In a small bowl, beat together the egg yolks, the lemon juice, the almond essence and 15 ml /1 tbls iced water. Sprinkle this over the flour mixture, tossing it with a fork until the pastry begins to hold together. Add a little more iced water if necessary.

Sweet pastry bites

4 When about three-quarters of the mixture holds together, lightly and quickly press the pastry together into a ball using a cupped hand. Wrap it in cling film and chill it in the refrigerator for 1 hour or more.
5 While the pastry is chilling, make the

pastry cream: pour the milk into a saucepan and add the vanilla pod. Bring it slowly to boiling point, cover the saucepan and set aside for 10 minutes to infuse.
6 In a large bowl, whisk together the egg yolks with the sugar until they are thick and light. Gradually whisk in the flour and the cornflour.

pastry and use it to line 72×4–5 cm /1½–2 in tart tins. Press the pastry gently into the flutes and prick the bases with a fork. Chill for 30 minutes.

10 While the pastry is relaxing, make the praline. Butter a baking sheet. In a small saucepan gently heat the sugar until it turns liquid, stirring constantly, then continue to cook it until it is light gold. Remove the pan from the heat and stir in the hazelnuts until they are coated with the caramel.

11 Pour the praline onto the baking sheet and leave until it is cold and hard, then break it into small pieces and grind to a powder in a blender. Store in a covered container in a cool place (not the refrigerator) until it is required.

12 Heat the oven to 190C /375F /gas 5. Place the tart shells on baking sheets and bake for 10 minutes, until set and golden. Leave to cool, then store them in airtight tins until they are required.

13 To assemble the tarts, first complete the chocolate praline: break the chocolate into the top pan of a double boiler and place it over simmering water until it has melted. Pour it into a small bowl and stir in the finely ground praline.

14 Make the glazed fruit tartlets, using half the baked tart shells. Spoon 2.5 ml /½ tsp chocolate praline into each shell, then cover with 2.5 ml /½ tsp pastry cream.

15 Top the pastry cream with fruit, varying the tarts as much as possible; for each tart use 3 seedless grape halves, or 3 black grape halves, or 1 apricot half, or 3 cherries, or 3 raspberries, or 1 lichee half, or 3 wild strawberries, or 2 large strawberry halves, or 1 banana slice, or 6–8 redcurrants.

16 Make the apricot glaze: in a small saucepan combine the apricot jam with 45 ml /3 tbls water and stir over a medium heat until the jam melts. Boil for 2–3 minutes to reduce slightly, then press the mixture through a fine sieve into a bowl. Add the Amaretto and brush the fruit tartlets with the glaze while it is still slightly warm. Leave them to set.

17 To make the iced tartlets, spoon 2.5 ml / ½ tsp chocolate praline into the remaining tart shells and cover with 5 ml /1 tsp pastry cream. Reserve these while you make the icings.

18 Make the chocolate icing: in a small saucepan combine the butter, sugar, chocolate and 60 ml /4 tbls water. Stir over a low heat until the chocolate melts and the mixture is smooth. When it starts to boil, stir in the vanilla essence, then remove the icing from the heat and leave it to cool slightly. Use while it is still warm.

19 While the chocolate icing is cooling, make the vanilla icing: combine the icing sugar, 60 ml /4 tbls water and the vanilla essence in the top pan of a double boiler. Heat over simmering water until the mixture is smooth and shiny. Stir in the cognac and a few drops of food colouring, if wished. Use while it is still warm.

20 To finish the iced tartlets, decorate them with swirls of contrasting-coloured icing: pour the chocolate icing from the tip of a teaspoon onto the tartlets, making zigzag patterns. Leave it to set for about 5 minutes, then pour on the vanilla icing as a contrast. Leave it to set.

7 Remove the vanilla pod and gradually pour the milk onto the egg mixture, whisking it well. Return the mixture to the pan and bring it to the boil over a moderate heat, stirring constantly. Simmer for 3 minutes, beating the mixture vigorously with a wooden spoon to disperse any lumps.

8 Remove the pan from the heat. Add the butter and beat for 1–2 minutes, until the cream starts to cool. Stir in the maraschino, the vanilla and almond essences, then pass the pastry cream through a sieve into a bowl. Cover it with a piece of greaseproof paper and leave it to cool, then chill it until it is required.

9 On a lightly floured board, roll out the

Chocolate-dipped candied peel

🕐🍴 2¾ hours, plus 2 days drying, then coating

Makes 30 sticks of peel
1 large orange
1 large lemon
100 g /4 oz granulated sugar
50 g /2 oz caster sugar
25 g /1 oz dark chocolate

1 Scrub the orange and the lemon and cut them into quarters. Scrape away the flesh, reserving it for another recipe. Cut the peel into long narrow strips.
2 Put the peel strips in a saucepan and cover them with cold water. Bring the water to the boil and then drain. Return the peel to the saucepan and cover it with cold water again. Bring to the boil, then simmer over a gentle heat for about 1½–2 hours until the peel is soft but not mushy. Top up with water if necessary.
3 Leave the peel to cool completely in the liquid, then drain.
4 Put the granulated sugar and 50 ml /2 fl oz water in a pan and stir over a gentle heat until the sugar has dissolved. Add the peel and simmer until the peel has absorbed the syrup.
5 Turn the peel onto a wire tray covered with greaseproof paper. Using tongs, separate the pieces of peel so they do not touch. Put the trays in an airing cupboard or warm place for 2 days until the peel feels almost dry.
6 Sift the caster sugar onto a plate and roll each piece of peel in the sugar. Store in an airtight container for up to 6 months.
7 To serve, melt the chocolate in a bowl over a saucepan of hot water. Dip one end of each piece of peel into the chocolate. Dry on non-stick paper. Peel dipped in chocolate can be kept for 1–2 weeks in an airtight container in a cool place.

● Grapefruit peel can be dried in the same way but change the water at least 3 times during the initial softening process to ensure the bitterness is removed.

Toffee-glazed fruits

🍴 15 minutes, plus 30 minutes cooling

Serves 6–8
oil, for greasing
100 g /4 oz strawberries
100 g /4 oz white grapes
1 small orange or tangerine
225 g /8 oz sugar

1 Lightly oil 2 baking trays. Without hulling the strawberries, wash and dry them on absorbent paper. Divide the grapes into sprigs of two. Peel the orange, remove all the pith and divide it into segments.
2 Put the sugar and 125 ml /4 fl oz water in a small saucepan and stir over a gentle heat until the sugar dissolves. Increase the heat,

bring to the boil and boil until the syrup is a pale golden colour. Then remove it from the heat quickly.
3 Use tongs to dip the orange segments into the syrup. Hold the strawberries and grapes by the stalks and dip them into the syrup. Put it onto the baking trays and refrigerate to harden the toffee. Place in paper cases and serve within 2 hours.

Orange-almond petits fours

🍴 25 minutes, plus cooling

Makes 20
butter, for greasing
2 egg whites
100 g /4 oz caster sugar
150 g /5 oz ground almonds
grated zest of 1 orange
a few drops sweet orange oil or essence
candied orange peel, for decoration

1 Heat the oven to 180C /350F /gas 4 and grease a baking tray.
2 Whisk the egg whites until they are stiff.
3 In a bowl mix together the caster sugar, the ground almonds and the orange zest until they are well combined. Add the orange oil or essence. Fold this carefully into the egg whites.
4 Fit a piping bag with a 15 mm /½ in star nozzle and spoon in the mixture. Pipe little rosettes onto the baking tray, pushing the nozzle down to flatten the biscuits. Place a tiny piece of candied orange peel in the centre of each biscuit.
5 Bake for 15 minutes, until the biscuits are firm and evenly coloured. Cool them on wire racks, then store the biscuits in an airtight container. They will keep for up to 3 weeks.

● Lemon flavouring may be used instead of orange, or the biscuits may be decorated with a flaked almond or piece of glacé cherry.

Toffee-glazed fruits and Chocolate-dipped candied peel

Summer fruit salad

🍴🍴 1¼ hours,
then 3–4 hours chilling

Serves 16

1.4 kg /3 lb strawberries, hulled and halved
4 kiwi fruit, peeled and sliced into rounds
6 oranges, pith and peel removed, cut into
  rounds
450 g /1 lb raspberries
4 peaches, peeled and sliced
4 nectarines, peeled and sliced
juice of 2 lemons
2 honeydew melons
700 ml /25 fl oz sweet sparkling white wine,
  such as Asti Spumante
100 ml /3½ fl oz Grand Marnier
sugar (optional)
mint leaves, to garnish

1 Put the strawberries, the kiwi fruit, the oranges, the raspberries, the peaches, and the nectarines into separate bowls.

2 Divide the lemon juice between the peach and the nectarine slices and toss them so they are well coated.

3 Halve the melons and discard the seeds. Using a melon baller, scoop out the flesh of the melons into another bowl.

4 Mix the wine and the Grand Marnier together and divide it equally among all the bowls of fruit. Add sugar to taste, if wished. Toss the fruit so it is well coated, then put the bowls in the refrigerator to chill for 3–4 hours. Chill a large rectangular serving dish (see note at the end).

5 To serve: remove each fruit from its bowl with a slotted spoon and arrange it in diagonal lines across the serving dish. Place complementary colours next to each other so it looks as attractive as possible. Sprinkle some of the macerating liquid over it if wished. Garnish the corners of the dish with sprigs of fresh mint leaves.

● If you do not have a large enough rectangular dish to accommodate all the fruit in lines, then mix the fruit in a glass bowl which has been chilled first.

Summer fruit salad — a glorious array of fresh, delicious fruit

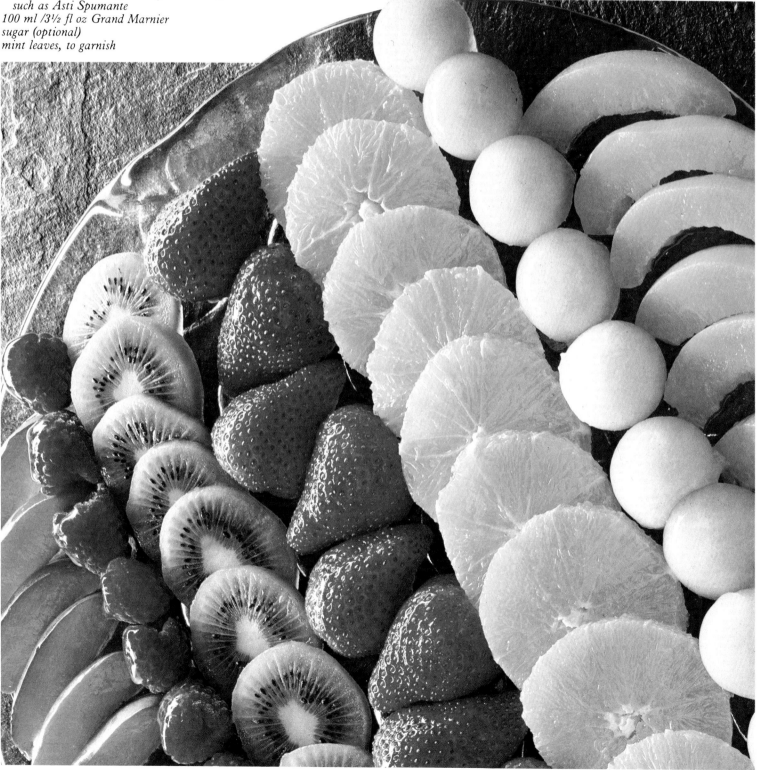

Rose wedding cake

⏱🍴🍴🍴 3 hours baking, plus 24 hours, 5 hours, then 1 hour decorating

Serves 24–48
100 g /4 oz flour
3 eggs
2 egg yolks
100 g /4 oz caster sugar
5 ml /1 tsp vanilla essence
50 g /2 oz butter
butter and flour, for the tins
To decorate
225 g /8 oz bought fondant icing
pink and yellow food colourings
300 g /10 oz sugar
700 g /1½ lb unsalted butter
1.4 kg /3 lb icing sugar, sifted
4 medium-sized egg yolks
2.5 ml /½ tsp lemon essence
225 g /8 oz apricot jam
ribbon, lace and silver leaves

1 Heat the oven to 170C /325F /gas 3. Grease a 23 cm /9 in deep square tin, line it with greaseproof paper, grease the paper and dust it lightly with flour.

2 Make up a double quantity of sponge mixture. Clarify the butter. Sift the flour.
3 In a bowl, over barely simmering water, whisk the eggs, egg yolks, caster sugar and vanilla essence until the mixture is light and thick.
4 Remove the bowl from the heat and whisk until it cools. Sift the flour and mix it in thoroughly.
5 Fold in the clarified butter.
6 Put the mixture in the prepared tin and bake for 1½ hours. Cool for 15 minutes, then turn it onto a rack and remove the paper. Increase the oven heat to 180C /350F /gas 4.
7 Prepare an 18 cm /7 in deep square tin. Make up a single batch of sponge mixture and bake it for 45 minutes. When cold, store both cakes for 24 hours.
8 Tint the fondant pale pink, then divide it in 3. Tint two of the batches again, making one darker than the other. Make 8 medium and 2 small pale roses; 2 large, 4 medium and 10 small middle-shade roses; 8 medium and 20 small dark roses (see method in Rose posy, page 61).
9 To make the butter cream, dissolve the sugar in 150 ml /5 fl oz water, then boil it until the syrup reaches 108C /220F.
10 In a large bowl, beat the unsalted butter

Rose wedding cake

until fluffy. Beat in half the icing sugar, then add the egg yolks, one at a time. Gradually beat in the rest of the icing sugar alternating it with the syrup.
11 Add 2 drops of pink colouring and lemon essence.
12 Cut the cakes horizontally and sandwich them together with ⅓ of the butter cream. Centre the larger cake, bottom upwards, on a silver cake board 30 cm /12 in square.
13 Place the smaller cake, bottom upwards, on a thin card 15–18 cm /6–7 in square.
14 Sieve the apricot jam into a pan, add 60 ml /4 tbls water and bring it to the boil. Cool it, then brush it over both cakes. Leave them for 30–60 minutes.
15 Coat both the cakes with butter cream, smoothing with a palette knife. Leave for 2–6 hours.
16 Tint the remaining butter cream to match the middle-shade roses and put it in a piping bag fitted with a medium-sized star nozzle.
17 Centre the small cake on top of the larger cake.
18 Pipe a row of shells as shown. Decorate with ribbons, lace and silver leaves.

Index